Pierre Macherey
and the Case of
Literary Production

Pierre Macherey and the Case of Literary Production

✦

Edited by Warren Montag
and Audrey Wasser

NORTHWESTERN UNIVERSITY PRESS
EVANSTON, ILLINOIS

Northwestern University Press
www.nupress.northwestern.edu

Printed in the United States of America

10 9 8 7 6 5 4 3 2 1

Library of Congress Cataloging-in-Publication Data

Names: Montag, Warren, editor. | Wasser, Audrey, editor.
Title: Pierre Macherey and the case of literary production / edited by Warren
    Montag and Audrey Wasser.
Description: Evanston, Illinois : Northwestern University Press, 2022. |
    Includes bibliographical references.
Identifiers: LCCN 2022011420 | ISBN 9780810145115 (paperback) |
    ISBN 9780810145122 (cloth) | ISBN 9780810145139 (ebook)
Subjects: LCSH: Macherey, Pierre. | Macherey, Pierre. Pour une théorie de la
    production littéraire. | Literature—History and criticism—Theory, etc. |
    Literature—Philosophy.
Classification: LCC PN45 .M3173 2022 | DDC 801.95—dc23/eng/20220308
LC record available at https://lccn.loc.gov/2022011420

CONTENTS

Introduction

✦

Warren Montag and Audrey Wasser

The recent publication in English translation of two of Pierre Macherey's most important and influential works, his contribution to *Reading Capital* (1965, trans. 2015) and *Hegel or Spinoza* (1979, trans. 2011), has served to call attention to the power and originality of Macherey's thought. *A Theory of Literary Production* (1966, trans. 1978; reissued 2006), however, available in translation for more than forty years, remains an unsettled text that continues to provoke disagreement about its basic positions. Far from consigning the book to a particular historical moment—specifically, the structuralist moment of the 1960s—its capacity to produce contradictory readings enabled it to survive this moment, and several others, as if some of its most important postulates were deferred at the outset, intelligible only under conditions that did not exist in 1966 or even in 1978. While the publication of some of Macherey's most important texts in translation is no more likely to eliminate the heterogeneous effects of *A Theory of Literary Production* than the appearance in 1990 of his second book on literature, *The Object of Literature* (under the title *À quoi pense la littérature? Exercises de philosophie littéraire*; trans. 1995), these texts taken together help clarify its arguments and, in doing so, distinguish the conflicts proper to it from those projected on it.

Another source of the ambiguity surrounding Macherey's first book for English-language readers is the lack of a comprehensive account of the theoretical conjuncture in which Macherey wrote (beyond vague notions of a structuralist or structural Marxist moment). Without understanding the stakes and objectives of what Macherey conceived as an intervention, English-language critics, commentators, and those who simply applied something of what Macherey wrote systematically overlooked essential aspects of his project and misread others. In part, this may be explained by the twelve-year gap between the publication of the French original in 1966 and its English translation in 1978. The interest elicited by the appearance of Althusser's *For Marx* and *Reading Capital* in English in 1969, and the collection of articles (including several on art and literature) published as *Lenin and Philosophy* in 1971, led readers who sought an "Althusserian" literary criticism to Macherey's text, which was originally published in Althusser's Théorie series. In the absence of an English translation, Terry Eagleton's presentation of Macherey's text in *Criticism and Ideology* (1976) took on an unusual importance and continued to shape the reception of Macherey's work long after it was translated, in part because of this work's conceptual and stylistic density, the difficulties of which Macherey himself later acknowledged. Eagleton's account of Macherey is itself a revealing exercise in philosophical and theoretical translation: it captures and often enlivens some of Macherey's most important theses (above all, those involving criticism as judgment) and, at the same time, blocks the apprehension of others (the entire constellation of theses mobilized to articulate the critique of interpretation).

Fredric Jameson also played a role in shaping what was visible of Macherey's work in the United States. The opening of *The Political Unconscious* (1981) devoted more than twenty-five pages to Althusser and Macherey's positions on interpretation, causality, and structure. Some commonalities between Jameson and Macherey's practices of reading are certainly worth noting here—for example, the "limitations" and "strategies of containment" that Jameson identifies and juxtaposes in his reading of other critics can be compared to the attention Macherey pays to the *décalage* exhibited in the literary work.[1] In this way, both thinkers arguably take as their object of study not an "object" in the traditional sense but a difference, a dislocation, or a discrepancy. Yet on the whole, Jameson's work represents a missed encounter with Macherey's. Althusser and Macherey's arguments are folded into what is broadly characterized as a Nietzschean, antihermeneutic tendency in post-structural French thought, while their specifically Spinozist commitments are largely unaddressed, as are Althusser's arguments about the unevenness of historical time. Of Macherey in particular, Jameson says very little, preferring to assimilate Macherey's position to Althusser's without recognizing the disagreements that unfolded between the two precisely over the role of literary interpretation in working out a concept of structure. The latter is represented by Macherey's essay "Literary Analysis: The Tomb of Structures" in part 2 of *A Theory of Literary Production*.[2]

Through these early and decontextualized readings, Macherey's work nevertheless played an important role in changing some basic assumptions concerning both the literary text and the act of reading. It often did so, however, indirectly, that is, in the form of an absent cause. While each decade after 1970 saw an increase in the number of references to Macherey, the effects of his work were significantly greater than the number of direct citations would indicate. On the one hand, the critique of normative approaches to literature, the negative consequences of which were on full display in the debates over the canon, together with his rejection of the postulate of the formal and thematic unity of the literary work, helped initiate a transformation of the very concepts of literature and the literary text. This critique allowed readers to look for the historicity of literary works, not in their relation to the world outside of them, but internally, immanent in both their form and their content, that is, in the impossibility of the coherence and consistency of these latter—an approach that in turn necessitated a decentering and reconceptualization of the very idea of the author, whose role as creator and proprietor had served as one of the most important guarantees of the ultimate unity of the work. This coincided with, but was not the same as, the transformations of basic concepts of literary studies wrought by early receptions of deconstruction and "la nouvelle critique."

On the other hand, Macherey's approach to the questions posed by literature remained only partially intelligible to readers. Readers of the English translation expected, and thought Macherey had provided, a more or less finished theory of literary production, when in fact the entire first, theoretical, section of the book is devoted to the more modest task of identifying and dismantling what Macherey called the *illusions* (rendered in English as "fallacies") that had so far prevented the development of a theory of literature, or of what he would call in the course of his exposition "literary production." The *illusions* he identifies all serve in different ways to deny or negate the complex reality of the literary work and the process of its production. The constitutive contradictions, conflicts, and discrepancies that every literary text displays are treated as superficial or inessential, whether as a puzzle needing only to be reassembled in its proper order or as mere surface phenomena, functions of the work's deep structure. In some cases, the unity of the text is restored with a reference to its origin in the mind of an author, or to the coherence of its historical moment. These approaches, despite the significant differences between them, share a conception of reading as an act of reduction. In one case, that to which texts must be reduced to be understood is internal to them, the essence to be recovered from the excrescence that surrounds it; in the other case, their meaning is contained in their external, spatiotemporal origin. Perhaps the most influential of Macherey's analyses was his account of the normative illusion, the act of judging works according to the degree of their deviation from a norm or ideal external to them. Criticism of this type tells us what a work is not and what it lacks in relation to an ideal invented by criticism. The positivity of the work is irrelevant to judgment whose concern is to apply an aesthetic legality (whose effects are not limited to the realm of literature) to decide whether a work has obeyed or violated its letter and spirit.

Macherey's insistence on the constitutive discrepancies of the literary text is a way of underscoring the text's irreducible materiality. And this attention to materiality necessarily extends to literary criticism itself. An analysis of the ways criticism denies the material existence of literature cannot in turn deny the material existence of the illusions that govern the practice of reading: to do so would mean simply inventing a new set of illusions to add to the old. Macherey's illusions, however, are neither pathologies of a perceiving subject nor insubstantial apparitions that will disappear in the light of knowledge. They are endowed with a necessity and with a function insofar as they are tied to ideology. And as Althusser wrote in "Marxism and Humanism" (1964), "Marx never believed that an ideology might be dissipated by a knowledge of it: for the knowledge of this ideology, as the knowledge of its conditions of possibility, of its structure, of its specific logic and of its practical role, within a given society, is simultaneously knowledge of the conditions of its necessity."[3] Without an understanding of what Macherey calls "illusions" as necessary, determinate, and endowed with a mass whose capacity to resist the force applied to it can be measured, there can be no explanation of their historical emergence, persistence, and function.

It is precisely the importance Macherey places on identifying, confronting, and dismantling illusions, however, that creates some of the most difficult challenges readers of *Theory* must face, with the result that part 1, "Some Elementary Concepts," remains simultaneously the most influential and least understood part of Macherey's work. From his perspective, only a thorough analysis of the "forms of illusion" can clear the way for the development of an adequate knowledge of the literary work, as well as of the process of what he will call literary production. Without confronting these illusions, it will be impossible to say something new, something that is not simply a variant of one of the illusions that govern our attempts to think about literature. English-speaking readers, however, expected that once Macherey had pointed out the fallacious assumptions of nearly every attempt at literary criticism, thereby dispensing with them as if they were errors that, once identified and corrected, would simply vanish, he would then proceed as expeditiously as possible to the presentation of a new theory with which to replace them. Despite the various theories readers attributed to him, no such theory appears here or anywhere else in his text. Instead, Macherey promises the reader "some"—that is, an as yet indeterminate number of—"elementary concepts," an examination of "some critics," and an analysis of "some texts," that is, literary texts (primarily those of Jules Verne). Not only does he insist that the few provisional concepts he offers do not constitute a theory; he refuses to give any assurances that a finished theory will arise from the starting point they provide.

Further, while a glance at the organization of the book's contents might make it appear as though Macherey follows the expected order of exposition, beginning with an account of a more or less completed theory in order then to apply it to certain critical texts (Lenin and assorted structuralist thinkers) and finally to the literary works of Jules Verne, the actual order of its development seems to be the reverse. The Crusoe and Borges essays are dated earlier than the first section of the book; the Verne essay was begun in 1964 and likely worked on concurrently with the theoretical sections. In a number of ways, the analysis of the literary texts seems necessarily to precede and make possible the distillation of certain elementary concepts, as if Macherey himself had followed the method he ascribes to Spinoza in the latter's *Tractatus*

Theologico-Politicus. Spinoza does not offer his theory of the interpretation of scripture until the seventh chapter, and therefore, according to Macherey, only after he had put into practice a theory that had yet to be stated in theoretical form. Even more strikingly, Macherey directs our attention away from the attempt to supply a theory (which rests on the supposition that theories will always arise where they are most needed), and instead to the necessity of clearing away the illusions that, in the case of literature, have prevented the articulation of concepts capable of constituting the literary work as an intelligible object of knowledge. To carry out this work, however, we must be able to identify the illusions *as* illusions, something that becomes possible only in the light of the new theory whose development the illusions have blocked: we are thus caught in a circle or suspended between the incompatible postulates of a paradox. For Macherey, however, while practice precedes the theory by which it is necessarily guided, the theory practice discovers already exists, but in the practical state, entirely immanent in the practice whose activity alone will allow theory to take a theoretical form. Thus concludes part 1, the theoretical section of *A Theory of Literary Production*.

The ability to dwell in and explore the paradoxes he encounters as he writes explains the experimental character of Macherey's writing and the thought that develops within and through it. Althusser once described his own work as a process of discovery, but a paradoxical discovery of what comes into existence only in and through writing itself.[4] Macherey's text is a perfect example of such discovery: his sentences constitute conceptual experiments, each burdened with the task of clearing an opening in the already occupied space of literary theory for the new arguments and concepts it bears. The act of clearing takes the form of drawing lines of demarcation that will prevent the assimilation of Macherey's theses into already existing notions of literature. We cannot forget that Macherey wrote in a moment of rapidly developing political struggles in which the relationship of forces was increasingly favorable to those, both workers and students, who were convinced that a revolutionary transformation of capitalist society was possible. Something of this is visible in Macherey's style, remarkable for its appropriation of literary language to produce a nonliterary knowledge of literature, pushing this language to the very limits of sense, and not infrequently using it to produce effects rather than convey ideas. There are moments at which he appears to have abandoned his position as author to permit the concatenation of voices around him to be heard, content to transmit a thought whose power he feels, even if its meaning is not entirely accessible to him. The epigrammatic and even fragmented character of section 1 is not the result of a decision on his part but a necessity imposed on him by the accelerating flow and density of historical time. Macherey's style operates by displacing, fracturing, and shattering what Althusser called the *evidences*, the obviousnesses of both academic and social life more generally. The fact that Macherey, as he explains in his postface to the 2014 edition of his first book (chapter 1 of the present volume), found himself unable to understand certain of the passages he had written nearly fifty years earlier is itself a validation of his decentering of the author by replacing the term "creation" (with its theological and individualizing connotations) with "production" (collective and publicly knowable).

The concluding sentence (two sentences in the English translation) of part 1 concentrates these notions in one of the dense phrases characteristic of Macherey's first book: "In this way, perhaps, the forms of illusion that have bound literary criticism to ideology may be exorcised: the illusion of the secret, the illusion of depth, the illusion of the rule, the illusion of harmony" (Alors peut-être pourront être exorcisées les formes d'illusion qui ont retenu jusqu'ici la critique littéraire dans les liens de l'idéologie: illusion du secret, illusion de la profondeur, illusion de la règle, illusion de l'harmonie) (113/236).[5] "Perhaps" reminds us that nothing guarantees the success of the attempt to displace these and other illusions, no matter how valid and compelling its arguments and criticisms; the extent to which it is able to diminish the power of the illusions that prevent us from producing a knowledge of literature is contingent on the play of forces in the conjuncture in which it operates. That Macherey describes this attempt (with a note of irony whose effects should be neither ignored nor allowed to mask the diverse operations at issue here) as "exorcism," a freeing of literary criticism from the theoretical equivalent of demonic possession, is significant. Every exorcism is in some sense deliverance from illusion, but from an illusion powerful enough that one, unable simply to dismiss it, must be delivered from it, and whose effects are very real and inscribed as much on the body as on the soul. To free literary criticism from the bonds of ideology requires more than the power of reason, more than persuasive argument. The possession that can be treated only by exorcism takes root in the body, and its corporeal effects are not always completely resolved, even in cases of exorcisms deemed successful.

The contradictions and conflicts that traversed the field of literary criticism and were heightened and intensified by developments in Marxism, psychoanalysis, and linguistics made it possible for Macherey in the course of his critical analysis to construct from the materials at hand a number of concepts sufficient to begin the project of a literary criticism whose aim was neither appreciation nor judgment nor interpretation, but a knowledge of the conditions of existence of literary texts and of something like literature. To register the material existence of the work, Macherey proposes in the remainder of the final sentence of part 1 that it be conceived as "decentered, displayed [exposée], determinate, complex." Known through these elementary concepts, whose existence marks the beginning or perhaps only the possibility of establishing a new theory and practice of literary criticism, "the work runs the risk of receiving its theory." Rejecting the theoretical voluntarism that denies the limits of what is possible at a given moment and mistakes regression for progress, Macherey turns his attention to what, setting aside the language of illusion—the language of what might be dissipated through disillusionment or disproven and therefore eliminated on rational grounds—we may now call the "obstacles" to a knowledge of literature through its causes. This term, often used with an accompanying adjective, "epistemological obstacles," was introduced into the history and philosophy of the sciences by Gaston Bachelard, a figure whose reflections on the history of physics and chemistry the Althusserians regarded as critical to the project of understanding Marx's theoretical revolution. The concept of the obstacle, like that of the rupture, was essential to Bachelard's lifelong project of developing a notion of the history of the sciences (in the plural) capable of registering and explaining the combined, uneven, and discontinuous development specific to a given science. To put it briefly: the history of scientific knowledge is the history of the errors and obstacles that it had to overcome to constitute itself as knowledge. These obstacles become intelligible only after the fact, that is, from the perspective made possible by their having been overcome, displaced by a new "problematic" characterized by a rationality proper to it.

Macherey refers to Bachelard only once in *A Theory of Literary Production*: when he argues that "either literary criticism is an art, completely determined by the pre-existence of a domain, the literary works, and finally reunited with them in the discovery of their truth, and as such it has no autonomous existence; or, it is a certain form of knowledge, and has an object, which is not a given but a product of literary criticism" (7). A literary criticism not content to remain "an art of reading," that is, an extension of the literary text itself, must through its own labor endow itself with "in Bachelard's words . . . the discursivity characteristic of true knowledge." Macherey thus situates his project at the point of a break or rupture, from the perspective of which the validity once extended to the prior forms of literary criticism has expired, and they can be recognized for what they are: not simply illusions, but obstacles, ossified and tenacious, blocking the way to a criticism capable of producing knowledge.

It is at this point that a problem common to Bachelard and Macherey emerges: what are the causes of the "tenacity" of the obstacles or illusions? What enables them to resist the force of even the most informed critique, whose objections cannot be answered from the perspective of the obstacle in question? And finally, by what means can they be displaced or dismantled? These questions are not directly posed by either philosopher, in part because they are preemptively excluded by notions that appear to have answered them. The explanations in both cases are remarkably similar: in Bachelard's case, they are ascribed to opinion, and, in Macherey's, to ideology. Both notions could be described as forms of illusion. In fact, Bachelard's definition of opinion or common knowledge as "needs translated into knowledge" is not far from the working definition of ideology in *A Theory of Literary Production*. Yet both terms are placeholders that, at the time of their writing, identify and keep open the place that at some point must be occupied by a fully realized concept, which does not yet exist. Macherey's references to ideology and to its role in ensuring the tenacity and solidity of the illusions or obstacles he enumerates in his text are references to a concept that, although necessary to his analysis, does not yet exist—that is, to an absence.

This absence does not indicate a failure on Macherey's part, nor is it a function of the work's design. The absence of an explanation of the obstacles or illusions through their causes in *Theory* is determinate and therefore intelligible. The key to understanding it lies in the history of the notion of ideology in the period from 1960 to 1975 in France, a brief history, but one in which the continued use of the word "ideology" masked the proliferation of different perspectives and different objects, and therefore a history composed of discontinuities and rapid breaks and mutations. We cannot undertake a study of this history here, but we wish to underscore that the specifically material character of the illusions Macherey describes in his book could not yet be understood or acknowledged from the perspective of the Althusserian notion of ideology as it existed in 1966, prior to its reformulation in "Ideology and the Ideological State Apparatuses" as well as in the wider text from which it was drawn, posthumously published as *On the Reproduction of Capitalism*. In these texts, ideology was grasped as immanent to the apparatuses and the practices, rituals, and discourses that constituted it.

Althusser's reworking of the concept of ideology in the years following the publication of *Theory* also allows us to read Macherey's critique of the normative illusion (*l'illusion normative*) in a new way. His description of the operation of norms in the study of literature was intimately tied to a growing body of work in the fields of psychoanalysis, sociology, and biology concerned with the concepts of norm, normality, and normalization, above all, that of Georges Canguilhem, whose book *The Normal and the Pathological* appeared the same year as *Theory*, in a revised and augmented edition. Macherey's book begins by recalling that literary criticism is not a unified activity but consists of two approaches not only different but antagonistic: a project whose aim is to explain literature though its causes and a project that renders judgment on literary texts, sometimes invoking explicit rules but more often applying to literature unstated norms that become fully intelligible only after the judgment is rendered. The second tendency in literary criticism is largely incompatible with the production of knowledge, insofar as it judges a work according to the degree to which it corresponds to the norm. Since no text exhibits the perfection prescribed by the norm, it may be said that criticism as judgment bases its decisions on the extent to which a given work deviates from or falls short of the norm, the extent to which it could have been better than it is. This approach, as Macherey tells us, begins with the gesture of rejection; it is more interested in what a text isn't than in what it is, referring it to an ideal whose unattainability condemns every work to failure. Much of this critique, as Macherey himself notes, is derived from Spinoza, specifically the arguments advanced in the appendix to *Ethics* I. The normative critic, however, is not content simply to invoke a set of norms and note the degree to which a given work deviates from its directives. Normative criticism is in fact a prolonged effort to improve the mass of literary texts by reducing the degree of their variation in relation to the norm and to each other in the interests of what might be called the standardization of literary forms.

At the same time, the norms at work in literary criticism as described by Macherey could not be entirely separated from the function of norms in the processes of subjection both within and outside of the educational apparatus. Althusser's notion of the interpellation of the individual as subject was derived in part from Kant's remarks on the subject position imputed to the individual by law: every legal person is assumed to be and is treated as the sole or at least primary cause of his or her actions. Given that no actually existing individual is self-determining, we can say that the imputation of responsibility in both the causal and moral senses amounts to the imposition of a norm according to which individuals are both understood and judged by the extent of their deviation from this norm. The literary text, especially insofar as it is considered the work of an author, understood in the larger legal sense as the doer of a deed, any deed, is the object of a judgment that determines the degree of its deviation from the ideal it arises from but can never fully attain.

Thus, the critic as judge is not a mere aesthete or "technician of taste," to use Macherey's phrase, who decides what is and is not fit for consumption before instructing the uninitiated in the proper means of appreciation. It is in the educational apparatus that the critic, invested with the right and power of judgment, determines which texts are truly literary, and of these, which are read, taught, and written about. Criticism appears to apply aesthetic norms through operations of exclusion and hierarchization; in fact, these norms are postulated retroactively as an attempt to rationalize operations linked more closely to the function of the university in capitalist societies than to aesthetic doctrine. Even when criticism claims to have freed itself from normative approaches to literature, it often shares with these approaches the objective of dematerializing and dehistoricizing (sometimes in the form of a historicism so restricted that it too serves as a means of exclusion) literary texts. As Macherey argues, the history of criticism is the history of its unceasing attempts to deny or repress the materiality of the text in order to avoid having to explain it through its causes.

We are now in a position to understand some of the difficulties readers of *A Theory of Literary Production* faced, above all the account of the act of reading that Macherey shared (and had developed in common) with Althusser, which the latter called "symptomatic reading." The difficulty of this account lay in part in its unfamiliar reference points (it perhaps owed more to Spinoza than to Freud or Lacan), but it was also a consequence of the fallacies outlined above, fallacies that became obstacles to reading, of which the most important were the fallacies of literary creation and authorial intention, as well as those of textual order, unity, and depth. Significantly for any understanding of Macherey's work that would place it uncomplicatedly in the context of structuralism, or even under the sign of Althusser's notion of structure, Macherey also drew a line of demarcation between two concepts of structure. He demonstrated that the concept of structure as applied to literature was in fact the site of two antagonistic notions: in one, structure was a synonym of order and harmony, initially hidden and revealed, if at all, only in the concluding moment at which the totality closes upon itself. In this view, every element in the text is assigned a function necessary to the constitution of the totality. From this conception of structure, Macherey separates out a second conception, produced in the interstices of the first: neither hidden in the work's interior nor serving as the principle of order, structure is the immanent or absent cause of the disorder specific to the work. In this way, Macherey did not simply apply Marxist and Spinozist-inflected notions of structure to literary analysis. Rather, he made literary analysis itself the privileged site of a full-fledged philosophical intervention in existing concepts of structure, structural causality, and structural necessity.

Fifty years later, as if on cue, the same positions with which Macherey engaged have been taken up again, raising questions and posing problems that, while irreducible to those that animated French philosophy and theory in the sixties, are not entirely separable from them. The critique of historicism, a renewed interest in formalism and in methods of reading, even the questions of the nature of the literary work (whether it may be understood as an object or rather as an activity or domain of research) and of the materiality of language itself have reappeared in ways that confer a new importance on *A Theory of Literary Production*. If much of this work proved resistant to interpretation, overlooked and unseen, in the French sixties and the Anglophone seventies, this may have been the case because its propositions and even its questions offered the beginning of a response to problems not yet posed as such, as if Macherey's work, after drifting through the theoretical void, would finally swerve into an encounter that would allow it to be read again and read differently.

The problematization of "the way we read now," in the last decade, which gave rise simultaneously to surface reading and distant reading, leads us back to Macherey's work, where the stated and unstated assumptions of these recent developments are explored in detail. The fact that the proponents of surface reading feel compelled to define their approach in opposition to Macherey and Althusser, even if their critique is directed against an imaginary Althusserianism, simply confirms the need for a return to *A Theory of Literary Production*, for a return to the letter of this text as well as a reconsideration of the mode of reading implied by such "returns," as Macherey himself explores in his essay on Althusser included in this volume. For these reasons, a collection devoted to new, historically and philosophically informed engagements with *A Theory of Literary Production*—that is to say, a collection that illuminates its many overlooked or misread parts and that puts them to work on contemporary problems—seems necessary to us. The contributions here are not limited to engagements with Macherey's text but include studies of literature and links to philosophy and theory that test the explanatory power of Macherey's theses. In addition to original work by a particularly distinguished group of scholars, the collection includes two recent and heretofore untranslated texts by Macherey: his postface to the new French edition of *A Theory of Literary Production* (2014) and "Reading Althusser," an analysis of the concept of symptomatic reading. Finally, we are pleased to present the most comprehensive interview ever conducted with Macherey, in which Macherey reflects on his experience at the École Normale Supérieure as Althusser's student, his practical and theoretical engagement with Marxism, his encounter with Spinoza, and the contexts of his work on literature.

The essays collected here intervene in contemporary debates in three major ways. First, as we mentioned, they grapple with the question of reading. The term "reading" has been at the center of a number of recent critical debates about the methods specific to our discipline, debates in which the term "symptomatic reading" has been put into play without the concept, as Althusser developed it, fully coming into view. For this reason, a careful examination of Althusser's reflections on the status of reading are an especially productive way into these debates. These reflections first have to be disentangled, however, from the projections that have been cast on them and from the roles they have been made to play in arguments that were not Althusser's own. The present collection does this work of disentanglement as it elaborates, through a reactivation of Macherey's work, what is most original about Althusser and Macherey's practice of reading. As a group, these essays extend Macherey's insights over and against the lines being drawn in contemporary methodological disputes.

Second, and relatedly, this collection intervenes in renewed debates over formalism, and over the politics of formal analysis. Our collection shows what Macherey's particular practice of a Marxist attention to form can contribute to these debates. It also makes the case for a materialist literary analysis, and it demonstrates how this analysis can contribute to contemporary work on race and on the politics of identification.

Finally, *Pierre Macherey and the Case of Literary Production* is addressed to scholars of Althusser and those concerned with the Althusserian legacy. Not only does it arrive on the heels of translations of Macherey's *Hegel or Spinoza* and the complete edition of *Reading Capital*, but it also joins major new critical studies of Althusser published in recent years. These studies, often influenced more or less directly by Macherey's reflections on the period of his collaboration with Althusser (1961–78), and on the relation of their project to the structuralism contemporaneous with it, succeeded in deepening our understanding of the Althusserian project, of its philosophical sources and engagements, and of the complexity of its relation to structuralism. This collection speaks to literary scholars in particular while highlighting the concerns these scholars share with philosophical audiences.

The first essay in the collection is a recent text written by Macherey himself. On the occasion of the French reissue of *A Theory of Literary Production* in 2014, Macherey composed a "postface" to the text, reconsidering his work after an interval of more than forty-five years. Here, with characteristic lucidity and scholarly humility, Macherey reflects on the historical and theoretical moment that led him to embark on such a polemical project, with Althusser's encouragement, at the age of twenty-eight. He describes the urgency with which he turned to literary problems, though he was trained as a philosopher, including his dissatisfaction with the contemporary practice of Marxist literary criticism. In this text we see clearly how Macherey's methods, which pit explication against interpretation and seek to trace out the complexity of literary discourse in lieu of extracting ideal meanings, were aimed at developing a materialist practice of literary criticism. This practice is made possible by the notion of literature as transformative labor, where literary production intervenes in, rather than reflects upon, the real. Ultimately, Macherey observes certain unresolved conflicts in his book, which he attributes to the demands of the theoretical conjuncture in which he was working. These include the demand for what Althusser called "scientific" rigor and for an elaboration of the "materialist dialect": the difficult articulation of causal determinism together with the mobility of dialectical becoming. Through his work on literature, Macherey was seeking to tackle the biggest philosophical problems of his generation, including the problem of how to do "philosophy" differently.

While *Reading Capital* opens with a problematization of the activity of reading, Macherey's *Theory of Literary Production*, in contrast, which extends the insights of *Reading Capital* in a literary direction, does not explicitly prioritize or theorize the term "reading." Audrey Wasser's essay, "Why Read, Macherey?," takes this lack of explicitness as a provocation to return to Macherey's text, seeking to draw out its unstated theory of reading. Following a discussion of Macherey's theory of criticism and the "illusions" at work in the production of knowledge about literary texts, she argues for a notion of reading as a kind of receptivity or resistance that remains inscribed in the activities of literary and critical writing, one that often appears in the guise of obstacles or contradictions in critical discourse. To develop this argument, she considers Macherey's work not only in light of the *Reading Capital* project and against Alain Badiou's early criticisms of treatments of the literary work as a determinate object, but also in relation to key insights of deconstruction. She puts forward the idea that, by examining the relationship between criticism and reading in Macherey's work, we might better understand the kind of knowledge produced in literary studies and the purchase this knowledge has on the real.

In "Spoken and Unspoken," Ellen Rooney argues that Macherey's text intervenes in a decisive way in contemporary arguments about surface reading, description, the post-critical, and the politics of reading. She links the belatedness of Macherey's intervention to the untimeliness of the reading process itself, which she describes as an event of reproduction with uncontrollable and unpredictable effects. In the context of contemporary debates, she shows how Macherey's work displaces both the seemingly neutral posture of reading as description, with its concomitant refusal to see the text as a theoretical object, and the inflated rhetorics of exposure and unveiling. Macherey refuses to make critique into an act of unveiling of hidden depths, and refuses, as Rooney puts it, to "make the unspoken the telos of reading." Instead, she maintains, he directs our attention to the relation between spoken and unspoken, a relation both contradictory and enabling, and the product of the inescapable work of reading.

Nathan Brown's essay, "Baudelaire's Shadow: On Poetic Determination," exemplifies and carries farther an approach to literary production and literary criticism theorized by Macherey, attempting to clarify and extend some of his major theoretical claims while also introducing the concept of "poetic determination." The latter Brown defines as the analysis of literary works at the specific level of their existence. Working through the emphasis in Macherey's *Theory of Literary Production* on the determination of the literary work, he asks what it means to say that literary writing involves, as Macherey claims, the "production of a tautology" and how a practice of literary criticism can respond to Macherey's double exigency to elaborate the work and yet leave the work as it is. To demonstrate the coherence of this apparent methodological paradox, he engages in an extended reading of Baudelaire's "Obsession," focusing in particular upon the first line of its concluding tercet, "Mais les ténèbres sont elles-même des toiles." Elaborating the conflicting sense of *toiles* in this line and demonstrating the defiguration of metaphor this entails, he draws from the reticence of Baudelaire's pivotal metaphor an account of how his work resists incorporation into the schemas of imagination or interpretation. Differentiating his approach from that of Walter Benjamin, Paul de Man, and Jean-Pierre Richard, he situates *les ténèbres* as a major Romantic signifier and reads the antimetaphorical dislocation of its figural sense as a key instance in which Romanticism is delimited by *Les fleurs du mal*.

In "What Is Materialist Analysis? Pierre Macherey's Spinozist Epistemology," Nick Nesbitt argues that Macherey's *Theory of Literary Production* should not be read as a work whose significance is limited to the realm of literary theory. According to Nesbitt, Macherey develops (in conjunction with Althusser) a radically new theory of materialism that starts with the acts of reading and writing in order to demonstrate that they have a material existence. Notions of reading as interpretation, based on the division of the literary text into surface and depth, interior and exterior, or of writing as the expression or representation of a historical reality or an authorial intention, represent an attempt to read a work by reducing it to something other than itself, whether inside or outside the work. Macherey compels us to ask what it is to read and write if we take the literary text as irreducible, as neither expression nor representation and lacking the hidden unity that criticism has been expected to retrieve. The answer, Nesbitt argues, is to be found in his engagement with the work of Spinoza and in the avowed Spinozism of Althusser, whose notion of symptomatic reading represents one of the first attempts to answer this question.

In "Blackness: N'est Pas?" David Marriott subtly draws out what he describes as "the evanescent structure of a *n'est pas*" that belongs to black being, a paradoxical and foundational effacement that "has to be thought of as more originary than either being or ideology." Interrogating a later essay by Macherey, "Figures of Interpellation in Althusser and Fanon," Marriott observes the revisions that Macherey brings to Althusser's notions of subjectivation and ideology. Yet by reading Fanon against Macherey and using the limitations of Macherey's argument to draw out the finer points of Fanon's analysis, Marriott argues for a structural, rather than experiential, understanding of the racial politics of interpellation. His focus on Fanon's reference to irony ultimately links the question of blackness to an interruption in language and being unthinkable in phenomenological terms, and gives new meaning to Macherey's treatment of the said and the unsaid in *A Theory of Literary Production*.

In "What Do We Mean When We Speak of the Surface of a Text?" Warren Montag points out that the proponents of surface reading reject approaches to the literary text that disregard the surface of the work in favor of deeper, hidden meanings. According to them, Althusser and Macherey are among the most important practitioners of a hermeneutics of suspicion that takes the surface as nothing more than a symptom, a necessarily false and misleading distortion of a truth hidden within the work. The problem with this undoubtedly overdetermined declaration is not so much that it is false, that Macherey argues exactly the opposite, namely that the text is a surface without depth, an exterior without an interior, and defines interpretation as a fallacy; the problem that haunts surface reading is, rather, the lack of a concept of the surface of a text. In the absence of such a concept, surface reading inevitably reproduces the opposition between appearance and essence, and between the apparent and the real, by confining this opposition to the surface of the text (thereby posing the question of whether such a surface is really a surface at all).

Operating on Spinoza's principle that "we have a true idea" that a concept (or concepts) of the surface of the text already exists, if only in the practical state, Montag approaches the question of the surface by asking what meanings and functions are currently attributed to it. At the moment Macherey rehabilitated the notion of surface (separating it from its semantic associations with superficiality and false appearances) as a way of excluding any reference to a textual depth, a number of his contemporaries were engaged in a similar enterprise—above all, Lacan and Deleuze. Macherey's discussion of surface is best understood as an intervention against theories of hidden meaning, hidden form or structure, and finally against the dominant notion of literature as reflection or mimesis. In each case, Macherey does not simply reject these concepts, but shows the contradictions at work within them. Finally, Spinoza's critique of the interpretation of scripture in the *Theological-Political Treatise* is thoroughly woven into Macherey's arguments and forms the condition of possibility of the concept of surface that emerges from his work.

In "Reading Althusser," translated here for the first time, Macherey applies the notion of symptomatic reading to Althusser's own treatment of the notion in the introductory section of *Reading Capital*. He begins by confronting one of the specters of Althusser, a remnant or revenant that determined, in part, the reading of his project. The idea that the progress of historical materialism or psychoanalysis depended on a "return to" Marx and Freud provoked a long series of critiques, many of which argued that Althusser sought to confine Marxism to a realm of theory from which practice had been all but excluded. In fact, Macherey maintains, in opposition, that the return to Marx is a return to an object that has never been present to theory, precisely because the practical element within which *Capital* took shape left its mark on the text itself in the form of absences, gaps, and fissures, that is, in what it cannot say in the course of saying what it says. To return to Marx is thus to return to the event it constitutes, an event unevenly developed and traversed by contradiction, and to place ourselves within it to think its discoveries and impasses.

To do so effectively, however, requires that we abandon a model of knowledge as vision and replace it, if provisionally, with the model of reading. Vision takes as its object the reality that is presented to it and which it must describe. The division of this reality into surface and depth or appearance and essence belongs to this model. To see only the surface is "partial vision"; to see into the depths is "complete vision." The notion of knowledge as reading prevents us from taking the object of analysis as given, ready to be known. Instead, reading is a process without origin or destination, "a circle that turns indefinitely around itself, producing difference in repeating itself (as one would say in Deleuze's language)." But if reading is always a reading of others reading others without end, it must be understood not simply as a decoding of what is read, but by the act of intervening in it by drawing lines of demarcation that transform it. A symptomatic reading refuses to overlook the disorder of texts, the absences that necessarily accompany what is present, and takes texts as constitutively incomplete, unfinished and unfinishable. It is here, in the interstices and fissures that are exhibited in the literal existence of the text, in the internal limits that separate it into discordant parts, that history is present, the absent cause that exists only in its effects.

The collection closes with a lively interview with Macherey, conducted by Joseph Serrano in 2019. Macherey describes his early philosophical training—including his first encounter with Spinoza and the beginnings of his relationship with Althusser—as well as his evolving ties to the French Communist Party, his thoughts on Althusser's relationship to Maoism, and the particular conditions that led him to write *A Theory of Literary Production*. The interview culminates with Macherey's reflections on his most recent work at the intersection of literature and philosophy, and on the ongoing importance of Althusser's thought.

Of particular interest to us is the role Macherey accords to the activity of reading in this narrative. He recounts how, as an undergraduate, he was fortuitously guided in a study of Spinoza's *Ethics* "*à la lettre*," which for him meant discovering an experience of the text as an event of thought rather than as a fixed doctrine. He describes the collective reading of Marx that Althusser spearheaded not as a simple return to the past but as an act of creative renewal and intervention in the present. In both cases, reading is portrayed as a dynamic act and as a mode of response to what is already dynamic in a text or system of thought. Considering Althusser's encounter with Maoism, Macherey goes on to show how the complexity of this encounter took the form of a close reading of Mao on the question of contradiction, from which Althusser drew key insight for his own analysis of conjunctures. Finally, Macherey relates his early turn to literature as a way of pushing against two reigning ideologies of the time: of structuralism in the social sciences and of reflection as a form of thought in Marxism. Macherey turned to literary study, we might say, as a way of setting one practice of reading against another, pitting a nonfinalist, materialist practice of reading against an idealist, reflective reading that relied on models of transcendence or depth. These two versions of reading arguably reappear in the confrontation Macherey sets up between two systems of thought in *Hegel or Spinoza*. In the conclusion of the interview, Macherey comments on a formula of Spinoza's of which Althusser was particularly fond: *habeo enim ideam veram* (for we have a true idea). Althusser's reading of this formula is an interesting caution against taking reading for granted as much as it is a call to reread the knots of contexts and conditions that give rise to all ideas.

Notes

1. Fredric Jameson, *The Political Unconscious: Narrative as a Socially Symbolic Act* (Ithaca, NY: Cornell University Press, 1982), 10. Thanks to the anonymous reader for pointing out this affinity.

2. For more on these disagreements, see Warren Montag, *Althusser and His Contemporaries* (Durham: Duke University Press, 2013), ch. 5, esp. 73–79.

3. Louis Althusser, "Marxism and Humanism," in *For Marx*, trans. Ben Brewster (New York: Verso, 2005), 230.

4. Louis Althusser, *Lettres à Franca (1961–1973)* (Paris: Stock/Imec, 1998), 200.

5. Translation modified, with reference given to the page number of the English (2006 edition) followed by the numbered paragraph of the French (2014 edition).

Postface to *A Theory of Literary Production*

✦

Pierre Macherey

A Theory of Literary Production was published in 1966 by Maspero in its Théorie series, which Althusser had created the previous year and in which *For Marx* had already appeared, as well as the two volumes of the collective work *Reading Capital*, to which I also contributed. Apart from one detailed and on the whole favorable review by Raymond Jean in *Le Monde*,[1] my rather atypical book was hardly acknowledged by the press, nor was it much commented on or reviewed by specialists of literature.[2] This didn't prevent it from reaching a fairly large public or from being translated, in whole or in part, into a number of other languages (German, English, Italian, Spanish, Japanese, Korean, etc.). In 1980, when it reached a sixth edition, fifteen thousand copies were circulating in France, which was more than respectable for a work of this kind. In 1985, Maspero removed it from its catalog, and Éditions La Découverte, which had taken over the publishing house from Maspero, did not put out another edition. For almost twenty-five years, then, it was unavailable in the original French, though it remained in circulation in other countries, in different languages from the one in which it had been written.[3] I am particularly grateful to Anthony Glinoer for proposing to republish the original version of this book in electronic form, in the Littérature series of La Bibliotheque Idéale des Sciences Sociales [Social Sciences Virtual Library],[4] which will allow it to embark on a new life perhaps and give it a new chance to put its claims to the test.

With the intention of introducing this book—the first I ever wrote—on the occasion of its reissue, I was led to reread it after an interval of more than forty-five years, which I must admit was a rather disconcerting experience. Yet I cannot say this distance made it so foreign to me that I could view it in a completely neutral, indifferent, and thus objective way. It has served for me as the point of departure for work that continued after it, work that may have followed different paths but never completely left this book behind, continuing along with it in a certain way, even if it wasn't clear to me exactly how. To account for, to try to understand, what I had originally wanted to do in this project, to evaluate to what degree I might have succeeded, is a difficult enterprise now, but at the same time an indispensable and even inevitable one: in effect, it forces me to articulate the relationship I have continued to maintain with literary questions, all while practicing and teaching philosophy these past forty years. A philosopher by training, I have worked in a discipline that, according to the way courses of study are defined in France, diverges from literature, even serves as a sort of rival discipline to it, or at least is not associated with it or seen as complementary to it in any way. At the time, I thus approached the problem of literature from outside, without any special preparation. This gave me a certain margin of freedom, but at the same time exposed me to the risks of amateurism, whose consequences I perceive today better than I did back then, when, borne along by the intoxication of the theoretical "moment" of the '60s, and encouraged by Althusser, I believed I could bring a new perspective to bear on questions of literature, all the newer because of the shift in terrain. I must admit that, returning to certain sentences I wrote under those conditions, I no longer fully grasp what it was I wanted to say, nor the reasons that made me formulate things thus, a fact that a fortiori prevents me from justifying myself completely on the subject, even as I assume responsibility for the project and for what resulted from it, under these conditions of a critical assessment of the book's contents, of its limitations, even of the insufficiencies of its realization.

In order to understand the nature of the rather bold enterprise I undertook in writing *A Theory of Literary Production*, we first have to consider it in context. When I wrote this book, what would later be called "literary theory," whose front-runners in France would be people like Roland Barthes and Gérard Genette, did not exist organically. New techniques of analysis, such as those showing how literature used artificial means to produce a "reality effect,"[5] for example, existed only in the state of preparatory sketches circulating among select initiates in avant-garde journals like *Tel Quel*[6] or *Change*.[7] Still dominant were explanatory models that relied either on a spiritualist aesthetics of the individual artist, who was credited with the power of rolling out his creations unconditionally in an ideal space in order to "express himself," or on a political aesthetics of engaged literature, Jean-Paul Sartre's legacy, where the writer was seen as intervening in specific contexts while still maintaining his freedom, so that his actions made manifest his pure "being-in-the-world." The latest representative of the Marxist current in aesthetics was Lucien Goldmann, who had introduced certain ideas of Georg Lukács's in France by showing the necessity of discerning the determining role of social groups behind the efforts of individual writers.[8] In this conjuncture marked by a certain imprecision—the laborers of the concept were not in abundant supply, and their interventions were still scattered— those who claimed to be adherents of Marxism were mired in the quarrel over realism, following the directives of the laughable Garaudy, who was officially responsible for the culture and philosophy of the PCF [the French Communist Party].[9] Their main concern was the question of how, and under what conditions, literature could come to "reflect" the real, and what value should be assigned to such reflections. Aragon, from the heart of the besieged fortress of his journal *Les lettres françaises* [*French Letters*] tried to make his voice heard on the subject, but years of allegiance to the party and to the party's propaganda had condemned him to a double language that prevented him from defining without ambiguity a line that would enable him to abandon the label of "realism" and the mass of false problems posed under its auspices.[10]

It was in this intellectual field, more or less well mapped out and in which it was not obvious how I should orient myself, that my intervention was situated. To characterize the latter, we can follow three different lines of analysis. The first, negative, line draws attention to the polemical aspect of my project, to the way it defined itself in relation to the adversaries it sought to oppose. The second takes the opposite approach, interrogating my work on the basis of the positive objectives it gave itself as it sought to pose the question of literature on new terrain: what was it that I was seeking to do, exactly? What different idea of the literary was I trying to put forward? The third examines the specific means I employed, more or less effectively and within certain limits, to give concrete form to this idea by detailing its implications, which were far from self-evident.

Let's begin with the first approach. What was I struggling against, exactly? What mode of apprehending the phenomenon of literature was I contesting? Retrospectively, it seems to me that what I was denouncing was, above all, submitting literature to an interpretive model based on the univocal—and by that fact reductive, simplifying—norm of meaning, the norm of the real presence of meaning, destined to be consumed as is, in its substantial plenitude. If we retain such an interpretive model, the province of a hermeneutics for which meaning is simply given, preexisting the modalities of its communication, then the work as a specific, textual organization becomes no more than the transmission of a content that transcends it. It possesses no reality in itself but at best serves as the support for a mystical, sacred revelation of the meaning that traverses the work and transfixes it. Against this way of approaching the productions of literature, which is, in the last instance, religious, I wrote:

> The work does not contain a meaning which it conceals by giving it a finished form. The necessity of the work is founded on the multiplicity of its meanings; to explain the work is to recognize and differentiate the principle of this diversity. The postulate of the unity of the work which, more or less explicitly, has always haunted the enterprise of criticism, must be denounced. (Part 1, 169/88)[11]

> The book is not the extension of a meaning; it is constructed from the incompatibility of multiple meanings, this being the most solid link by which it is attached to reality, in a tense and ever-renewed confrontation. (Part 1, 172/89)

On this basis, I hoped to direct critical attention to what, within a work, serves as the index not of a presence but of an absence, an absence that constitutes the work in its materiality—that is to say, in its irreducible complexity. This index is what I called the "lack" [*défaut*] in the work, meaning that the work is meaningful not by reason of what it says or represents in the manner of a content to be transmitted, but because it reveals a limit that is impossible to cross, a limit the work runs up against and against which, in a certain sense, it shatters. The space of literature is one where conflicts of meaning play out, and far from proposing imaginary resolutions for these conflicts, the work gives these conflicts free rein while making them visible, or rather legible, providing a site for the elaboration of lacunary assemblages, where what is empty makes possible the comprehension of what is full. What is given to be read in a literary work, insofar as we refrain from reducing the work to a simple and univocal communication of a "meaning," is thus less what the work says than what it does not say and what it is prevented from saying, even in the guise of a latent meaning awaiting the conditions of its actualization. What it does not say, it does not say at all, or rather says it in the form of the "not-at-all," in the form of a radical impossibility whose consequences it deploys across the folds and erasures of its text, a text that is consequently never adequate to itself or to what it wants to say, the latter being exactly what it does not succeed in saying. Following this logic to its conclusion, we could say that literature practices, above all, the cultivation of a non-sense, of the failure of the advent of sense, a sense whose center it refuses to penetrate, approaching it instead from the periphery, from the knot formed by the conflictual network that makes it exist in its complexity, in its disparateness and fragmentation, or in its dissemination, to put it in Derrida's terms. "Closed and interminable, complete and endlessly re-beginning, coiled around an absent center that it can neither conceal nor reveal, diffuse and gathered together: the discourse of the work" (Part 1, 54/30).

Of course, it wasn't possible for me to remain with this inadequate conception of literature. I had to go farther to show that this "lack" constitutive of the literary work, the lack preventing it from being completely in accord with itself and existing in the form of a harmonious totality, was positively (and here I arrive at the second approach to my work) and paradoxically what permitted the work to be made while being unmade, while being dispersed. The work is made when it constructs, with a maximum degree of precision, the incompatibility or conflict on which it is built and which defines its true element. Rereading my book today, I am struck by a sentence that is rendered a bit enigmatic by its evasiveness, but which reminds me of what preoccupied me most with respect to literature: "In every book, something happens" (Part 1, 82/46).

What I wanted to point out, to put front and center, was what "happens" in a book, insofar as the latter genuinely bears the marks of the literary and thus cannot be reduced to a repository of information, a catalog of impressions, or an account of various opinions. In other words, I sought to valorize a conception of the literary work that was not static but dynamic, one that identified the work as the site or terrain of the unfolding of an active process from which it derives the necessity proper to it. The work, far from fixing this process, grasps it in the course of its trajectory, in the activity of its unfolding, an activity that continues with the reader who perpetuates it in turn, exposing it to his own point of view in a way that is both free and determined, yet without being constrained or closed off. This is why the literary work—and this is its essential characteristic—is never completely identical with itself, and it is precisely this noncoincidence that gives it its value:[12] it is as if, within the very limits imposed by its textual inscription, it moves, thereby opening a transformative perspective on a process through which, by virtue of traversing or at least attempting to traverse it, it participates in the movements of the real world. Consequently, what interested me in literary works was the set of tensions that simultaneously tore them apart and animated them from within, projecting them toward something else—but what?—that wasn't easy to identify; and it was this difficulty, testifying to an essential ambiguity, that stimulated my interest in literature and its unevenly developed productions. These, I wrote, "go beyond, or fall short of, the distinction between the true and the false" (Part 1, 116/64), a feature that distinguishes literature from other discursive formations, particularly from scientific knowledge, for which the verification of truth is crucial.

To put it in slightly different terms, what I sought to capture was a literariness in act, one that could not be confused with the mute forms of a canvas painting. This is why, when I put forward the notion of "literary production," the reference to production was supposed to work on two fronts: if, on the one hand, it underscored the necessity of relating the literary work to the conditions under which it was produced (and reproduced), which was indispensable for dispelling once and for all the mirage of meaning and of meaning's creative spontaneity, it seemed on the other hand to point to the productive and, as I said earlier, transformational dimension of the literary work, insofar as the work is more than a cultural artifact, evidence of an epoch whose image it only has to register with more or less accuracy. Instead of aiming to reveal a block of meaning that is supposed to lie behind the work and support it, I sought to follow the divergent lines that originated within the work itself, lines whose very entanglement was the best indication of their purchase, however indirect, on historical reality, whose instability and mutability they revealed. Since I wanted to offer an analysis of works that foregrounded this productivity, that grasped it in its course, it was no accident that the main literary examples I chose were Balzac and Verne. These two writers were particularly sensitive to the ongoing transformations of their epoch,[13] and they undertook, employing the means of fictional narrativity, to accompany these mutations by situating themselves at their margins, to reconstruct their contingent and unpredictable course, partly opened, dangerously, onto the unknown.

When I consider my arguments now, rereading my work, it seems to me that this was the direction I was going in, instinctively and even intuitively, as it were. But at the time, in the context proper to the "Marxist" culture reconceptualized by Althusser, and responding to the desire for "scientificity," if I may put it that way, a desire evinced by the reference to Theory with a capital *T*, in whose name a materialist explanation was pitted against the claims of hermeneutics, which we openly scorned for its idealism. Now, this return to an explanatory paradigm that was supposed to yield privileged access to scientific knowledge was grounded in what I would be tempted today to call an act of faith—a prejudice in favor of a total theory of causality. And consequently, even if this aspect of the notion of production was not, ultimately, my main concern, I was led to place a strong emphasis on the realization of the work in the sense of a strict determinism, one whose rigidity makes it difficult to grasp the mobility proper to the processes at work, which are by definition unstable. Without being fully conscious of it, I was confronting an aporia inherent in the project of the "materialist dialectic," a project that faced an insoluble dilemma between the following: either to think the dialectic on the basis of materialism, and thus to refer it to a causal determinism, or to think materialism on the "basis" of the dialectic (but here the term "base" or "basis" becomes inadequate) and thus to open the possibility of a mobility without assignable end, one that prioritizes becoming over being, whose materiality and the weight attached to it are dissolved. I remember when Althusser reviewed the manuscript of my book to prepare it for publication, at the time preoccupied for strategic reasons with returning the dialectic to the orbit of materialism to prevent its assimilation into bourgeois thought, he had added, in a few well-chosen places, the adjective "determinate" so that things would be perfectly clear in this regard.[14] There was a difficulty there, to say the least, that I was not able to surmount, and which marks the limits within which my project remained enclosed.

Now we come to the third approach to my work, concerning neither the position I opposed nor my larger objectives, but the means I employed to put into operation a different conception of the literary. Above all, what was at stake for me was to apprehend literature as an activity and a labor, which in turn led to an evacuation or at least a modification of the metaphor of the mirror, which otherwise restricts literature to a contemplative and ultimately passive role. Now, a labor, a real activity of production, cannot be accomplished without material to be labored on. To say that literature intervenes in the world, however, to say that it contributes to transforming the world instead of contentedly leaving it in the state it is in, still leaves open the question of where this intervention is situated and on what objects it leaves its mark. In other words, to claim that literature intervenes directly in the "real" instead of creating more or less faithful representations of it doesn't really bring anything new to the table, because when we take the "real" as a given totality, we are already dealing with an abstraction, a fiction lacking effective content. To say that the world is real is ultimately a pleonasm devoid of meaning. What I was seeking was thus, above all, to identify where and how literature grasps the composite whole that constitutes a historical world in its becoming, grasps it in order to penetrate to its depths and make it the object of its labor. Since the question was that of the object on which literature acts, it seemed to me that this object—and this was the hypothesis on which my entire inquiry rested—was ideology: the diverse set of discourses and representations that spontaneously constitute, to use Marx's expression from *The German Ideology*, the "language of social life." To put it otherwise: for me, the function of literature consisted not in adding yet another layer of superstructure—and in the Marxist vulgate, literature, or art in general, is no more than one more superstructure added to the others, to the juridical, political, religious, etc.—but in grabbing hold, in some way, of this specific sphere of collective existence that a superstructure is, this more or less coherent system of representations that accompanies its unfolding. It does this not to repeat or reiterate it but to submit it to a test, to press it, in a concrete sense, to explode it into its *disjecta membra*, even if this means gathering up the pieces later, freely and at a distance, to recompose them.

In short, what literature allows us to see is not the world, the human soul, or social life as such as immediate realities, but the body of representations through which these "realities" are grasped, always partially, obliquely, and with some distortion, because they exist in the service of particular interests and in the proximity of the play of social conflicts. Literature is not one representation among others, but a certain manner of staging those representations already imposed by history, the result being to loosen the grip, even in certain cases to decompose, the established order by means of which, at any given moment, appearances are imposed as incontrovertible truths. In my book, I used the metaphor of the broken mirror to underscore the critical, demystifying function of literature, a function that, under certain conditions, produces not beautiful works of art that conform to ideal models but a gap, distance, or play that allows these works to contest the given and its representations, to question their validity and, by doing so, to shed light on them.

> Within the work, a relation of contestation is instituted, and not merely a relation of contiguity, between the work and its ideological content. (Part 2, 52/138)

> The spontaneous ideology in which men live (spontaneous not in the way it is produced but in what men believe they have access to) is not simply reflected in the mirror of a book; it is shattered in this mirror, sent back, turned inside out, insofar as being set-into-work gives it a status that differs from a state of consciousness. By nature disdaining the naïve view of the world, art, or at least literature, makes myth and illusion into visible objects. (Part 2, 74/148–49)

> A work takes shape against an ideology as much as on the basis of
> one. Implicitly, it contributes to denouncing it, or at least to tracing
> its limits. . . . Its function is to present ideology in a form that is not
> itself ideological (Part 2, 75–76/149)[15]

As I followed this line of thought, it seemed to me possible to attribute to
literature a certain kind of knowledge: if, in Althusser's terms, ideology "represents the imaginary relationship of individuals to their material conditions
of existence,"[16] a definition that confers on ideology a certain material existence, then we can conceive of literature as penetrating this existence in a way
that reveals its underside, thus shattering it. Far from simply repeating the
imaginary relationship of individuals to their material conditions of existence
and thereby confirming the appearance of things as they are, decorating them
with the prestige of art and rendering them easier to digest, it shakes up this
relationship by interrogating it, exposing its fault lines, pointing to its inconsistencies. It makes this relationship appear *as* imaginary. This perspective led
me to emphasize the negativity at work in the labor of literature, a labor that
works to disturb rather than reflect the self-representation of the established
order. Consequently, the particular form of knowledge that literature offers,
by means of the labor proper to it, is not of a contemplative or descriptive
kind. Literature prepares us to see things otherwise, catalyzing the process
of their transformation: not by photographing reality, which in the best of
cases would imply that literature has a documentary value, but by revealing
the cracks in systems of perception and interpretation that normally give us
access to things. If literature is knowledge, it is a knowledge that is also a
practice: instead of reflecting from a distance, it is a specific manner of acting on, and in, the drama of the world. This orientation owes a lot to Brecht.
    Restoring a cognitive dimension to the literary has several consequences, one
being to remove literature from the exclusive jurisdiction of the aesthetic, where
supposedly beautiful works are granted a special status, valorized because they
are well made and they impress us with their perfect coherence. In addition,
the hierarchy traditionally separating major and minor literature ceases to be
relevant, and we come to consider that what is specific to literature is not only
visible in the margins of the institution but has at its disposal a kind of surfeit of
visibility. It is in this spirit that I undertook my study "Jules Verne: The Faulty
Narrative" [included in *A Theory of Literary Production*], and this at a time
when Verne had been consigned to the category of adventure novel, ghettoized
as children's literature, and however surprising it might seem to us today, his
oeuvre was still far from being considered a classic in its own right, one that
could be published in the prestigious Pléiade collection. It was representative
of what Deleuze calls a "minor" literature, all the more revealing of what literature is insofar as it sheds light on this institution from its margins, not from
its center, and in that way refutes the myth of "Literature" as an unconditioned
entity existing in and for itself, propped up by a repertory of eternal models.

In the work I have subsequently dedicated to literature, in particular my book *The Object of Literature*,[17] published twenty-five years after *A Theory of Literary Production*, I turned my attention to the relation between literature and philosophy, which led me to put forward the notion of a "literary philosophy." I wanted to depart from the hermeneutic program, from a treatment of literature or of the literary text as an object on which philosophy reflects in order to appropriate its meaning. The notion of a "literary philosophy" raised the question of how one could philosophize *with* literature, alongside it, or in its vicinity, and of what kind of philosophy would come out of this practice, which was by definition marginal. According to this notion, literature is not simply philosophy in a different form, philosophy transcribed into a different language by means of an operation that leaves it fundamentally unchanged. Rather, literature becomes a provocation to practice philosophy differently, to begin differently, to construct a new philosophical relation, even, one that would modify where and how philosophical speculation take place because it deprives these speculations of their purely speculative character. Philosophizing with literature is, above all, not philosophizing *on* literature, tacking onto it prefabricated categories that distort its free play by directing its movements, that level its uneven surface with abstractions and return it to the order of the already known. Nor is it looking for scraps of philosophy that can be easily lifted out of works of literature because they have an added-on existence to begin with. Rather, it entails what I called "exercises in literary philosophy": embarking on reading works that are called literary partly out of convention, without claiming to elucidate their ultimate meaning—because an "ultimate meaning" is precisely what they do not have—and from this reading derive the impulse to do philosophy otherwise, yet without replacing the existing ways philosophers, who are themselves writers of a singular type, work. It accompanies them in their work without promising to complete or perfect it. It means offering different orientations, or new ways of posing traditional philosophical problems without being able to offer solutions—to the extent philosophical problems are meant to be resolved, which is far from certain.

In short, I did not have to take off my "philosopher's" hat in order to concern myself with literature. Literature has always interested me for reasons that transcend, and in a certain way transgress, the distinction and the hierarchy of genres. That's why my approach has been atypical, and as such, perilous, from the beginning: it was practiced in the spirit of inquiry, and I cannot affirm with certainty whether or not it has led somewhere. To use an expression that Althusser was fond of: my goal was to "shake things up" [*faire bouger les choses*]. It's not up to me to determine the extent to which this goal has been realized.

July 2012

*Translated by Warren
Montag and Audrey Wasser*

Notes

This postface was written for the 2014 edition of *Pour une théorie de la production littéraire* (Lyon: ENS Éditions, 2014). Open-access at https://books .openedition.org/enseditions/628. —Trans.

1. Raymond Jean, "Deux regards sur l'écriture: Création ou production?," *Le Monde*, November 8, 1967. —Trans.

2. In a September 14, 1966, letter to Franca Madonia, Althusser notes: "P. Macherey's book on literature will come out in the collection in November: it will be surprising." *Lettres à Franca (1961–1973)* (Paris: Stock/Imec, 1998), 714.

3. Routledge recently published a new English paperback edition in the Routledge Classics series [in 2006. —Trans.].

4. Bibliothèque Idéale des Sciences Sociales (Bi2S) is a collection of electronic and print reprints of important works of philosophy and the social sciences, published by Éditions ENS de Lyon. The reprints are all accompanied by new scholarly prefaces (*Pour une théorie* is prefaced by Anthony Glinoer), and many include additional new commentaries (such as Macherey's own postface), translations, or interviews with the authors. The collection is available on the web at Open Edition Books: http://books.openedition.org/enseditions/177. —Trans.

5. Macherey is referring to Roland Barthes's 1968 essay by this name, reprinted in *The Rustle of Language*, trans. Richard Howard, ed. François Wahl (Berkeley: University of California Press, 1989), 141–48. —Trans.

6. *Tel Quel* (1960–82) was a literary journal published by Éditions du Seuil, as well as an intellectual movement in its own right, with a number of associated intellectuals and activities. Philippe Sollers was a founding member; subsequent collaborators included Roland Barthes and Julia Kristeva. The journal was structuralist and Maoist in orientation, and published work by Roland Barthes, Georges Bataille, Jacques Derrida, Michel Foucault, Gérard Genette, Bernard-Henri Lévy, Nathalie Sarraute, and Tzvetan Todorov, among others. —Trans.

7. *Change* (1967–83), a literary journal likewise published by Éditions du Seuil, was founded by Jean-Pierre Faye following a split in the editorial board of *Tel Quel*. *Change* denounced what it saw as right-wing tendencies at *Tel Quel*, and opposed the structuralism of the latter with more dynamic models drawn from Chomskyan linguistics. —Trans.

8. See, notably, Lucien Goldmann, *Pour une sociologie du roman* (Paris: Gallimard, 1964). —Trans.

9. Roger Garaudy (1913–2012) was a philosopher, resistance fighter, and leader in the PCF in the 1960s, expelled in 1970. He subsequently became a Holocaust denier, and in 1998 was found guilty by the French government of denial of crimes against humanity and incitement to racial hatred. —Trans.

10. Louis Aragon was a poet, intellectual, and longtime member of the PCF. A leading artist of the Dada and surrealist movements in the 1920s, Aragon turned later to socialist realism as a tool of social critique. From 1953 to 1972, Aragon was the director of *French Letters*, a literary journal that had originated as a clandestine publication of the French Resistance and continued after the war with support from the PCF. —Trans.

11. All translations of *Pour une théorie de la production littéraire* are modified, with references given to the numbered paragraphs of the French (2014 edition) followed by page numbers of the English translation (2006 edition). —Trans.

12. This had been suggested to me by my reading of Jorge Luis Borges, whose work obsessively turns around the idea of a suspended, incomplete, indefinitely deferred identity. In the margins of the remarkable story "The Garden of Forking Paths" from *Fictions*, I noted, "Each book remains profoundly different from itself because it implies an indefinite possibility of 'bifurcations'" (Part 3, 213/279).

13. I would point out that the term "epoch" is a technical one in Macherey's work: in "Lenin, Critic of Tolstoy," for example, Macherey demonstrates how the historical "epoch" of 1861–1905 in Russia is not given as an object of knowledge but must be constructed on the basis of careful analysis. —Trans.

14. For example, when I read in my work, "The literary work gives the measure of a difference, makes visible a determinate absence" (Part 1, 171/89). Or "The work exists above all by its determinate absences, by what it does not say, by its relation to what is other than itself" (Part 1, 118/172). I am almost certain it was Althusser who turned those "absences" into "determinate absences," wanting to prevent them from foundering in the *Abgrund* of the unknown and indefinite, in other words of the negative, which eludes "science" and its causal explanations.

15. This analysis, like the one referred to in notes 12 and 14, was presented in the conclusion of my study of the critical texts Lenin devoted to the work of Tolstoy.

16. Macherey substitutes the term "material" for "real" in this quotation, combining two theses of Althusser's from "Ideology and Ideological State Apparatuses." In the first, Althusser writes, "Ideology represents the imaginary relationship of individuals to their real conditions of existence"; in the second, "Ideology has a material existence." From Louis Althusser, *On the Reproduction of Capitalism: Ideology and Ideological State Apparatuses*, trans. G. M. Goshgarian (New York: Verso, 2014), 256–58. —Trans.

17. This work represents the thesis that Macherey defended in 1991 for his *docteur ès Lettres*. Literally, the French title *À quoi pense la littérature?* means "What is literature thinking about?" —Trans.

Why Read, Macherey?

✦

Audrey Wasser

When, in *Reading Capital*, Althusser held up Marx's *Capital* as an object for philosophy, he held it up under the sign of *reading*. In so doing, he proposed reading as an activity proper to philosophy, if not as a new understanding altogether of philosophy's proper activity. No doubt this is a surprising gesture if we are used to thinking about reading as an inherently literary activity, and less so a philosophical one. It may be all the more surprising that Macherey, whose *Theory of Literary Production* set to work the collective insights of *Reading Capital* on a series of questions about the nature of literature, did not announce as his project the elaboration of a theory of reading. Reading is not absent from his discussion—it appears occasionally in disparaging references to a "simple reading" or a "facile reader"—but other terms and concepts take center stage.

What does *reading* name, then, in this nexus of texts from 1965–66, if it designates an activity shared by philosophers and literary critics alike? And what does it fall short of naming? Answering these questions will return us to the letter of *A Theory of Literary Production* to elaborate a theory of reading, a theory that belongs to this text even where the text does not explicitly state it, much as Althusser sought to divulge the philosophy that belonged to Marx's text without being uttered in it. Is there a theory of reading present in Macherey's text, in other words, in the very form of its being unstated? In a 1976 interview, Macherey remarked that he wanted *A Theory of Literary Production* to speak to teachers and students of literature, to those engaged in practical problems of reading and writing about literary texts.[1] Those of us whose disciplinary formation is indeed literary—as mine is—might wonder, further, what insights this philosopher writing in 1966 has to offer literary scholars, especially to scholars in the present, and to those of us working in the specific conditions of the American university. What do we stand to gain from this philosopher telling us about reading, and what do we glimpse in his own reading practices?

"Reading" is not Macherey's central term, but "criticism" is, a fact that may be surprising given a glance at his book title, one that would seem to anticipate strong claims about the nature of the literary as such, or at least about the production rather than the reception of literary texts. At least this is true for the English title *A Theory of Literary Production*. The French *Pour une théorie de la production littéraire* does not announce a full-blown theory but suggests, more accurately, that the book will take on the preparatory and critical work of clearing the ground for such a theory.[2] Macherey does not begin with claims about the nature of literature, though he will arrive at them by the end of his argument. Instead, he begins with a question: not "What is literature?" but "What is literary criticism?"

    What he signals in this opening, then, is not the advent of a theory of literature but the unfolding of an inquiry into how the literary object is appropriated and reproduced in critical discourse. *A Theory of Literary Production* is, first and foremost, a theory of literary criticism. In other words, it investigates a practice of responding to literary works that surely involves a certain activity of reading without being reducible to it. My goal in what follows is to bring out the difference between reading and criticism that remains largely unstated in Macherey's argument; I do so by demonstrating that reading, for Macherey, can function neither as a mere synonym for criticism—that is, the difference between reading and criticism is not simply terminological—nor as a wholly opposed activity, such that we could always pit a good criticism against a bad reading. Rather, what goes by the name "reading" needs to be grasped as a necessary moment within critical practice, one that calls out for its own theory. In the end, I situate this particular treatment of reading not only in light of the *Reading Capital* project, but also in relation to some of the most developed theories of reading in literary studies, namely those of Paul de Man.

A Theory of Critical Production

Throughout *A Theory of Literary Production*, Macherey takes care to distinguish between the passive apprehension of a literary text and the positive construction of knowledge about it (106/58).[3] "Criticism," done the right way, is his name for a productive activity, an activity that produces at least two things: it gives rise to a critical discourse *about* a literary object, and it gives rise to a literary object *within* this discourse, insofar as this object is able to serve as an object of knowledge.

    With the question of criticism at the fore, Macherey begins by diagnosing three major illusions governing critical practice. These illusions—or fallacies, as the English translator calls them—all serve as obstacles to critical knowledge. Most important for our purposes, they throw into relief Macherey's positive claims about how literary criticism should be carried out. The "empiricist fallacy," first of all, confuses the object of criticism with an empirically given fact and the task of criticism with the "art or technique" of approaching said fact (3/5). The truth of a work is assumed to be given, to lie in wait for the critic; criticism becomes the art of accurate description, smoothing the way for a reading that is only a passive consumption (22/15). The second fallacy, the "normative fallacy," evaluates the literary work by holding it up to an external standard, as if the critic were writing "Could do better" in the work's margins (28/18). In this way, the empiricist and the normative critic are mirror images of one another: the empiricist conflates a description of the work with the work itself and pushes aside the distinctiveness of critical knowledge. The normative critic, conversely, conflates the actual literary work with an ideal model or standard, pushing aside the distinctiveness of the work as it is (here Macherey speaks of a "marriage of criticism with its model" (31/19). The normative critic ultimately makes a kind of empiricist mistake, though, by failing to question the givenness of his models (39/21).[4]

Finally, the third fallacy, the "interpretive fallacy," substitutes a unitary kernel of meaning for the multiple and discordant forms of expression of the actual work, ignoring the real complexity of the text in favor of a truth supposedly buried in its depths. Employing a Platonistic and moralizing dichotomy that pits the falseness of appearance against the truth of interiority, the interpretive critic seeks to replace the language of the text with a discourse that is not its own (162/85), performing, in this way, a version of what Cleanth Brooks called the "heresy of paraphrase."[5]

In Macherey's catalog of critical fallacies, then, we see that what is obscured is either the reality of the literary work in its textual complexity (here, the normative and the interpretive) or the reality of the operations that give rise to the work, including the operation of criticism itself (the empiricist). Against the normative and interpretive fallacies—against the abstraction of ideal and unitary models—Macherey seeks a criticism that grasps the work as a concrete reality. Against the empiricist fallacy—against the illusion of givenness—Macherey advocates for a criticism that examines the specific and complex processes that give rise to a work as an object of knowledge, processes in which, he argues, the critic herself participates.

The aim of literary criticism—this is Macherey's argument—is to explain how a literary work is produced. It is, therefore, the task of the literary critic to establish the chain of reasons and events by which a work comes into being. These reasons and events include what is usually meant by "social context," but they extend beyond it to include images, languages, and other books:[6] the contours of the work, he writes, are carved out by "the allusive presence of other books against which it is constructed" (172/89). And more generally, "the work has its beginning in a break with the usual ways of speaking and writing" (109/60). I use both "reasons" and "events" as synonyms for "conditions" because Macherey the Spinoza scholar follows a rationalist line of investigation here, treating the conditions of a work as something that must themselves be rationally constructed. The critic must decide what is relevant, in other words; she articulates the conditions of the work in a discourse that differs from the actual work just as the definition of a triangle differs from an actual triangle. Indeed, Macherey describes the very notion of condition as "profoundly misunderstood," for a condition is often taken "in the empirical sense" rather than as a "rational principle" by means of which the work is known and measured (103/55–56). As Macherey understands it, a condition marks the limit and the specific difference that makes a thing available to thought. The elaboration of a literary work's production, criticism entails the positive knowledge of this difference.

In this way, literary study finds its affinity with rationalist philosophy, sharing in the idea that to explicate something is to address the necessary chain of reasons and events that determines it.[7] On this point, Spinoza's treatment of "adequate ideas" is instructive. Whereas the classical conception of a "true" idea refers to an agreement between the idea and an object external to it, an "adequate" idea, for Spinoza, refers to the formation of the idea itself, which should encompass the formation of its object and describe the causes of that object.[8] More concisely, as Spinoza puts it, in an adequate idea "the knowledge of an effect depends on, and involves, the knowledge of the cause."[9] Macherey explains the stakes of Spinoza's notion of adequation: "The essential function of the category of *adequatio* is to break with the conception of knowledge as representation."[10] Instead of the idea as the mirror of an object, we have "the intrinsic determination of the relation of the idea to itself" (63). "Adequate" literary criticism, then, we might say, does not mirror its literary object but elaborates the process of its object's formation, and in so doing, it attains to its own powers of knowing.

The Persistence of the Category of the Work

Here it is worth pausing to emphasize the fact that, while Macherey sees the task of criticism as concerned with the *production* of the work, he likewise asserts its concern with the production of the *work*. Criticism should not, in other words, seek to dissolve the work into the process of its becoming. In this regard, too, the title *A Theory of Literary Production* may be somewhat misleading insofar it seems to emphasize process over product. To put a finer point on the issue, I turn to an early criticism of Macherey's work, one put forth by Alain Badiou in 1965: specifically, criticism of Macherey's essay "Lenin, Critic of Tolstoy" ("Lénine critique de Tolstoï"), included in *A Theory of Literary Production*, and first published in *La Pensée* 121, June 1965. While I have no interest in adjudicating the debate that arose between Badiou and Macherey at this moment, I do want to use Badiou's comments to shed light on Macherey's insistence that we need to keep in view *both* the conditions of the work *and* the work itself as a determinate object.

In "The Autonomy of the Aesthetic Process," Badiou lays out a series of theses that push against Macherey's position, precisely in favor of asserting, in its place, the primacy of process over product. Badiou begins by pointing to what he thinks is a major oversight in Macherey's argument, writing, "I see a sign of [its] pre-theoretical character in the fact that Macherey maintains the work as *pertinent unity* of critical study."[11] The persistence of the work as a unit of analysis, he argues, leads Macherey to pose the question of the work's *relation* to ideology, and especially of how we pass from ideology to the aesthetic. Thus he writes that "literary theory remains for Macherey the description of a relation; that is, the relating of the work's being . . . with its (ideological or historical) outside" (35). In Badiou's eyes, the whole problem of relation can be—and should be—avoided if we grant autonomy to what he calls "the aesthetic mode of production." Doing so means rejecting all heterogeneous elements from our analysis of the aesthetic. For, Badiou argues, aesthetic practice is incapable of taking up and aestheticizing heterogeneous elements—elements such as ideological statements, for example, which are produced by ideological modes of production and are made known by theories of ideologies. Instead, it must be the case that aesthetic practice labors on elements that are already aesthetic (37). The process is uniform with itself, in its starting point as well as in its destination. The upshot of Badiou's argument is that the work as a determinate entity disappears into the homogeneity of the aesthetic process.

From Macherey's perspective, however—and despite Badiou's well-known determination to hold the rationalist line—to insist on the homogeneity of a process in this way is still to remain within the bounds of empiricism. It makes no difference that what is at stake is the givenness of a process rather than the givenness of a particular fact, if no attempt is made to account for the genesis of that process, and if there is no analysis of the transformations internal to it. By contrast, Macherey underscores precisely those transformations at work in aesthetic practice. Such transformations turn out to be key, moreover, in conceiving of aesthetic practice as labor. For in Macherey's view (following Althusser's on this point), an artwork labors on its initial conditions as well as on the necessarily heterogeneous materials that constitute it. He writes:

> The work is the product of a labor, and thus of an art. . . . The writer, as the laborer of his text, does not manufacture the materials with which he works. Neither does he find them spontaneously pre-disposed, stray pieces, available for constructing whatever edifice: these elements are not neutral and transparent. . . . [Rather] they have a sort of specific weight, a particular force, which means that even as they are mixed and put to use in an ensemble, they retain a certain autonomy and may go so far as to reclaim a life unto themselves. (83–84/47)[12]

What are the writer's materials? Let us suppose they are languages, images, affects, and ideas; turns of phrase, tropes, generic conventions; everything that belongs to the social production of language and everything that has been inscribed in "the history of forms," as Macherey calls it (84/47). This material is heterogeneous to aesthetic practice because neither is it created out of thin air by an artist-God, nor is it without its own place in the wider, historical real. At the same time, this material must submit to a transformative labor if a work of literature is to have a mode of existence distinct from a conversation in the street.

At stake here is an entirely different conception of autonomy from the one in Badiou's article. For Macherey, "autonomous" does not mean "homogeneous," but very nearly the opposite: "autonomous" describes an operation that takes up, works on, and transforms heterogeneous material. Consider what Macherey has to say about the "autonomy" of the production of knowledge: "We must . . . restore to it its rightful autonomy (this does not mean its independence), its proper dimension. We must recognize its power to produce the new, thus effectively to transform reality as it is given. We must consider it, not as an instrument, but as a labor. At a minimum this supposes the existence of three distinct terms: material, means, and product" (7/7).[13] What Macherey says here of the critical knowledge of the work is equally true of the work itself. In both cases, granting autonomy to a process means acknowledging its power to transform a given reality and produce something new. Citing "material, means, and product," Macherey draws on Althusser's arguments about theoretical practice in *For Marx* and *Reading Capital*, where knowledge is likewise construed as the result of a transformative labor. That is, he follows Althusser's assertion that knowledge "is constituted by a structure which combines . . . the type of object (raw material) on which it labours, the theoretical means of production available (its theory, its method and its technique, experimental or otherwise) and the historical relations (both theoretical, ideological and social) in which it produces."[14]

Accordingly, in his analysis of literary production—as in his analysis of the production of critical discourse—Macherey distinguishes the materials and the process of production from the finished product, retaining all three categories in order to think their difference. Let me reiterate this point: Macherey's emphasis on literary *production* does not entail a rejection of the literary *work*. In fact, as we have seen, it is precisely the work's determinate nature that makes it available to critical inquiry. "The work is determined," Macherey writes. "It is itself and nothing else. . . . Thus stabilised, if not, as we shall see, immobilised, the work becomes a theoretical fact" (79/45). Again, the determination of a work with respect to a set of conditions is what is taken up in critical knowledge.

When critics (Badiou or others) want to insist on aesthetic production or aesthetic experience over the formal determinations of a work, they often end up championing a kind of process without a difference: a process that differs neither from what is given in initial materials or conditions nor from what is produced. But what are the consequences of viewing literary production or literary reception as pure activity, and as activity for its own sake? At bottom, it entails detaching these processes from their historical and material circumstances and disconnecting them from their concrete effects. For what is meant by "determination," in Macherey's argument, is the affirmation of a work's situatedness in time and place, its necessary insertion into a network of relations, and its ability to produce real effects. We might say that the work's determination can be grasped only when we acknowledge the work's difference and exteriority from the process that gives rise to it, as well as from the process that receives it.

Here, too, in the way he thinks about determination, Macherey follows Spinoza. Like Spinoza, he conceives of determination both negatively and positively: a work is determined in the negative sense insofar as it is bound, limited, and inserted into history rather than expressing the free will of a divine creator. But it is determined in a positive sense insofar as its existence entails a power to transform its conditions, a transformation capable of producing unforeseeable effects.[15] In this sense, a work maintains a relation to its conditions precisely in order to differ from those conditions. Thus Macherey can write, "*In every book, something happens.* . . . With respect to its initial givens, every book constitutes an event, a surprise." At the same time, this surprise is not without relation, for "in every work one can find the indices of this internal rupture, of this decentering that reveals the dependence of the work on its distinct conditions of possibility" (82/46).[16]

When Macherey speaks of "indices of rupture," he locates us at the threshold of a theory of reading. Thus far, we have traced the argument that every work maintains a relation to its conditions—specifically, a differential relation—and we have argued that such a relation makes the work available to critical knowledge. We have not yet addressed the question of whether and by what means this relation is visible, or rather legible, in the literary text. This question is my concern in the next section, where I turn to Macherey's implicit theory of reading and its affinities with Althusser's work as well as deconstructive approaches.

The Resistance of Reading

In the preceding section, I made a case for the role of determination in Macherey's analysis. Interestingly, it is precisely this notion of determination that Macherey now claims to find dissatisfying. In his postface to the 2014 edition of *A Theory of Literary Production* (see the preceding chapter of this book), he cites Althusser as being responsible for having inserted the term *déterminé* at strategic points in his manuscript, and he argues that the term points to an impasse present in his thinking at the time. This impasse arose from the conflicting demands of the theoretical moment: on the one hand, the demand to think the dialectic on the basis of materialism, and hence according to a causal network of determinate entities; on the other hand, the demand to think materialism on the basis of the dialectic, and hence according to a kind of "mobility" or becoming. Macherey observes, in other words, a conflict in his own thinking between determination and becoming, or between literary form and literary production.

Despite these protestations, I have maintained that determination remains necessary to Macherey's argument. And I want to propose, now, a certain notion of *reading* as what allows us to think the passage between production and work. Earlier, we saw Macherey use the term "reading" in a pejorative sense when he wanted to describe a sheer following along of the literary text, a passive appreciation or a "simple reading" as distinct from "theoretical knowledge" (99/54). This sense of reading corresponds with the empiricist fallacy of taking the work as given. The corrective to this fallacy involves actively constructing the work as an object of knowledge, and yet Macherey goes on to argue that this corrective must equally avoid the normative and interpretive fallacies of wanting the work to be other than it is. We thus arrive at "the essential difficulty of critical activity," as Macherey calls it (166/86), criticism's "double demand": "The work must be elaborated, treated, for without this it will never be a theoretical fact, an object of knowledge; but it must also be *left* as it is, if we are to achieve a theoretical judgment and avoid value judgments. It must be at once constructed and maintained within its own limits" (168/87).

Between an appreciation that doubles the text as it is and a criticism that confronts the text with the production of a new discourse lies an intermediary activity, one that ought to go by the name "reading." Macherey does not make this argument, but he may have a version of it in mind when he concludes part 1 of *A Theory of Literary Production* by insisting on what it means "to read truly, to know how to read and to know what reading is" (236/113). So that whereas he begins part 1 with the question of criticism, he ends with a statement about reading. Between these bookends, Macherey arrives at what I can only describe as an ontological thesis about the work itself: "The necessity of the work is founded on the multiplicity of its meanings," he writes (169/88). "The structure of the work . . . is this internal dislocation [*décalage*], this caesura, by means of which the work corresponds to a reality that is equally incomplete, one it makes visible without reflecting. The literary work gives the measure of a difference" (171/89).[17] The work gives the measure of a difference in the real, in other words, by means of its own internal difference. Reading encounters this difference inhering in the text itself, a structural difference that yields multiple meanings. To register this difference, really to *read* it, is not yet to do the work of criticism, because it is not yet to *know* something. Neither is it to follow along a line of narrative, or a line of explicit claims the text is making. For reading is struck by multiple lines at once; the difference it encounters may be a difference between the text's explicit claims and its implicit practice, or between its logical assertions and the consistency of its poetic figures.[18]

This internal difference of a text, which Macherey also calls a "discrepancy" (*décalage*), cannot be stated in the form of a proposition, nor can it be represented conceptually, which is why I suggest it does not attain to the status of knowledge. This difference cannot be stated or represented, not for any sort of mystical reasons but for logical ones. For every explicit statement, Macherey argues, there is something else implicit, "because in order to say anything, there are other things you must not say" (184/95). To bring the unsaid into the realm of the said succeeds only in leaving new things unsaid; we risk producing what Gilles Deleuze describes in *The Logic of Sense* as an "infinite regress" of explicit proposition and implicit sense.[19] If we turn to *Reading Capital*, we find that Althusser's own treatment of reading considers the possibility of just such an infinite regress and manages to propose an exit from it. Reading Marx reading Smith, Althusser draws the said and the unsaid together onto the same terrain; just as Macherey does, he treats the said and the unsaid as necessary effects of one another. Thus he describes a "non-vision" that inhabits vision from within: "It is a form of vision and hence has a necessary relationship with vision."[20] Or in Macherey's terms, "meaning is in the relation of the explicit to the implicit" (191/97). In this way, both thinkers suggest that it is the relation *between* said and unsaid, between vision and blindness, that needs to be read. In other words, they suggest that the object of a reading is not a particular sentence or even a text made up of sentences, but a differential relation. This relation is both the internal complexity of a work and the external rupture of the work with existing ideas, images, and languages.

At times this differential relation seems to belong to a first reading as a kind of glitch or obstacle encountered by a reader, an obstacle that calls out for a critical response. Macherey writes: "What, in the work, solicits explication is not that false simplicity lent to it by the seeming unity of its meaning, but the presence of a relation, or of an opposition, between elements of its exposition. . . . This conflict . . . makes it possible to detect the inscription of an *otherness* in the work" (172/89).[21] Reading installs itself in this otherness, an otherness that, again, cannot be conceptualized but that asks for conceptualization. Because what is *in* the work is not the same as knowledge *about* the work (42/23),[22] criticism here discovers its vocation.

At other times, this differential relation seems to belong to critical discourse itself, emerging as a series of gaps or contradictions in this discourse. Now recall that for Macherey, criticism's task is not simply to describe a literary object—what Althusser would call the pretense of an "innocent" reading—but to produce a *new* discourse. The newness or autonomy of critical discourse is the mark of its status as genuine knowledge. For "to know is thus not to discover a hidden meaning, to reconstitute something latent or overlooked. It is to construct something new, an addition to the reality from which it begins and of which it has something different to say" (5/6). And yet by setting up criticism as autonomous in this way, Macherey runs into a potential problem, that of a possible nonrelation between criticism and literary text. Perhaps unsurprisingly, he runs into a version of one of the most enduring problems of philosophical rationalism: that of a possible nonrelation of the idea to the real it claims to take as its object. The internal coherence of the rational order, in other words, is precisely what raises the question of its purchase on the material real. In literary terms, again, this problem takes the form of a certain self-sealing quality of literary criticism, a criticism that would enclose within itself "the principles of its own veridicity," as Terry Eagleton has put it, instead of being subject to external criteria. Along these lines, Eagleton has argued that Macherey's "theory of literary language [and by extension, his theory of criticism] is vulnerable to exactly the same charges as Althusser's trust in the self-validatory protocols of scientific knowledge."[23] Eagleton accuses Macherey of a kind of critical "formalism" in a way that echoes the oft-repeated charges of a "scientism" or a "theoreticism" in Althusser's work.

Against this mistrust of an autonomous critical discourse, I want to argue, ultimately, that the internal verification of criticism—as well as its internal refutation, for the two are one and the same—is exactly what we need and what I want to foreground at this point in my discussion. For what is at stake is the very ability of criticism to "read" itself, and thus to produce a "critique" of itself. What is at stake, in other words, is nothing short of the possibility of literary theory, this particular theory that is neither an anthropology, nor a sociology, nor a politics, but the theoretical elaboration of a critical discourse that is bound to the practice of reading.[24] And the difficulty of the endeavor of literary theory, as well as of criticism, is by and large inescapable insofar as both are steeped in the vertiginous task of using language to describe the workings of language. In philosophical terms, theory and criticism both confront a problem of immanence—for their medium is the same as the mark at which they aim—and both confront a problem of what lines of demarcation can be drawn within a situation of immanence. I propose we follow Althusser here by acknowledging that a certain nonknowledge, blindness, or failure inheres within critical discourse and, moreover, that such failure is constitutive of this discourse. *Reading*, then, would be the name for the resistance to criticism: for the blindness that inheres in vision and for those gaps and contradictions that necessarily make up the fabric of critical discourse. These gaps and contradictions mark, within criticism, the persistence of the literary text as a real object.

I can elaborate this argument in the following way: *reading* marks the receptivity of criticism, its encounter with the literary text as a real object, while *criticism* smooths over the disarticulations of the literary text with the production of a new discourse. It might be helpful here to think of critical discourse along the lines of what Paul de Man calls the "narration of an understanding" of a text or an "allegory of reading."[25] De Man argues that what we tend to call the "understanding" of a text implicates, in fact, another act of language, the production of a discourse that narrates our understanding of a text, a story replete with its own protagonists, dramatic conflicts, and successful resolutions. In this sense, literary criticism does not even have to be written, for in de Man's terms, "there are always two texts, regardless of whether they are actually written out or not."[26] Underlying de Man's claims is a perspective quite close to Macherey's own: that acts of knowing are inscribed in language and produced through acts of language, where they take up and transform linguistic elements that already exist. What de Man and Macherey both seek to show, then, is the way our knowledge of literary texts is not spontaneous but produced, and produced as a series of linguistic operations.

Where de Man employs the term "reading" to emphasize the immanence of such operations, Macherey focuses instead on the term "criticism" to underscore their autonomy: his concern is to advocate for the autonomy of a knowledge that emerges in an encounter with literary texts, a knowledge that remains truly unforeseeable in advance. Ultimately, Macherey wants to bring out the productive and transformative power of literary texts themselves—so that what is at stake for him is not just the production *of* literature by linguistic and other social forces, but also a production *by* literature of something else, something affected by literature's determinate reality. We can see this idea becoming more explicit in his later work, from the question "How does literature act?" in "For a Theory of Literary Reproduction" (1994) to the claim that literature "gives us to think" something, in *Proust entre littérature et philosophie* (2013).[27] Still, reading remains a necessary moment within criticism, a wedge against the closure of criticism and a link to the complex reality of the work.

Why do we read? we might ask Macherey, just as we might pose the question for ourselves. We read, I would venture to say, because we have the capacity to be affected by language that is not of our own making. We read because our thoughts are not created ex nihilo but occasioned: they intervene in complex networks of ideas that have come before them, and by intervening in these networks, they come to know themselves and their own ability. To read is to think in situation, and to think in situations of language, by means of operations that transform ideas and texts rather than simply create them. What Macherey's treatment of reading shows us, without yet being stated directly, is precisely this capacity to be affected that inheres in our power of knowing and is provoked by the real complexity of things. What his theory of criticism shows us, more explicitly, is that our response to literary texts does not have to be a shadow or a self-effacing pedagogy. Rather, it constitutes a productive activity in its own right, a form of knowledge with its own history and a unique capacity to join forces with other discursive forms of knowledge.

A Theory of Literary Production also shows us something quite timely, perhaps, if we consider the current state of literary studies in higher education and the degree of autonomy we have managed to retain, or perhaps are still seeking, as critics and teachers of literature. We are often asked to design classes or teach texts that appeal to students or administrators, which means that we are asked to appeal to what students and administrators already know, or to what they already want. Macherey's arguments about the autonomy of critical knowledge might speak directly to the autonomy, or lack thereof, of our discipline within the university. And it is significant that his arguments about the task of criticism are intimately bound up with a thesis about the nature of literature itself. He argues that every work begins with a rupture with existing ideas and forms of language, a rupture that prevents the work from being assimilable to anything else, at least if we hope to know it (109/60). Because of its determinate, and ultimately formal, nature, what a work of literature says has not been said anywhere else. What it gives us to think, in other words, is not patiently waiting for us like candy to be unwrapped, nor does it correspond to our already formed ideals and expectations. It is something we construct through a loving sort of labor, when we are open to what we have not yet thought, on the basis of a textual encounter. The most precious thing we have to offer our students is perhaps this encounter, this experience, and this surprise.

Notes

1. "An Interview with Pierre Macherey," ed. and trans. Colin Mercer and Jean Radford, *Red Letters 5* (Summer 1977): 4.

2. As Warren Montag has pointed out in *Louis Althusser* (New York: Palgrave, 2003), 50.

3. The first number refers to the numbered paragraph of *Pour une théorie de la production littéraire* (2014), the second to the page number of the English translation (2006). All translations modified. While elegant, Geoffrey Wall's translation too often obscures Macherey's meaning, especially its philosophical import.

4. Macherey also describes the normative fallacy as working in a "prophetic" mode (33/19), insofar as it projects an ideal against which the work will be measured and attempts to mediate between the two. He likely has in mind Spinoza's study of scripture and the way it describes the prophets of the Old Testament mediating between the word of God and the images and signs by which this word could be apprehended (see the *Theological-Political Treatise*, in *The Collected Works of Spinoza*, vol. 2, ed. and trans. Edwin Curley [Princeton, NJ: Princeton University Press, 2016], esp. 84, 95–98). In philosophical terms, normative criticism is idealist and teleological: idealist insofar as it substitutes an ideal for the real unfolding of the literary work, and teleological insofar as it moves through the work with the goal of approaching this ideal.

5. Cleanth Brooks, *The Well Wrought Urn: Studies in the Structure of Poetry* (New York: Harcourt, 1947), 192–214.

6. I mention this because Macherey is often identified as a "literary sociologist," no doubt because of his association with the Sociology of Literature Project at the University of Essex (1976–2001). Much less commented on is the way he theorizes literary form primarily as an intralinguistic phenomenon.

7. We can also see how Macherey's insistence on the need to understand the work in terms of the conditions that give rise to it allows us to position his

arguments alongside other attempts to think together structure and genesis, a problem that concerned so many French philosophers in the mid-sixties. Looking back to Jean Hyppolite's *Genesis and Structure of Hegel's "Phenomenology of Spirit"* (1946), and passing from Michel Foucault's investigations into the "archaeology" of epistemological structures in *The Order of Things* (1966), to Gilles Deleuze's search for the genesis of representation in *Difference and Repetition* (1968), to Jacques Derrida's work on Edmund Husserl, especially "Genesis and Structure in Phenomenology" (1967), this problem held in its grip an entire generation of thinkers, who sought in different ways to complicate the gains of structuralism and conceptual formalism. Here, however, of key importance is the manner in which Macherey approaches these problems through a specifically rationalist and, more specifically, Spinozist lens.

8. Spinoza, Letter 60 to Tschirnhaus, in *The Collected Works of Spinoza*, vol. 2, ed. and trans. Edwin Curley (Princeton, NJ: Princeton University Press, 2016), 432–33.

9. Spinoza, *Ethics*, in *The Collected Works of Spinoza*, vol. 1, ed. and trans. Edwin Curley (Princeton, NJ: Princeton University Press, 1985), book I, axiom 4.

10. Macherey, *Hegel or Spinoza*, 60.

11. Alain Badiou, "The Autonomy of the Aesthetic Process," trans. Bruno Bosteels, *Radical Philosophy* 178 (March/April 2013): 34.

12. "L'œuvre est le produit d'un travail, et ainsi d'un art. . . . Ouvrier de son texte, l'écrivain, en particulier, ne fabrique pas les matériaux avec lesquels il travaille. Il ne les trouve pas non plus spontanément disposés, pièces errantes, libres d'aider à l'édification de n'importe quel échafaudage: ce ne sont pas des éléments neutres, transparents. . . . [I]ls ont comme un poids spécifique, une force propre, qui fait que, même utilisés et mélangés dans un ensemble, ils conservent une certaine autonomie et peuvent aller dans certains cas jusqu'à reprendre leur vie propre."

13. "Il faut lui restituer toute son autonomie (cela ne veut pas dire: son indépendance), sa dimension propre: il faut lui reconnaître le pouvoir de produire du nouveau, donc de transformer effectivement la réalité telle qu'elle lui est donnée. Il faut le considérer non comme un instrument, mais comme un travail: ce qui suppose au moins l'existence de trois termes effectivement distincts, matière, moyen et produit."

14. Louis Althusser, Étienne Balibar, Roger Establet, Pierre Macherey, and Jacques Rancière, *Reading Capital: The Complete Edition*, trans. Ben Brewster and David Fernbach (New York: Verso, 2015), 42.

15. I have in mind here the detailed discussion of determination in Spinoza's *Ethics* that Macherey lays out in chapter 4, "Omnis Determinatio est Negatio," in *Hegel or Spinoza*, esp. 172–73. I am also intentionally echoing Spinoza's foundational definition of freedom and determination: "That thing is called free which exists from the necessity of its nature alone, and is determined to act by itself alone. But a thing is called necessary, or rather compelled, which is determined by another to exist and to operate in a certain and determinate manner" (Spinoza, *Ethics* I, D7, trans. modified). Here "determination" does not run contrary to what Spinoza calls freedom, for it is ascribed to free and necessary beings alike. Moreover, the term is not used in the purely negative sense of "external limitation," but in the positive sense of the deployment of a thing's power to exist and

to act. Jason Read helpfully points out the use of the term "operation" in this definition in his discussion of what "theoretical practice," in Macherey's hands, owes to Spinoza's philosophy. Jason Read, "The Order and Connection of Ideas: Theoretical Practice in Macherey's Turn to Spinoza," *Rethinking Marxism* 19, no. 4 (2007): 516.

16. "En tout livre il se passe quelque chose . . . tout livre constitue par rapport à certaines de ses données initiales un événement, une surprise. En toute oeuvre on peut trouver l'indice de cette rupture intérieure, de ce décentrement, qui manifeste sa dépendance par rapport à des conditions distinctes de possibilité."

17. I describe in detail what it means for a work to be constituted through an operation of difference in my book *The Work of Difference: Modernism, Romanticism, and the Production of Literary Form* (New York: Fordham University Press, 2016).

18. Macherey seems to have in mind this discrepancy between a text's explicit claims and its implicit practice when he opens his chapter on "Implicit and Explicit" with an epigraph from Descartes: "In order to ascertain their real opinions, I ought to take cognizance of what they practiced rather than of what they said. . . . [V]ery many are not aware of what it is that they really believe, for as the act of mind by which a thing is believed is different from that by which we know we believe it, the one act is often found without the other (Descartes, *Disourse on Method* III; quoted in *A Theory of Literary Production* 177/91). Just as the act of believing differs from knowledge of that belief, so does the poetic act of a literary text differ from the statements the text can offer about itself. The implication here is that literary texts lack full knowledge of their own inner workings, or at least that they cannot *say* in one and the same breath what it is they *do*.

19. Gilles Deleuze, *The Logic of Sense*, trans. Mark Lester with Charles Stivale (New York: Columbia University Press, 1990), 28.

20. Althusser, *Reading Capital*, 19.

21. "Ce qui en l'oeuvre sollicite l'explication, ce n'est pas cette fausse simplicité que lui donne l'unité apparente de son sens: mais la présence en elle d'un rapport, ou d'une opposition, entre des éléments de l'exposition ou des niveaux de composition, ce caractère disparate qui montre qu'elle est édifiée sur un conflit de sens; ce conflit permet de déceler en l'oeuvre l'inscription d'une alterité."

22. "On ne cherchera pas *dans* l'oeuvre les éléments d'un savoir sur l'oeuvre." This sentence was omitted from the English translation.

23. Terry Eagleton, "Pierre Macherey and the Theory of Literary Production," *Minnesota Review* 5 (Fall 1975): 142.

24. Compare Ellen Rooney, "Form and Contentment," *Modern Language Quarterly* 61, no. 1 (2000): 26.

25. Paul de Man, "The Rhetoric of Blindness," in *Blindness and Insight: Essays in the Rhetoric of Contemporary Criticism* (Minneapolis: University of Minnesota Press, 1983), 108; *Allegories of Reading: Figural Language in Rousseau, Nietzsche, Rilke, and Proust* (New Haven, CT: Yale University Press, 1979), 72–77.

26. Paul de Man, "Anthropomorphism and Trope in the Lyric," in *The Rhetoric of Romanticism* (New York: Columbia University Press, 1984), 260.

27. Pierre Macherey, "For a Theory of Literary Reproduction," in *In a Materialist Way: Selected Essays*, trans. Ted Stolze (New York: Verso, 1998), 42; *Proust entre littérature et philosophie* (Paris: Éditions Amsterdam, 2013), ch. 1.

Spoken and Unspoken

Ellen Rooney

> The speech of the book comes from a certain silence, a matter which it endows with form, a ground on which it traces a figure.
>
> —Pierre Macherey, "The Spoken and the Unspoken"

> There is no guarantee that the figures in a truly recursive figure would fit together at all.
>
> —Barbara Johnson, *The Feminist Difference*

Some Elementary Concepts and the Reading Effect

The politics of literature names a problematic as capacious, riven, and venerable as any in literary studies. It encompasses radically incompatible arguments, from celebrations of *littérature engagée,* or committed literature, to the veneration of its nemesis, the autonomous work of art, alongside multiple alternative conjunctures emerging from various historical moments, traditions, and genres. These last include, of course, genres of literary theory and critique that find their primary investments elsewhere but either imply a politics of literature or extend their purview to this topic as the question (inevitably) arises; for example, reader response criticism was not born in a political idiom, but it proved highly adaptable when adopted for projects of political critique.

In no respect an artifact of our particular political moment or even of a slightly longer durée reaching back to the 1960s and the decisive impacts of social movements and their cultural critiques on literary studies, the "politics of literature" arguably appears as a site of contestation in tandem with the emergence in the eighteenth century of the modern European sense of literature as such. As Raymond Williams reminds us in his gloss on this deceptively "simple" word, the historical specification and narrowing of the connotation of the term "literature" were themselves bound up in fundamentally political transformations: "The sense of 'a nation' having 'a literature' is a crucial social and cultural, probably also political, development."[1] The instantiation of the literary as a distinctive mode of writing is coeval with the problem of the politics of literature.

Such an "always already" political concept of literature may itself be inconceivable without the foundational notion of the canon(ical), the coherence of a tradition seen as radiating from its original works to be realized across time and territory. And in the wake of canon building comes contestation. Canon wars, conflicts over the curriculum and its reach, its exclusions and inclusions, the possibilities of reforming, opening, and extending "the" tradition are on any account a critical component of the thinking of the politics of literature across the latter half of the twentieth century and well into the twenty-first. The currently very powerful definition of literature as storytelling and the significant consensus on the power and importance of telling diverse and challenging stories have if anything grown in influence in recent years, even as the concept of "narrative" becomes omnipresent across fields, disciplines, and political and social contexts. This expansive, culture-wide account of and attention to narrative has led both to celebration—we are convinced that it is essential to tell one's story, to uncover missing narratives—and to profound suspicion, as struggles to "control the narrative" or mount counternarratives, and the sometimes perverse relation between potent narratives and disinformation become impossible to ignore. The word "narrative" paradoxically serves both as an indication of the revelation of essential truths and as a synonym for "spin," "cover story," or simply "lie."

But even in periods of intense canon revision, efforts to think the politics of literature are not limited to reworking the canonical, that is, to questions of *what* we ought to read, our tradition or curricula. Indeed, I would argue that the question of *how* to read, or what it is we do when we read, has a political salience independent of the interrogation, expansion, or rebuilding of any specific canon. Not that these two concerns are opposed to one another or never at work in tandem. Indeed, when any proposal for canon revision moves beyond the argument that some particular "great" work has been overlooked, excluded or omitted (and this movement seems all but inevitable), it invariably provokes some interrogation of the terms of inclusion, the principles of evaluation—sometimes silently at play, sometimes emphatically enforced—that established the inside and the outside of canonicity in the first place. The problematic of the politics of literature then becomes a matter of the politics of reading in another sense, that is, a question of what it is to read.[2]

In his "For a Theory of Literary Reproduction," Pierre Macherey approaches the question of the politics of literature obliquely, not by any thematic route or through particular content but by means of the questions of history, action, and the specificity of literature—that is, first, its historical specificity, its concrete connection to a given time and place, but ultimately, its specificity as a mode of textuality, a historical form. While he acknowledges the impulse to answer the (political) question "How does literature act?" by insisting on its profound address to its immediate context, even by privileging it as a form or mode of political intervention, Macherey's conclusion—his answer to the question of action—points in quite a different direction.[3] The literary work is distinguished by its peculiar temporality—indeed, by a trajectory in which its production is a consequence of its reproduction, that is, of its reading, as though it had only in fact actually been "produced by being reproduced" (48).

Macherey sees in this distinction and the emphasis of reproduction an account of "the very notion of the literary work," one that moves beyond the notion of literature as "a collection of finished works, produced in turn, then once and for all recorded within a repertoire, in order to be offered next to the consumption of readers to whom is entrusted the task of ensuring its reception" (50). Neither a "a collection of monuments," nor even of minimally "finished things" to be "inventoried as a purely empirical factual reality," the "palimpsest" of the literary emerges only in the event of reading, in the reproduction of the work, in a futurity not simply present in any "original" work at the moment of its composition. Only in its reproduction—indeed, its plural reproductions, and its "indefinite possibility of variation" (47)—does literature produce its effects. As Macherey observes, "If one takes this hypothesis seriously, one must go so far as to say that works are not at all 'produced' as such, but begin to exist only from the moment they are 'reproduced'" (47). These processes of reproduction are the site of any imaginable politics of literature, and they are processes that inevitably depart from any historical origin, itself a kind of fiction that ultimately obscures the emergence of writing from reading. "There is no first writing which is not also a rewriting, just as there is perhaps no reading which is not already a rereading" (49). And at every moment of this interminable process, there is the operation of the unspoken.

The politics of rereading are immediately foregrounded in Barbara Johnson's "Lesbian Spectacles: Reading *Sula*, *Passing*, *Thelma and Louise* and *The Accused*"; they take the form of the problematic of "reading *as a*." In this brief piece, Johnson takes up literary and cinematic works immediately legible as entangled with questions of canons and traditions. That said, these two novels, authored by African American women writers Toni Morrison and Nella Larsen, were, by the time of Johnson's commentary, canonical works, while the films she addresses were in some ways controversial but widely commented upon cinematic texts centering on women's agency, phallocentrism, and sexual violence, themes that were implanted at the center of cultural analysis by the same kinds of aesthetic and critical challenges that had earlier affirmed Morrison and Larsen's stature in the canon.

Johnson's intervention, then, is not to advocate for these works, to secure their value or repair neglect: her reading depends upon their currency and our familiarity with them (and to some extent with their historical reception). Rather, she performs a kind of reading experiment, one that begins in uncertainty. She writes: "It is hard to pin down the origins of a reading effect."[4] Johnson offers this quiet observation about the reading effect's resistance to origin stories, precise mapping, or fixity, that is, to being "pinned down," in the course of reporting on just such orphaned and therefore elusive effects. Johnson proposes in this essay to don "lesbian spectacles" and read "explicitly as a lesbian," something she had not previously undertaken in her career as a justly celebrated critic, a self-described slow reader. She notes that this interpretative project, explicitly tethered to an identity or positionality, contributes to the effort to undermine the "fiction of universality." (This is often one of the consequences of canon revision, though not universally.) But Johnson is nonetheless exquisitely attuned to its risks—that of reproducing either "media induced images" or "idealizations" of "what a lesbian is . . . or what a lesbian *should* be" (157). The figure of the spectacles—an aid to vision that in this case makes a kind of spectacle of (a) lesbian desire, both in the texts Johnson addresses and in her responses to them, her reading—underscores the conventional yet real, felt yet ideological, unconscious yet political quality of even such a deliberately "personal" or "particular" undertaking. (She speaks cautiously of her "particular desire structure" to elude the temptation to overgeneralize or idealize [157].) Rather than diminish the challenges of her project, Johnson insists upon the divided and paradoxical nature of her elaborately reflexive yet not fully controlled or programmatic reading: "I needed a way of catching myself in the act of reading as a lesbian without having intended to" (157).

Johnson evokes this kind of interpretative or analytical contortion elsewhere in her work. In "Nothing Fails Like Success," concerned with the possibility that even as destabilizing a theoretical intervention as deconstruction may become overly familiar and so mechanical or rote, she argues that "the impossible but necessary task of the reader is to set herself up to be surprised."[5] In the case of "Lesbian Spectacles," the surprising results of her experiment are quite disappointing to its subject, not least from a political perspective: in the course of her readings, Johnson discovers her erotic attraction to a powerful yet phallocentric femininity, the psychoanalytic figure of the "phallic mother" who wields authority "within a patriarchal institution," a woman who succeeds in its power structures and so ultimately validates its workings. (The example is the deputy district attorney played by Kelly McGinnis in *The Accused*.)

Johnson ruefully concludes, "So much for reading with the unconscious" (163). She argues that her efforts to read with political intent and genuine openness to the unexpected or unscripted, inherent in "making [her] own erotic unconscious participate in [her] reading project," "far from guaranteeing some sort of radical or liberating breakthrough, brings [her] face to face with the political incorrectness of [her] own fantasy life" (163). These results are not only personally disconcerting but politically and intellectually disturbing and surprising (perhaps in a way that resonates with the "bad surprise" that Eve Sedgwick analyzes in her account of paranoid reading). In the course of trying to surprise herself in the act of reading, to come "face to face" with her own libidinal investments, and to "explain to [her]self why [she] felt that way," Johnson discloses what she calls a "real disjunction" between politics and the (her own?) unconscious, a dislocation realized—made real—in and by the reading subject reading. Rendered symptomatic by her own scrupulous interpretative practice, Johnson's ultimate view of reading "spectacles" remains productively ambiguous, if not blurred. We are all aware of the stubbornness of (even inconvenient) desires and of the association of politics with the will to change. What "remains," Johnson concludes, is a haunting question, that "of knowing what the unconscious changes and what politics repeat" (164).

In "The Political Fallacy," Sandra Macpherson asks, "What kind of action is literary criticism?"[6] By way of beginning to answer, she reports that Joseph North's *Literary Criticism: A Concise Political History* "tells us up front. It's political action" (1214). If we take Johnson's spectacular experiment as exemplary for a project of critical or symptomatic reading, it undeniably warns us against mistaking what is up front for the whole story (a point Macpherson herself will also make). But even if we accept—or promote—the premise that literary criticism cannot help but appear (in the strong sense of that term) as "political action" of some kind, Johnson's readings dilate a startling range of disruptive contingencies, contingencies that pertain first to the literary and film texts she considers; second, to her own subjectivity, its grounds, the plasticity of its textual encounters, and the blind spots that it seems to entail; and finally, to the status of reading and so of politics as such. Taken together, all of these uncertainties—and the potential surprises they may harbor—leave any calculation of the consequences of a political action that takes the form of reading very much in question. Macpherson views such contingencies as dashing the causal arguments that are essential to launch or defend almost any such "aesthetic-political project." "Skeptical that there are any necessary political effects to [Cleanth] Brooks's—or anyone else's literary ontology" (1218), she proposes the notion of the "political fallacy" to gloss the failed (and perhaps misbegotten) efforts to bind our readings of literary forms to particular political effects. These kinds of questions seem especially fraught when such a reading, one in the service or interests of (particular) forms of political change, simultaneously argues that part of its distinctive *value* lies in its non- or even antiprogrammatic orientation: when reading proposes as its "necessary task" that it "set [itself] up to be surprised," how can it simultaneously align itself with a political aim, any political aim? Alternatively, what political intervention attaches itself to surprise as a specifically political value?

Peggy Kamuf has suggested that a possible intervention into debates concerning "the subject of reading," one that would originate in "what deconstruction has understood about reading, unreadability, writing, the unsaturability of context, the divisibility of the letter, and so forth," might put forth a "delirious" or "'mad' thesis, to wit, that reading disorder was a general condition because no one ever really *knows* how to read."[7] This is just the kind of not knowing evoked by Johnson's interrogative conclusion, in the surprise of her readings—their powerful and unanticipated forms of both discontinuity and repetition—and in the contingencies of both reading and politics her analysis simultaneously enacts, suffers, and exacerbates. Where does such a form or practice of the contingency of reading, this delirious reading effect or disorder, emerge in the context of the debates on the politics of reading that today go by the name of the post-critical? Would its apparently inescapable repetitions congeal and so stall any action? Or is it a kind of counteraction, incompatible with the reduction of reading to "information extraction" (2) or even communication, and so an avatar of what I will be calling the contingency of critique? Where is such contingency spoken? and how?

The Reading Effects of the Critique of the Critique of Critique

> Insidious Questions: When we are confronted with any manifestation which someone has permitted us to see, we may ask: what is it meant to conceal? What is it meant to draw our attention from? What prejudices does it seek to raise? and again, how far does the subtlety of the dissimulation go? and in what respect is the man mistaken?
>
> —Nietzsche, *Dawn of Day*

> This is where their *surprise* lies (*there can be no taking hold without surprise*).
>
> —Louis Althusser, "The Underground Current of the Materialist Encounter"

"The Spoken and the Unspoken" is chapter 15 of Pierre Macherey's *A Theory of Literary Production*, part of the opening section of the volume, which is titled "Some Elementary Concepts." This very brief section of the book, only five pages in length, may seem an unlikely text to bring to bear on current debates around the problematic of reading and what has been generalized—and sometimes celebrated—as the advent of the post-critical or post-critique. Macherey goes almost entirely unmentioned in many of the best-known post-critical interventions in these arguments, such as Stephen Best and Sharon Marcus's "Surface Reading: An Introduction" or Eve Sedgwick's "Paranoid Reading and Reparative Reading, or, You're So Paranoid, You Probably Think This Essay Is About You." This is true despite the fact that even in a chapter title as terse (though also potentially elusive) as "The Spoken and the Unspoken," Macherey seems to signal a relation to literature, criticism, and critique that would be all too tempting a target for post-critical commentators. The fascination of the "unspoken" could, it seems, be easily aligned with the "suspicious," "paranoid," both politically self-aggrandizing (faux heroic) *and* politically ineffectual (or "critiquey") mode of reading that is the nearest opponent of post-critique projects and practices. As Best and Marcus observe, the forms of critique or "symptomatic reading" that they present as both out of date and "out of steam" (in Bruno Latour's sense) are marked by their sustained attention to what a text represses, excludes, or simply doesn't say. Symptomatic reading privileges a latent meaning or absent cause, "significant truths" that "are not immediately apprehensible and may be veiled or invisible."[8] Macherey's distinction between the spoken and the unspoken appears to signal just such an interpretative project of unveiling, and the opening "Some Elementary Concepts" portion of *A Theory of Literary Production* features other similarly inviting targets—consider "Implicit and Explicit" (chapter 14) or "Depth and Complexity" (chapter 18)—for what I think we can only call (despite many disclaimers) a post-critical *critique*, that is, the "suspicious" exposure of the latent structure of this allegedly hegemonic preference for reading for the absent cause.

Macherey does make two brief appearances in Rita Felski's *Limits of Critique*, one of which is of particular interest, in part because it perhaps explains the more general absence of references to his work from the debate. Early in the book, during Felski's discussion of "The Stakes of Suspicion," Macherey is paired with Fredric Jameson (a literary theorist with whom he shares relatively little, though both are Marxists) and named as one of the developers of an "influential model of symptomatic reading" emerging "at the high point of Althusserian thought in the early 1980s."[9] But Felski doesn't pursue this brief observation in any detail, turning instead to a general characterization of the theoretical whirlwind that provided the context for her work in feminist theory as a young scholar writing her dissertation: "Vocabularies proliferated and changed with an often bewildering speed; performativity and the panopticon, the mirror stage and the *mise en abyme*, interpellation and *l'écriture féminine*" (19). Not a scene in which much was left unspoken.

Macherey's second appearance is more puzzling, however, coming as it does after his previous placement—however much in passing—as one of the developers of the practice of symptomatic reading that is itself the major "symptom" of the limits of critique in Felski's literary critical history. Indeed, rather than figuring as a historical avatar of the limits of critique, Macherey's role in the chapter that examines the reading practice Felski dubs "Digging Down and Standing Back" is transmuted, almost rewritten as its opposite: he stands in here for theorists belatedly "striving to divest the symptom of its traditional associations with depth and a hidden core of meaning." At this point, Felksi cites him directly:

> In Pierre Macherey's influential *A Theory of Literary Production*, translated in 1975 [*sic*], there are already signs of equivocation.

Insisting that "the work is not as it appears to be," drawing on the language of mystification and deception, invoking the latent knowledge encrypted in the unconscious of the work, much of Macherey's argument seems to endorse a familiar division between surface illusion and deeper truth. At other points, however, Macherey insists that the goal of his analysis is to short-circuit any kind of analytical apparatus that opposes appearance to reality. The work, he writes, cannot conceal anything: "Meaning is not buried in its depths, masked or disguised. It is not a question of hunting it down with interpretation. It is not in the work but by its side, on its margins." Here we see the critic eager to cast off the mantle of archaeologist and to discard the premises of depth interpretation.[10]

It is doubtful that Felski means her characterization of Macherey as "equivocating" in *A Theory of Literary Production* to suggest that he writes with the intention to deceive or mislead his readers. Indeed, I'm not sure "the critic" she describes as so "eager to cast off the mantle of archaeologist" is literally meant to reference the French theorist at all, as opposed to figuring a generic type of belated, mildly embarrassed, and perhaps less than persuasive effort to "discard the premises of depth interpretation" (68) that she recalls from the 1980s and 90s. The timing, after all, is a bit off. As Felski notes, Macherey's work was translated into English in the 1970s—1978, as it happens. But *A Theory of Literary Production* was first published in 1966, just a year after *Reading Capital*, the text in which Althusser's essay, "From *Capital* to Marx's Philosophy," proposes a new practice of a reading both "guilty" and "symptomatic" that he locates in Marx's own practice in *Capital* itself. Both theorists oppose the model of depth in their original work on reading; neither has a need to equivocate or cast off earlier formulations a decade and more later. Felski's micro-narrative lands more effectively as a fable of shifting times and theoretical positions than as a reading of Macherey, which is in keeping with her intention to characterize a problematic rather than propose close readings; as such, it may not reveal much about the emergence or moment of the specific problematic of "symptomatic reading." But it does tell us something about the time of reading effects themselves and their relation to critiques of critique and about the status accorded Macherey's text and others more or less like it, in an encounter that is no more bound by literal chronologies or original intentions than the disordered and unpredictable process that leads Johnson to the question of what politics repeats.

It is from this perspective—one that negotiates with the untimeliness of reading rather than grieves its disorderliness and leaps—that "The Spoken and the Unspoken" bears in startling ways on current debates around the problematic of reading and what has been generally characterized as the advent of the post-critical, not least as a moment in the history of reading sans depth. Literary scholars have been working (really rather intensively) for

(much) more than twenty years, at least since Eve Sedgwick's original intervention on behalf of the notion of reparative reading, on the Althusserian
question "What is it to read?" (That query dates to the 1960s, as do many
challenges to the "canon."). Our efforts have generated an impressive number of distinctive answers to this question: formulations such as reparative
reading, reading for form, distant reading, as well as symptomatic, surface,
suspicious, and susceptible reading, to name a few. Macherey's concepts of
the spoken and the unspoken in this chapter appear to me directly to address
some of the key arguments emerging from the multifarious challenges to
critique that the reading debates have fostered. These challenges are sometimes aligned with Sedgwick's invocation of the reparative, which is in many
respects the least hostile to the work of critique. (She points out the intimacy
of the powerfully paranoid, strong theory, and reparative effects in David
Miller's *The Novel and the Police*, for example.) But post-critical challenges
have also frequently been keyed to Stephen Best and Sharon Marcus's arguments for "surface reading," Heather Love's vision of "thin" description, or
Felski's interrogation of "suspicious" reading. I happily stipulate that these
theorists have important differences among them, which we should honor. As
I noted above, Sedgwick presents paranoid and reparative readings as entangled and even mutually entailed, such that her exceptionally "strong" reading
of the paranoid could be argued to establish it as *the* enabling condition for
reparative work. But I think it fair to argue that all these challenges to the
work of symptomatic reading or critique have been recruited in the service
of the proposition, most explicit in the privileging of surface and description
(which is most developed in Best and Marcus, and to some extent, Heather
Love), that criticism ought to attend to what the text itself tells us, to what
it speaks, its "spoken," in Macherey's idiom. As Best and Marcus put it in
their "Surface Reading: An Introduction," under the rubric of "*Attention to
surface as a practice of critical description*,"

> This focus assumes that texts can reveal their own truths because
> texts mediate themselves; what we think theory brings to texts (form,
> structure, meaning) is already present in them. Description sees no
> need to translate the text into a theoretical or historical metalanguage
> in order to make the text meaningful. The purpose of criticism is thus
> a relatively modest one: to indicate what the text says about itself.[11]

This kind of argument, whether on behalf of description, surface reading,
or the post-critical, disavows what is variously called paranoid, symptomatic, or suspicious reading—or, more simply, critique. These disavowed and
sometimes abjected reading practices are deemed problematic, dated, or pernicious for the heterogeneous reasons I cited just above: not every surface
reading privileges the same critique as it launches its post-critical program.
But one through line in the various arguments is the claim that challenges

symptomatic readings on the grounds that they "rewrite" their texts in other
(theoretical or political or formal) languages and thus claim to disclose what
the text does not say, what it conceals or mystifies, rather than record its visible surface or plain sense, its spoken. Fredric Jameson's work *The Political
Unconscious: Narrative as a Socially Symbolic Act* may provide the starkest
positive assertion of this view of critical method: "Interpretation is here construed as an essentially allegorical act, which consists in rewriting a given text
in terms of a particular interpretive master code."[12] On Jameson's account,
this masterful intervention unmasks the deep structure of the text's historical
deformation, what he names its political unconscious.

In the face of this kind of consciously allegorical practice, Best and Marcus
insist that we ought to interpret the text in the terms that *it* proffers, that is,
"indicate what the text says about itself."[13] In the broadly "post-critical"
view, interpretation ought not to rewrite the spoken in its own terms, burrow
beneath it, or strip it away. It ought not to master or trivialize or dismiss the
spoken by exposing it as mystification, a feint, a merely conscious gesture
of concealment whose significance or aesthetic effect secretly resides elsewhere, that is, whose significance is in some respect unconscious or latent,
hidden or repressed, suppressed or deep: in a word, Macherey's word, unspoken. Intimacy with and respect for the text—which are ethical and affective
imperatives, with decided political overtones—require submission and atten-
tiveness to and accurate description of the spoken. The post-critical argues
that the unspoken ought not to *displace* the spoken.

Of course, this post-critical account of the work of critique or reading—
both as a description and a prescription—has many opponents. My gloss on
this conjuncture may appear to be only too obviously the work of one such,
which it most certainly is. But all the same, I do not want to move too quickly
to characterize resistance to the post-critical—or the critique of this critique of
critique—as a form of sheer advocacy for the unspoken. (Or as a return to or
endorsement of a Jamesonian account of interpretation as fundamentally or
essentially allegory.) More particularly, the logic of allegory or of suspicious
reading as a stripping away of a veil to reveal the hidden kernel of meaning,
"a penetration of appearances in order to appropriate some secret; a negative
corroding criticism by which the work is destroyed or dismantled to reveal
the centre around which it has been built," is not the logic of the relation
Macherey establishes or proposes between the spoken and the unspoken.[14]
("Must we go over this again"? he sighs.) On the contrary, Macherey refuses
the temptation to make the unspoken the telos of reading. The unspoken is
not a hidden truth, a foundation obscured by mere appearances, a covert
meaning to be ruthlessly exposed by "suspicious and aggressive attacks" or,
indeed, even by scrupulous, modest, and tender rewriting.[15]

Macherey does not call on us to expose the unspoken. Rather, he *couples*
the spoken and the unspoken. Across the length of "Elementary Concepts,"
we find the spoken and the unspoken in the company of other salient pairs,

including "front and back," "explanation and interpretation," "implicit and explicit," "interior and exterior," and "depth and complexity." These couplings shift the terms of the discussion away from the problematic that avidly opposes the spoken to the unspoken—or the reader to the text, the past to the present, the inside to the outside, theory to criticism—whether in order to champion what it can then describe as "evident, perceptible, [and] apprehensible in texts," along with the "accurate knowledge" we may be able to produce about them, *or* to trumpet its disclosure of the hidden and, on those grounds, the core meaning of a work.[16] For his part, Macherey is interested in thinking (perhaps we should say reading) the *relation* between the spoken and the unspoken.

This insistence on relationality, Macherey's theorization of this pairing, may clarify elements of the ongoing debate. Might the quarrel over "what is it to read?" (as Althusser frames it) in fact amount to an argument about how a reading that insists on the relation of the spoken to the unspoken legitimates itself? If it can legitimate itself? If our attention shifts to the coupling of spoken and unspoken, how should we characterize the terrain on which they meet? The terms that enable their encounter? Or rather, their emergence, each in a distinctive form, from that very encounter, and perhaps without a reader having intended any such eruption? Macherey's refusal and displacement of the mischaracterization of the unspoken as a hidden depth incites many questions: How would a reading establish *the* unspoken of a particular text as *its* unspoken? How can we persuade another reader that this unspoken in some respect belongs to the text—is not an indulgent or even aggressive "rewriting"—precisely by virtue of its relation to the spoken? Is this relation "close"? Is it "deep"? And who is the other reader? For whom must the coupling of spoken and unspoken be translated into a kind of necessity?

Macherey's coupling does not dismiss (or erase or transcend) the spoken, but it does nevertheless undo the possibility of the spoken as original, unitary or "centred," "a self-sufficient totality" (51, 53), in his phrase—that is, as legible in its own idiom, outside, before, or even beneath any relation to its unspoken. In the place of this premise that the text may speak for itself, he proposes a concept of autonomy that is itself relational. How might the "autonomy" that Macherey insists inevitably accompanies writing as such and "establishes the difference which brings it into being, by establishing relations to that which it is not" (53) displace the fantasy of "independence" in which the text announces its essential unity and imperviousness, its priority? He argues that the "difference between two autonomous realities already constitutes a kind of relationship" and that such differences "are a continuously sustained, elaborated, and recapitulated process" and "display a very precise mode of relationship, non-empirical, but none the less real, because they are the product of a certain labor" (53). Would the unspoken in this problematic emerge as the impetus and practice of such sustaining labor, of reading as such? Might the relation of the spoken to the unspoken be the "reparative" at work?

As a formula or trope, "the critique of the critique of critique" points in two directions. On the one hand, it figures the possibility that there is no limit to critique. This would mean both that there is no outside, a neutral space from which one might mount a noncritical (or acritical?) challenge to the operations of critique, escape its "critiquey" moods, or transcend its insistence on difference as intrinsic to reading. From this perspective, critique *inevitably* engenders or inspires more critique: it is generically an open-ended text; it cannot come to a halt—or be evaded. The phrase thus hopes to capture the effort to "break" with critique—to disclose any polemic against the break of critique (its distance or even aggression) as itself a critical "break"— and thus to bind that effort back into a specifically critical relation to its object. On this account, the critique of critique is always also itself critique; as Heather Love writes of Eve Sedgwick's "Paranoid Reading, Reparative Reading," no doubt a work that systematically exposes the weaknesses and limits of paranoid reading or critique and argues for a reparative practice: "For one thing, Sedgwick acknowledges throughout the essay the benefits of paranoid reading. For another, the essay is not only reparative, it is paranoid."[17] (I will bracket the question of how successful or persuasive this move may be in particular cases, for the moment, and acknowledge the fact that post-critical polemic has certainly anticipated this move and frequently attempts to defend against it in various ways.)

And yet, the syntagm "the critique of the critique of critique" also animates the often observed capacity of linguistic repetition—a rose is a rose is a rose—to unhinge signification and disrupt the "self-sameness" that common sense tells us repetition ought to instantiate and even guarantee. (We see this effect dramatically at work in Althusser and Balibar's *Reading Capital*, as well as in Gertrude Stein.) In this analysis, repetition ineluctably insinuates difference alongside the claims to sameness and fidelity, which is to say it initiates a reading effect.[18] Reproduction is the nonoriginal origin of reading. The repetition of critique (of the critique of critique) insists on sameness, we might even say to the letter; and yet, it "simultaneously" (Macherey's term), in the same gesture, with the very same words, institutes difference. Theorizing this self-contradictory, even oxymoronic, mode of relationality is Macherey's object.

I think we might be able to extend what I have called Macherey's insistence on this contradictory and productive relationality. The apparent incompatibility between the self-avowedly "descriptive" or surface reading— loyal, modest, and deferential to the text's spoken—on the one hand, and the symptomatic reading, which insists that one's reading always (willy-nilly) illuminates some form of distinctive relation between the spoken and the unspoken, on the other, can itself be read symptomatically—or, if that term remains affectively disturbing and too tightly bound to "suspicion" and "aggression," we might simply say it can be reread. Rather than accept the oppositional account, one in which "the way we read now" (as Marcus and

Best phrase it) breaks with the (very long, not merely generational) history of critique, we could ask: Where might the post-critical and critique (or symptomatic reading) claim the same ground? Does symptomatic reading have the capacity to reveal *both* the relation of the spoken and the unspoken of the literary text and of its own discourse, that is, to make its own reading practice an element of its analysis—rather than assuming the humble and so eerily silent and silencing agent of textual self-sameness? Would this claim then entail a relation between the spoken and the unspoken of critique that the literary text works in turn to expose—in a kind of reversal that the post-critical in some sense sets out to celebrate, however problematically it makes its case? For its part, does the post-critical as theoretical intervention—which it is undoubtedly, even to those who insist it is not simply more critique but a different interpretative, affective, and even ethical stance—dream that it might elude the unspoken, that is, elude the relation between its spoken and its unspoken, and somehow think itself? And where is the humility in that?

The Tweets Speak for Themselves, or, "It Cannot Itself Think Itself" (Althusser)

With deep gratitude to former White House press secretary Sean Spicer (many press secretaries ago now, which is reason for celebration in itself), I will assume that the absurdity of the notion that the tweets speak for themselves can be stipulated. For the moment, I will also stipulate that even the most cautious and deliberately post-critical "description" entails a relation between the spoken and the unspoken that it (often explicitly) disavows: every imaginable text and interpretation resembles a tweet in this one respect: it does not speak for itself. (Tweetuality is in this sense a subspecies of textuality.) This is one of Althusser's overarching claims in his essay in *Reading Capital*, when he theorizes the "productivity" of knowledge and/as reading, the "surprise" that disrupts our expectation that history or scientific knowledge will unfold as continuity, and the "play on words" that reading (and all thought) inevitably encounters.[19] Althusser concludes that textuality "cannot itself think itself" (33), and his work promises no closure on or exemption from this observation: his tireless insistence on the unfinished, incomplete, and provisional nature of his own work makes this point without reservation. In Macherey's idiom, no reading practice eludes the unspoken in its relation to the spoken, even one that apparently "limits itself to seizing hold of something already given."[20] Those who imagine otherwise are, in Nirvana Tanoukhi's words, "new objectivists," seeking somehow to "read without reading."[21] We should consider the possibility that this "objectivist" posture—one in which reading is imperceptible, modestly withdrawn into the shadow of description, committed only to echoing the spoken—has enormous appeal in the present to the very forces that a self-conscious objectivism claims it seeks to derail.

I have elaborated this particular argument elsewhere, but here I want to consider the distinctive terms in which Macherey negotiates it in "The Spoken and the Unspoken." How does his account of the relation between the spoken and the unspoken enact or bear out the claim that the text cannot itself think itself? What motivates (to borrow the term Tanoukhi introduces to problematize some of the puzzling methodological and ethical claims of "new objectivists") Macherey's insistence on this relation? And how does his intervention—in defiance of the fact that it dates to 1966—seem to propose a critique of the post-critical *avant la lettre*? How does his argument proleptically respond to the effects of descriptive and surface reading and so require us to return to the question of the "times," the "now" and its articulation with the relation of the spoken to the unspoken? I will consider just three moments in Macherey's argument: first, his stress on the productivity of reading, a strict counterpart to the "literary production" his book as a whole theorizes; second, his (perhaps surprising, given the polemical lines drawn in our moment) concern to preserve the text, indeed, to discredit forms of reading that *substitute* (his term) something else for what he defines as the difference or specificity of the text—its singularity, its status as an encounter, its historicality as an event; and finally, his privileging of the relation of the text to otherness.[22]

These claims are mutually entailed. The failure to recognize the text as always caught up in a contradictory relationality to otherness[23]—the complex conditions from which it emerges into any existence whatsoever—engenders the failure to locate its specificity and so in a way leaves no alternative but to "translate" it into something else. (Macherey takes "translate" in a narrow, negative sense that I don't think would be widely endorsed today, when it has taken on a much broader meaning.)[24] *This* kind of translation, which Macherey condemns, has a decided resonance with the notion of masterful rewriting that surface and descriptive reading object to so strenuously. But it may result, in Macherey's view, in a text that is in fact "abolished" (17). Such "deciphering" not only "resolve[s] the problem in a way that simply gets rid of it" but also forgets—erases might be the better term—that the contradictory relationality that emerges both in literary texts and literary readings is itself a temporary achievement and artifice: "The transparency of the book is always retrospective, and it is only ever a moment rather than a defining characteristic of the narrative" (37, 38).

Working from the other side, this means that the specificity and hence significance of the text can be preserved only by revealing its emergence in alterity, from and as difference, in relationality and, I would argue, as contingent: revealing its relation to what it is not, to what it does not say, and to the stubborn fact that "in order to say anything, there are other things which must not be said" (85). This not said or absence is not a hidden content to be exposed but an enabling condition and an effect, inevitably, as the insistence on mutual determination announces, a disorderly one. The "silence,"

"matter," and "ground" to which the spoken owes its distinctiveness establish
that the text "is not self-sufficient; it is necessarily accompanied by a certain
absence, without which it would not exist"; the "origin of the reading effect"
is in fact a debt to this inescapable companion (85). No account of this relation can be proposed save from the distance of yet another relation, from a
difference through which the spoken and the unspoken necessarily emerge:
"Although the work is self-sufficient, it does not contain or engender its own
theory; it does not *know* itself" (84).

"Productivity" is Macherey's term for the work of the literary text emerging from these relations, its working through of these (for it) unnamable
relations, and also his term for the theoretically situated work of reading the
text (in this, he strongly resembles Althusser). Productivity is everywhere in
his argument, both the trace of difference and its source. Literary criticism
is "a certain form of knowledge, and has an object, which is not a given but
a product of literary criticism. To this object literary criticism applies a certain effort of transformation. . . . What can be said *of* the work can never
be confused with what the work itself is saying" (7). Productivity forges an
unanticipated or contingent discourse, one marked by an "irreducible difference" from the literary work—no context can predict its trajectory—and
it is through this radical difference that it constitutes what Macherey calls
the specificity of the text, which I take to mean that it generates new textual
forms along with their capacity to surprise. Form and surprise are coextensive here. This is a reading effect.

The Reading Effect

> Critical discourse does not attempt to complete the book, for
> theory begins from that incompleteness which is so radical
> that it cannot be located.
>
> —Pierre Macherey

The productivity of reading for Macherey derives from the fact that the text
is a theoretical object, not an empirical given: "Objects of any rational investigation have no prior existence but are thought into being" (5). He disputes
the notion that one might reach the object by some neutral (and, at least
implicitly, more modest or ethical) path in surprisingly contemporary terms,
terms that insist that all criticism, by its very existence, "immediately dis-
sents from the empiricist fallacy; it aspires to indicate a possible alternative
to the given" (5). A conscious effort to evade this dissensus is of little use.
"Conceivably, a certain type of criticism proposes a modest translation of
a work, but even with this minimum of transformation, so scrupulous and
restrained, it is seeking to replace what is by *something else*" (15). In this
account, an ideology of description is doomed to misconstrue the way "the

work is determined: it is itself and nothing else" (40); it ironically risks falling into the very allegorical problematic that it generally ranges itself against, by models derived from what Macherey calls "normative" and "empirical" fallacies. The contemporary post-critical polemic argues that description defends the spoken and thus accounts for its text closely, even intimately; the self-restraint of descriptive practice allows us to be surprised by its accounts. Macherey sees this as an evasion: the paradox of the reading effect is that to light up the *specificity* of the text, the manner in which it is precisely and surprisingly itself, the "critic, employing a new language, brings out a *difference* within the work by demonstrating that it is *other than it is*" (7). The relation that gives the work—and every reading of it—a distinctive form is not a matter of its own coherence, unity, or self-sameness, "entirely premeditated" or "deriving monolithically from a unique and simple conception" or model (41). Indeed,

> The writer, as the producer of a text, does not manufacture the materials with which he works. Neither does he stumble across them; they are not neutral, transparent components that have the grace to vanish, to disappear into the totality to which they contribute, giving it substance and adopting its forms . . . they have a sort of specific weight, a peculiar power, which means that even when they are used and blended into a totality, they retain a certain autonomy and may, in some cases, resume their particular life. Not because there is some absolute and transcendent logic of aesthetic facts, but because their real inscription in a history of forms means that they cannot be defined exclusively by their immediate function in a specific work. (41–42)

This inscription registers the displacement of immediacy and a relation to the unspoken, and as such, it has a markedly open or unfixed character, one resistant to exclusive definition: the raw materials of any writing or reading practice must be found or inherited or borrowed or stolen, potentially with different consequences in each instance. Function is at best a partial gloss on meaning, and "absolute and transcendent logic" and its idealizations are dismissed. The negative formulation "lack of transparency" can underwrite multiple forms and intensities of opacity, "weight," and resistance; the power of the materials themselves is "peculiar"—odd, strange, out of the ordinary; and while they possess only a "certain," not definitively named "autonomy," they "may, in some cases, resume their particular life." Though of course, in some cases, they may not.

We might interpret this relative lack of programmatic clarity at the very moment that figures the making or the "manufacture" of the text as a kind of indeterminacy at the origin—the origin of the literary work itself and therefore of all manner of reading effects. (We might even want to valorize this as an achievement, an effort to evade the degradation that Johnson warns befalls "any radically innovative thought [once it] becomes an -ism" and so loses "groundbreaking force" and becomes "more simplistic, more dogmatic, and ultimately more conservative, at which time its power becomes institutional rather and analytical."[25]) But I would suggest that Macherey's insistence on the relation of the spoken to the unspoken is underwritten by—and so puts into play—a kind of Althusserian overdetermination, one that emerges in the actual encounter of reading when that encounter is understood as a productive moment, situated but contingent, real and yet unpredictable, when "we experience the inevitable as surprise and vice versa" (43): the arrival of the necessary in the formal guise of surprise. Such an experience is not unmediated, and it entails labor: "The necessity of the work is not an initial datum, but a product" (42); it is not the trace of an intention, captured and immobilized, infinitely repeatable and for that very reason defined as knowledge, but an action whose appearance and final effects remain impossible to guarantee.

    This productivity is part of the reason that Macherey insists that the critic "employ[s] 'new language' in order to demonstrate the difference of the work" in its relation to that which is "*other than it is*." This other language is itself produced by reading, in a practice that shares in or repeats the productivity of the literary (though not by repeating its own language), similarly emerging from relations that are in turn transformed *by its appearance*, not unilaterally privileged as its preexisting ground, context, intention, or cause. The critic's language literally cannot repeat the language of the text; that is the nature of its "historicality," as Peggy Kamuf has called it. Emerging in another scene, critique, too, borrows, finds, or steals its materials as they appear to hand rather than in any ideal form and must therefore manage their "specific weights" and "peculiar," mediated powers. (Recall the twofold nature of the claims of "the critique of the critique of critique.") More crucially, the critic's language can only hope to account for literary language by training its attention just to one side: neither digging deeper, tearing away, nor looking through will suffice. Symptomatic reading, as Timothy Bewes argues for what he calls "reading with the grain," situates (insinuates?) itself "alongside" the text.[26]

    Macherey warns us that "what can be said of the work can never be confused with what the work itself is saying" (7). Form is silent. (Hamlet/*Hamlet* does not say "Iambic pentameter, that is the question.") "A knowledge of the work is not elaborated within the work, but supposes a distance between knowledge and its object: to know what the writer is saying, it is not enough to *let him speak*, for his speech is hollow and can never be completed at its own level" (84). What can be said of the work discloses its relation to what it does not say, the relation of its spoken to its unspoken, and the striations or otherness this relation leaves behind, evidence of its complex, contradictory production. Macherey calls these marks "diversity," "unevenness, "disparity," "superimposition," "splitting," and "incompletion," and he stresses that the contradictory forces within the text work simultaneously on one another and on the whole, which is defined not by its coherence or unity, but by the specificity of its dislocations and difference(s). Paradoxically, oxymoronically, the text is itself, but it is never self-identical, a "self-sufficient totality." "Autonomous" but never "independent," "no book ever arrives unaccompanied: it is a figure against a background of other formations" (53), of its rereading. It figures only through those relations.

On the account I have been elaborating so far, Macherey defines both reading and writing as productive but argues that they "are not equivalent and reversible operations. Let us avoid confusing them" (13). By reversible, he seems to mean that the critic does not walk back over the track of the text in reverse, repeating it backward, as it were. Such a practice—could it be applied to any imaginable text—would simply collapse into that text, no longer able to locate the relation of spoken to unspoken or any relationality whatsoever. Such a process would presume the possibility of a reading that repeats without wandering, that suffers no belatedness or distinction, and responds to no intervening reading or other reader (to what we once studied as critical history). But "when the critic speaks he is not repeating, reproducing, or remaking [the work]; neither is he illuminating its dark corners, filling its margins with annotations specifying that which was never specific" (84). Rejecting reversal and "equivalence" and the notion of reading as an imitation or copy, Machereyan reading produces the relation between the spoken and the unspoken, thus giving *both* form; reading is the process that delineates their *simultaneous formation*. This is a process to be thought in a kind of radical present, but never as immediacy. If the work in fact "*manifests*, uncovers, what it cannot say" (rather than veiling it), Macherey argues, "this silence gives it life" (84). Reading characterizes that manifestation in concrete forms, indeed, by giving them form. Reading does not "pass across" (86) from the unspoken to the spoken or "dispel" the spoken by wielding the unspoken. The unspoken is not beneath the spoken, not hidden or veiled; it is not belated, trailing behind the spoken only to arrive as its negation, but present at its first appearance—which is not to say it is the source of the spoken but that it comes into existence in concert with it. It can never replace the spoken, which would in fact entail its own erasure, but makes its formation legible. This is the reading effect.

Coda, or, Darkness Visible

Why, the post-critical demands, can't the text speak its unspoken? Why is it helpless to articulate the silences from which it emerges, to speak to its own omissions, to expose its not said and its critical relation to that silence? Surely, the venerable "text itself" knows better than any other reading or readers, from other, however "productive" terrains, the terms of its own emergence, operations, and play? Why does (symptomatic) reading jealously claim all canniness and condemn the text as blinded by its own light? Why does Macherey insist that "although the work is self-sufficient, it does not contain or engender its own theory: it does not *know* itself" (84, original italics)?

First, and categorically: symptomatic reading is not uncannily knowing. Exactly insofar as it is productive—that is, takes form—it too is blind, silent as to its own silence and its necessary relation to an unspoken other, the difference that constitutes its ground, form, matter. The relation of the spoken to the unspoken is an ineluctable structure. It marks every imaginable text with contingency. As Macherey puts it, "It is impossible to dissemble the truth of language" (89); we work in the very space that our work struggles to illuminate.

Practically speaking, in any (and every) given case, this means that the structure of the relation of the spoken to the unspoken remains. Self-reflection may of course examine a particular, singular silence and so displace it. As Bewes argues (and puts into revelatory practice), "A generous reading is always, in part, a reading of ourselves reading. The thought it produces is never transferable, recognizable, paraphrasable, applicable, expoundable, or illustratable—meaning that it cannot be detached either from the text itself or from the moment of reading. What we read for—our objective in reading—is that which in the text enables the present reading."[27] And in the process of disclosing that enabling moment in the text, a new question immediately arises about the conditions of the emergence of that very self-reflection, and so a new relation to the unspoken—to that otherness in the present moment that enables our reading—is born. (This is *not* a regression without end because each singular encounter may constitute an event, disseminating effects, effects that need not be permanent to be real; this is a topic for another time.) We might narrate this recurrence of the unspoken as a historical belatedness that we can never overcome or as a futurity that we can never fully anticipate or predict or a structural blindness that repeats in uncanny new forms. But the impossibility of dissembling our relation to what must remain unintentional because unspeakable is the condition of literary production *as* productive. (The same conditions pertain to theoretical production.) This impossibility constitutes the contingency that we perpetually encounter in reading, even as we knowingly seek to read from a position that could realize our desires or found political action. Critique is an encounter with the relation that in a single gesture "makes visible" and "makes invisible" (88) in every text, a mode of reading that is symptomatic in both senses of the term: revealing its own untimely symptom in its very revelation of the formation of the literary.

Notes

1. Raymond Williams, *Keywords: A Vocabulary of Culture and Society* (Oxford: Oxford University Press, 1985), 185.

2. See Louis Althusser and Etienne Balibar, *Reading Capital*, trans. Ben Brewster (London: Verso, 1979).

3. Pierre Macherey, "For a Theory of Literary Reproduction," in *In a Materialist Way: Selected Essays*, edited by Warren Montag (London: Verso, 1998), 42.

4. Barbara Johnson, "Lesbian Spectacles: Reading *Sula, Passing, Thelma and Louise* and *The Accused*," in *The Feminist Difference: Literature, Psychoanalysis, Race, and Gender* (Cambridge, MA: Harvard University Press, 1998), 157.

5. Barbara Johnson, "Nothing Fails like Success," in *A World of Difference* (Baltimore: Johns Hopkins University Press, 1987), 15.

6. Sandra Macpherson, "The Political Fallacy," *PMLA* 132, no. 5 (2017): 1214.

7. Peggy Kamuf, "Comes a Letter in the Mail: Ellipses of Reading," *differences* 28, no. 1 (2017): 3.

8. Stephen Best and Sharon Marcus, "Surface Reading: An Introduction," in "The Way We Read Now," edited by Marcus and Best, special issue of *Representations* 108 (2009): 3–4.

9. Rita Felski, *The Limits of Critique* (Chicago: University of Chicago Press, 2015), 19.

10. Felski, *The Limits of Critique*, 67–68.

11. Best and Marcus, "Surface Reading," 11.

12. Fredric Jameson, *The Political Unconscious: Narrative as a Socially Symbolic Act* (Ithaca, NY: Cornell University Press, 1982), 10.

13. Best and Marcus, "Surface Reading," 11.

14. Macherey, *A Theory of Literary Production*, 51.

15. Best and Marcus, "Surface Reading," 11.

16. Best and Marcus, "Surface Reading," 9, 17.

17. Heather Love, "Truth and Consequences: On Paranoid Reading," *Criticism* 52, no. 2 (2010): 238.

18. See Audrey Wasser, "How Anything Can Be Different from What It Is: Tautology in Stein's *The Making of Americans*," in *The Work of Difference: Modernism, Romanticism, and the Production of Literary Form* (New York: Fordham University Press, 2016): 139–59.

19. Althusser and Balibar, *Reading Capital*, 24, 45, 41.

20. Macherey, *A Theory of Literary Production*, 51.

21. Nirvana Tanoukhi, "Surprise Me If You Can," *PMLA* 131, no. 5 (2016): 1423.

22. See Wasser, "Why Read, Macherey?"

23. Macherey, *A Theory of Literary Production*, 38.

24. For example, see recent work by Emily Apter, "Untranslatability and the Geopolitics of Reading," *PMLA* 134.1 (2019): 194–200, *Against World Literature: On the Politics of Untranslatability* (London: Verso, 2013), and *The Translation Zone: A New Comparative Literature* (Princeton: Princeton University Press, 2006); Barbara Cassin, ed. *Dictionary of Untranslatables: A Philosophical Lexicon*, edited with Emily Apter, Jacques Lezra, and Michael Wood (Princeton: Princeton University Press, 2014); and Gayatri Spivak, "Translating as Culture" and "Translating into English," in *An Aesthetic Education in the Era of Globalization* (Cambridge: Harvard University Press, 2012): 241–55 and 256–74.

25. Johnson, "Nothing Fails like Success," 1.

26. Timothy Bewes, "Reading against the Grain," *differences* 21, no. 3 (2010).

27. Bewes, "Reading against the Grain," 28.

Baudelaire's Shadow

On Poetic Determination

Nathan Brown

J'avais devant les yeux les ténèbres.
> —Hugo, "Au bord de l'infini"

Peut-on déchirer des ténèbres
Plus denses que la poix, sans matin et sans soir,
Sans astres, sans éclairs funèbres?
> —Baudelaire, "L'Irréparable"

Paul de Man's classic essay, "Anthropomorphism and Trope in the Lyric," turns around the relation between two sonnets by Baudelaire: "Correspondences" and "Obsession."[1] De Man positions "Obsession" as Baudelaire's own *lyrical reading* of "Correspondences," through which the impersonal, third-person discourse of that poem is transformed into the rhetoric of first-person expression. According to de Man, this transformation also performs a "defensive motion of understanding" (261), a hermeneutic reduction of figural ambiguity through the recuperation of subjective address and "the reconciliation of knowledge with phenomenal, aesthetic experience" (258). On this basis, de Man offers the rather withering judgment that "'Obsession' translates 'Correspondances' into intelligibility, the least one can hope for in a successful reading" (259). "We all perfectly and quickly understand 'Obsession,'" he writes, but this understanding "leaves 'Correspondances' as thoroughly incomprehensible as it always was" (261). For de Man, "Correspondences" resists interpretation, while "Obsession" transforms the earlier poem's mysterious tropes into a series of readily legible lyric figures.

In what follows I show how the final tercet of "Obsession" resists de Man's assimilation of the poem to forthright understanding. But first I frame the conceptual and critical stakes of my approach to Baudelaire's poem through the work of a theorist whose protocols of reading are quite different, though his concerns are in some ways proximate. Whereas de Man's work foregrounds the *indeterminacy* of literary signification, Pierre Macherey, in

A Theory of Literary Production, foregrounds the *determinacy* of the literary work. "The work is determined," he tells us. "It is itself and nothing other. The moment this is understood, it becomes the object of rational study."[2] Yet this claim, which seems antithetical to the protocols of deconstructive reading, also depends for Macherey upon what he calls "the real complexity" of the work, "the *distance* that separates its several meanings" (45). Indeed, Macherey will argue that "the necessity of the work is founded upon the multiplicity of its meanings" and also that "the work exists above all through its determinate absences, through what it does not say, through its relation to what it is not" (79, 148). Macherey's characterization of literature thus involves a tension between what he calls the "determinacy" and "necessity" of the work and its disparate significations, these being held together by distances and absences that constitute the work's complexity. For Macherey, the work "is itself and nothing other" (46) *because* it means several things and *because* of what it does not say. Indeed, he refers to the production of literature as "the production of a tautology" (50), essentially claiming that the work is what it is because it is not what it is not. Confronted with this avowed tautology, the critic is then saddled with a paradoxical task: "The work must be elaborated, *treated*, or else it will never be a theoretical fact, an object of knowledge; but it must also be *left* as it is, or else one will bring to bear upon it a value judgment and not a theoretical judgment" (79). What are we to make, in critical practice, of this curious double exigency: we must elaborate the work while also leaving it as it is?

I am interested above all in exploring the implications of the concept of *determination* for literary criticism—in part because it may enable us to avoid the apparent self-evidence of reference to "form." The problem with such a reference is that it tends to suppose the form of the work is simply there, that it can be studied as given. But form is not only a determination of the work; it is itself the effect of a process of determination. *How* is form determined? This is also to ask, How is it indeterminate? How is form constituted by a field of determination in which it attains a particular existence, as the form of just *this* work (or *as* this work), rather than as a more general category into which works are fitted, or in which they participate? Attending to such questions requires a materialist approach to form, in which it is considered as immanent to particular works rather than as a template to which they are fitted or a pattern that may be abstracted from their material instantiation.

In Hegel's *Science of Logic*, determination involves *mediated particularity*. Whereas pure being is shown at the opening of the *Logic* to be without determination, determinate *existence* involves a movement of individuation that negates the indeterminacy of pure being. If, according to Macherey, "the work exists above all through its determinate absences" (148), it does so through such a movement of negative individuation. What the work does not say is constitutive of what it is—of the selective, negative particularity of its existence. One might reflect upon how difficult it is to grasp—or perhaps rather to discuss—the literary work at a level addressed to its existence, its determinate being. What would it entail to *analyze* the existence of the work, to "elaborate" it as Macherey would like us to do, while also leaving it as it is? To address the work *as it exists* would be to study the mediation of its particularity through the relation between what it is and what it is not. When we speak of literary form, I wonder if we do not miss the problem of literary determination situated at this level. Form determines, but it is also the abstraction through which we address the *result* of a process of determination, the "formation" of the work.

Consider how the literary-critical distinction between form and content is troubled by attention to the materiality of poetic language. The material inscription of the poem evades the distinction between form and content, falling into neither category. This has something to do with the peculiar function of poetic signs. Their arrangement (form) both determines their meaning (content) and depends on their inscription (matter). But to treat signs *as* material units, and thereby to register the physical arrangement that determines their content, is to perceive them as strangely contentless. This paradoxical structure constitutes the *ex-istence* of poetic signs, which is irreducible to either physical facticity or ideal sense. Attention to poetic determination thus involves addressing poetic language within the medium of this irreducibility, thinking "determination" as the field of mediations among form, content, and matter that constitutes the existence of the poem (rather than its meaning, or its form, or its material inscription). Poetic determination is neither prior to nor subsequent to form, content, or matter, but is rather the complex composition of their mediating articulation, as this is constructed by literary-critical knowledge. If we read for this reticent dimension of poetic language, we will find that instances of poetic indeterminacy do not dissolve the determination of the poem but rather display it. Indeterminacy is not the undoing of poetic determination but the mark of its insistence. This is the way of approaching literary works Macherey's theory foregrounds.

As I deploy the term, "poetic determination" is the field of literary/critical mediation in which the writing and the reading of literary works are reciprocally constitutive, the field of mediation in which the literary object is constructed as an object of critical knowledge. To address literary works through their critical construction is not to relativize the claims of literary-critical knowledge, but rather to establish the field of determination in which claims about the object can be rigorously situated and considered. Thus, the study of poetic determination is the study of the work within the field of its critical construction: the determination of the work is considered at the crux of its written constitution and its constitution as read. The work *exists*, exceeding its material inscription, at this crux, and "determination" is the category in terms of which we can study this dimension of the poetic work and its critical reception.

Returning to Baudelaire, I want to consider how "the production of a tautology" functions in the final tercet of "Obsession," and how poetic determination here articulates, divides, and dislocates a major figural locus not only in *Les fleurs du mal* but also in nineteenth-century French poetry more broadly. Macherey claims that "what the work does not say, it *manifests*, it lays bare, in its every letter: it is made of nothing other. This silence gives it its existence" (84). I will show that it is the manifest silence of Baudelaire's poem which lays bare the specificity of its existence, registering the peculiar reticence of this dimension of poetic language.

Sont elles-mêmes des toiles

The attentive reader of Baudelaire's "Obsession" encounters an interpretive crux at the end of the first line of the poem's final tercet:

Mais les ténèbres sont elles-mêmes des toiles
Où vivent, jaillissant de mon oeil par milliers,
Des êtres disparus aux regards familiers.[3]

The significance of the word *toiles* is particularly crucial in the first line, since it serves as the vehicle of a metaphor for which *ténèbres* is the tenor. A major signifier not only in *Les fleurs du mal* but in the Romantic tradition that precedes it, *les ténèbres* links an exterior, phenomenal condition of darkness or shadow with an interior spiritual or intellectual condition of doubt, ignorance, incertitude, or unease, potentially fusing these "exterior" and "interior" senses in the medium of a general *obscurity*. This synthesis of phenomenal and spiritual shadow is also drawn into relation, through connotation, with the liturgical Office des Ténèbres and thus with the extinguishing, one by one, of the candles illuminating a church, with the singing of Lamentations and the recitation of Psalms. It is unambiguous that, through the rhetoric of metaphor, the sense of this major Romantic signifier (*ténèbres*) is *determined* by the word *toiles*: "les ténèbres *sont elles-mêmes* des toiles." But the meaning of this determination itself is ambiguous. This ambiguity requires us to register, elaborate, and begin to theorize the complex dialectic of indeterminacy and determination at issue in this line and this tercet.

Most generally, the noun *toile* denotes a woven textile, a fabric. More specifically, it may refer to an artist's canvas (or, by synecdoche, a painting), or to a tapestry (as in *la toile de Pénélope*), or to a theater backdrop (*toile de fond*). In these cases the word denotes the fabric of an artistic composition, the surface *upon* which one paints, *within* which one weaves a scene, or *before* which a scene is enacted. The term might also refer to the canvas of a sail. But *toile* can also denote a spider's web, as in *toile d'araignée*, and thus a network of filaments woven by an arachnid, rather than a human being, upon which living prey, rather than artistic compositions, are captured. In this case, the mesh of the textile is both a home and a trap, and we can see how these connotations may be figuratively associated with the fabric of artistic representation, as in Maya Deren's *Meshes of the Afternoon* or the funeral shroud Penelope weaves and unravels, detaining the suitors and linking death, mourning, and capture with the duplicity of artistic making and unmaking. One might then seek a synthetic meaning of the metaphor determining "ténèbres" as "des toiles": a symbol combining the artist/spider as the figure of a constructive yet obscure making, *poiesis*, at once domestic and uncanny, dangerous and sustaining, natural and surreal, intentional and unconscious—as in Joanne Kyger's *The Tapestry and the Web*:

> and what am I?
> a flower
> a deer
> a spider waiting
>   for the breeze to
>   speed my weaving
>
> the reverie of
>
> memory past
> what I know.[4]

The role Kyger attributes to her lyric speaker—a spider waiting as it weaves the reverie of memory—is attributed by Gilles Deleuze to the narrator of Proust's *In Search of Lost Time*: "The Search is not constructed like a cathedral or like a gown, but like a web. The spider-Narrator, whose web is the Search being spun, being woven by each thread stirred by one sign or another: the web and the spider, the web and the body are one and the same machine."[5] But before leaping to this kind of synthetic, symbolic reading of the figure, let us remain for now at the level of denotation, where we confront an ordinary interpretive ambiguity whose complexities we need to consider before constructing an adequate approach to the final tercet of the poem and to the figural determination of *ténèbres*.

The ambiguity of denotative reference is foregrounded if we consider the problem of translation. In my view, *des toiles* could most plausibly be translated by either "canvases" or "webs," and the problem is that these are *equally* plausible. In her prose translation, Francis Scarfe chooses "canvases," as do Walter Martin, William Aggeler, Roy Campell, and J. E. Tiball, among others. Cyril Scott opts for "veils," but the French is not *voiles*, which would also have rhymed with *étoiles* in the previous stanza and might have served as an apt figure for "les ténèbres." Jack Squire translates *toiles* as "curtain," but that corresponds more closely to *le voile* or *le rideau*. James McGowan gives

us "screen," but this usage is perhaps overdetermined by the anachronistic
context of cinema. Richard Howard's translation avoids the problem by not
translating the word at all. He offers:

> Yet even shadows have their shapes which live
> where I imagine them to be, the hordes
> of vanished souls whose eyes acknowledge mine.[6]

Here the place of *des toiles* is occupied by "their shapes," which has little to
do with the semantic field of the French term. In her book *Dead Time*, Elissa
Marder offers a more direct translation of the first line of the tercet: "The
shadows are themselves canvases."[7] I think that works, and I translate the
two tercets of the sonnet as follows:

> How you would please me, o night! without these stars
> Whose light speaks a language we know!
> For I seek the void, and the black, and the bare!
>
> But the shadows are themselves canvases
> Where live, bursting from my eye by thousands,
> Those vanished beings with familiar gazes. (225)

The choice of "canvases" would seem confirmed by an earlier draft in which
se peint has been crossed out and replaced with *vivent* (figure 4.1). Pichois
conjectures that Baudelaire had erased *se peint* without completing the verb,
arguing rather too forcefully that "without doubt" Baudelaire would have
written "Où se peignent," or "where are painted."[8]

In his essay, de Man argues that given the existence of this previous draft,
"'peint' confirms the reading of 'toiles' as the device by means of which
painters or dramatists project the space or stage of representation" (258).
De Man asserts that "the metaphoric crossing between perception and hallucination . . . occurs [in the final tercet] by means of the paraphernalia of
painting, which is also that of recollection and re-cognition, as the recov-
ery, to the senses, of what seemed to be forever beyond experience" (258).
So, for de Man, a lot hinges upon the "paraphernalia of painting" in the
poem. Yet Baudelaire in fact *erases* the verb *peint*, eliminating it from the
published version of the sonnet. While de Man's reference to a draft secures
the determinacy of his reading, Baudelaire's erasure actually emphasizes the
indeterminate denotation of the noun *toiles*, as does the word with which he
replaces *peint*—*vivent*—indicating that something *lives* on these canvases or,
perhaps more likely, webs. The verb *vivent sustains* the indeterminate denotation of *toiles*, and we might note the curious effect whereby the indeterminacy
of denotative reference, and thus of translation, indicates the determinacy
of the French signifier itself. The word in the poem is *toiles*. Because of its

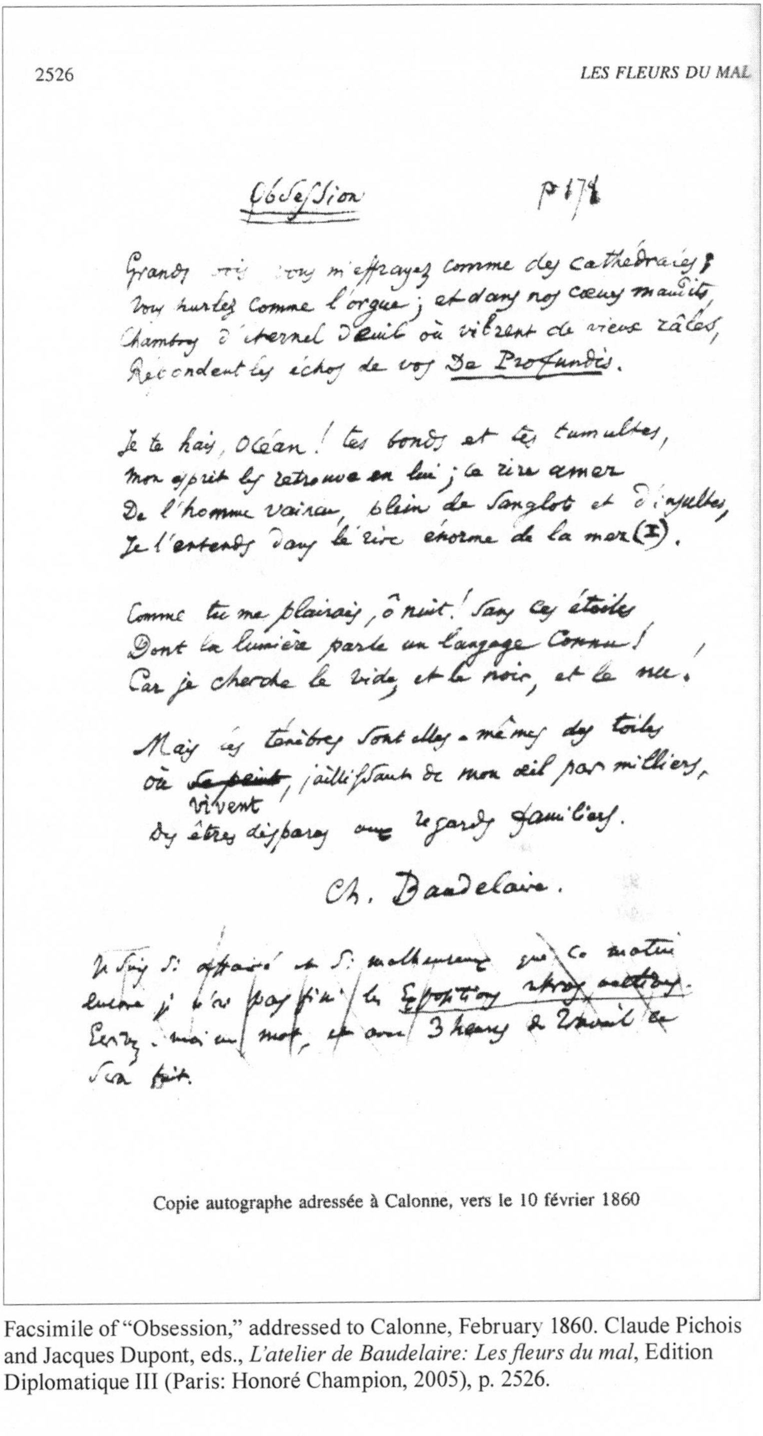

2526 *LES FLEURS DU MAL*

Obsession p 178

Grands bois, vous m'effrayez comme des cathédrales;
Vous hurlez comme l'orgue; et dans nos cœurs maudits,
Chambres d'éternel deuil où vibrent de vieux râles,
Répondent les échos de vos De Profundis.

Je te hais, Océan! tes bonds et tes tumultes,
Mon esprit les retrouve en lui; ce rire amer
De l'homme vaincu, plein de sanglots et d'insultes,
Je l'entends dans le rire énorme de la mer (I).

Comme tu me plairais, ô nuit! sans ces étoiles
Dont la lumière parle un langage connu!
Car je cherche le vide, et le noir, et le nu!

Mais les ténèbres sont elles-mêmes des toiles
Où ~~se peint~~ vivent, jaillissant de mon œil par milliers,
Des êtres disparus aux regards familiers.

Ch. Baudelaire.

Je suis si affairé et si malheureux que ce matin encore je n'ai pas fini les Expositions [illegible] mais un mot, et avec 3 heures de travail ce sera fait.

Copie autographe adressée à Calonne, vers le 10 février 1860

Facsimile of "Obsession," addressed to Calonne, February 1860. Claude Pichois and Jacques Dupont, eds., *L'atelier de Baudelaire: Les fleurs du mal*, Edition Diplomatique III (Paris: Honoré Champion, 2005), p. 2526.

complex indeterminacy, it cannot be translated or replaced by an apparently synonymous French word. If one understands that the word *could* mean either "canvases" or "webs," that is an indeterminacy introduced by the poem's reception, and a divided determinacy introduced by interpretation— not by the poem. The poem merely presents a signifier, there in its place, and the poet only decides on the word, not its interpretation. Insofar as one *necessarily* introduces indeterminacy into this determinacy, one is a "hypocrite lecteur" (8).

The ambiguity of denotative reference emphasizes the inadequacy of translation to the *connotative* field of the word. And this inadequacy, in turn, shows the obvious inadequacy of approaching poetic language through denotative reference. The *poetic* usage of *toiles* in this passage is specific insofar as it not only includes the connotative field of the word but shifts it beyond the lexical determinations of the dictionary, requiring a construction of the sense of the word, and thus the figure, at the level of the poem. This figural sense should also be weighed, I would argue, within the larger field of sense constituted by *Les fleurs du mal*—that is, at the level of the literary work. And here we touch upon Macherey's suggestive reference to weaving in his characterization of the power of literary language to distinguish itself from the usage of words in ordinary language: "Weaving them into the relations of a text, it makes of words something other than words, and, once torn from their ordinary connections and inaugurated into a different order, a new 'reality' emerges" (50). What we have to construct, through critical activity, is the "new reality" constituted by the final tercet of "Obsession," rather than merely the meaning of the words with which it is woven. With Macherey's own metaphor in mind (*tissant*) we might be tempted to suggest that the weaving of the word *toiles* into the poem figures the function of poetic language itself. But before we can consider such an understanding of the metaphor, we first have to work *with* the words that are woven, situating them within the referential field of the work.

If we begin to reconstruct the weaving of words through *Les fleurs du mal*, we find that Baudelaire uses the plural noun *toiles* only twice in the volume, once in "Obsession" and once in "Sepulcher," where it also rhymes with *étoiles*:

> À l'heure où les chastes étoiles
> Ferment leurs yeux appesantis,
> L'araignée y fera ses toiles,
> Et la vipère ses petits.

> At the hour when the chaste stars
> Close their heavy eyes,
> There shall the spider make her webs,
> And the viper her brood. (206–207)

Here *toiles* does indeed refer to the webs of a spider, weaving these under a sky in which the stars have closed their eyes. "Sepulcher" precedes "Obsession" by eight poems in the 1861 edition, and their proximity links the spider's webs of the former poem to the usage of *toiles* in the latter—especially since the fourth "Spleen" poem, located immediately before "Obsession," refers to spiders tightening their filaments (*ses filets*) at the bottom of the speaker's brain. Yet in "Music," the poem just prior to "Sepulcher," the word *toile* clearly refers to a sail (204–5), and "canvas" is the contextually clear sense of the word in each of the six other instances in which Baudelaire uses the singular noun.[9]

So if we can in fact read *des toiles* as canvases, webs, or the canvas-web of the artist-spider, we can now consider what would be at stake in deciding between these. If we decide on "canvases," the poem ends with the gazes of "vanished beings" leaping from paintings—and Baudelaire was certainly obsessed with the tenebrous glint of oil paint. If we read *toiles* as "webs," the poem ends in a disturbing figuration of the familiar gazes of vanished beings as the eyes of thousands of spiders, or their prey, suddenly bursting from the speaker's own gaze—and this is a superb Baudelairian figure for the psychology of obsession. If we decide on the synthetic resolution of "canvas" and "web" through the implicit image of the artist-spider, this figure would unify the act of looking at a painting with that of weaving a poem, and the difficult adequacy of the compound figure to this complex sense would testify, once again, that Baudelaire is an artist equal to the demands of his obsessions. The synthesis of *making* the poem with *looking at* a painting would then double the synthesis of production and reception implicit in the image of "familiar gazes" bursting *from* the gaze of the speaker. We could say that the poem ends with the glint of mediation between phenomenal reception and production, oil paint and spider's eye, in the uncanny familiarity of shadows. The thematics of mediation are themselves *rhetorically* mediated by a split figure held together by a single word (*toiles*).

But if we *can* move from two possible referents to a figure synthesizing them, *should* we do so? What if the indeterminacy of Baudelaire's poetic usage is itself crucial to its meaning? What if the denotative split itself, suspended prior to dialectical integration, *is* the vehicle of the metaphor?—an especially pressing question considering that its tenor, *ténèbres*, signifies not only sensory obscurity but also cognitive irresolution. Irresolvable semantic ambiguity *itself*, rather than its dialectical resolution, would be an aptly *negative* figure of shadows, or of darkness, or of doubt. But not that, even if we read indeterminacy of reference *as* the meaning of the metaphor, we reimpose referential determination. We read indeterminacy itself as the vehicle of the metaphor. Noting this dialectical structure, spiraling outward our interpretive efforts, let us tarry further with the potential field of "meaning" the final tercet of "Obsession" opens and participates in within *Les fleurs du mal*. Then we can attempt to approach the determination of Baudelaire's poetic

language in a manner that does not give way to an infinite process of dialectical displacement, concealed by the apparent resolution of interpretive
decision.

Mais les ténèbres

If the interpretive ambiguity of *toiles* involves a hermeneutic dialectic of
indeterminacy and determination, this very dialectic, and the problem of
mediation it involves, is also a major theme of the poem's final tercets. The
speaker *seeks* the indeterminacy of absolute negation:

> How you please me, o night! without these stars
> Whose light speaks a language we know!
> For I seek the void, and the black, and the bare!

But what he finds is the mitigated indeterminacy of shadows or darkness
mediating between the well-known language of the constellations and the
nothingness of the absolute void: "Mais les ténèbres sont elles-mêmes des
toiles." *Ténèbres* would seem to signify the phenomenal and spiritual *determinacy* of mediating negation: dark*ness*, or shadows, or doubt—a medium
of obscurity that is not an absolute absence of light but rather a lack of it, in
which *relative* darkness is itself a source of reflexive uncertainty, a *delimited*
region of darkness evoking an unseen sensible form. The figuration of *les
ténèbres* by *des toiles* determines the void through mediation, constituting a
bounded space where the chiasmus of phenomenal productivity and reception is delimited from the groundless howling of great woods, the enormous
laughter of the sea, and the absolute negation of the void, the black, and the
bare: figures of the sublime we encounter in the poem's two quatrains and
first tercet. What remains of the banished stars is not nothing, but the *trace* of
their absence, the familiar gazes of vanished beings. The registration of their
residual existence requires a spontaneous faculty of perception that *makes*
them appear within the locus of their disappearance, yet still surprises the
perceiver through the involuntary suddenness of this productive activity.

As in Hegel's *Logic*, the problem of the relation between absolute negation (pure being *or* pure nothingness) and the negativity of finite determinacy,
mediation, runs through *Les fleurs du mal*. But when Hegel reclaims the true
as the whole, through Absolute Knowledge or the Idea, the movement of the
concept comes to include all contradictions in the plenitude of *infinite* mediation, rendering the absolute determinate rather than void. The Absolute, for
Hegel, is not "the void, and the black, and the bare"; it must be produced
through mediation. Does Baudelaire's poetry, and the metaphor we have been
studying, move toward such a determinacy of the absolute? Is Baudelaire a
poet of determinate infinity, recovered through mediation, or is he a poet

of the finitude of all determinacy? How is the contradiction between these potential poetic commitments itself mediated in *Les fleurs du mal*?

The composition of the book involves a testing of possible poetic stances, of declarative and affective inclinations frequently ironized as poses, through the mutually destabilizing relationship of different moods or personae mobilized in the volume. But it also involves a recursive clarification and sharpening of certain norms. For example, although we veer between infernal abasement and heavenly elevation (Spleen and Ideal), in "Hymn to Beauty" the attribution of Beauty's origin to either God or Satan is a matter of *indifference*, since it is the advent of Beauty's singular qualities—"rhythm, fragrance, glimmer"—that "opens the door / Of an Infinite that I love and have never known" (62–63). Beauty opens the door of an Infinite but does not render it fully attainable; it is a "glimmer" rather than a blinding sun or an ideal form, and this is a privileged term (*lueur*) for the phenomenal experience of fleeting singularities in *Les fleurs du mal*. Yet this word also designates the maliciously gleaming eyes of the old man in "The Seven Old Men," a gleam that portends his auto-multiplication into a potentially infinite series of doubles. The bad infinity of this repetition, which horrifies the speaker, leaves his soul like a barge without sails "upon a monstrous and unbounded sea!" (265). Here a fleeting phenomenal singularity (*lueur*) portends a potentially infinite replication of identity that cancels phenomenal particularity, giving way to an unbearably boundless indeterminacy. Yet to render this conversion of singularity into boundlessness *in a poem* is to determine it through the bounded negation of that boundlessness. Neither pure negation ("the void, and the black, and the bare") nor phenomenal singularity (the malicious glimmer of an eye) can be inscribed directly in the poem. To be evoked, absolute indeterminacy, pure singularity, or infinite repetition have to undergo the shadowy determinacy of mediation: the formal boundedness of the poem, the material inscription of writing, the receptive production of meaning.

Ténèbres—whether it means shadows, darkness, or spiritual doubt—is one among the names in *Les fleurs du mal* for the determinacy of mediation, the imperfection of the absolute, against which the poem may strain but which it cannot escape. Like Baudelaire's allegorical swan, dying of thirst beside a "waterless gutter," the poet is a malcontent who twists a "convulsive neck" toward the sky "as if addressing reproaches to God" (257). In "Correspondences," phenomenal singularities, read as signs, mingle in a "shadowy and profound unity," and certain "scents" are said to partake of the "expansion of infinite things" (23). But in "The Swan" ("Le Cygne"), the "forests of symbols" evoked as the temple of nature in "Correspondences" become "the forest of my mind's exile," wherein the poet thinks "of starving orphans parched as flowers," "of the captives, of the vanquished . . . and of many more" (259). Baudelaire's poetic achievement reaches its pinnacle not with the attainment of the infinitely harmonious mediation sounded in "Correspondences," but in the voice of a speaker "oppressed by an image" of a dirty swan whose "mad gestures" are "like exiles, ridiculous and sublime / And gnawed by an insatiable desire!" (257). This is the insatiable desire for the void, the black, and the bare the poet seeks: a desire for infinite negation that in fact gives way to the finitude of determinate existence. Like the Infinite beyond the open door in "Hymn to Beauty," or the "thousands" of vanished beings mentioned in "Obsession," the "many more" evoked at the end of "The Swan" can only be gestured toward; they cannot *all* be included within the finitude of the poem's determinacy. The movement from the penultimate to the final stanza of "Obsession"—from "For I seek" to "But"—suggests that Baudelaire is a poet of finite determinacy. The *grammatical situation* of his shadows confirms that they are not a determinate figure of the Infinite, but a concession to the finitude of determinacy. It is the grammar of the poem's final sentence that positions the sense of its metaphorical rhetoric. *Mais* is in this sense the most important word in the poem—not an absolute negation, but a mediating qualification—and it would be an aptly deflationary claim to place it among the most important words in Baudelaire's *oeuvre*. All indeterminacy to which a poem gives rise is produced by its concession to determinacy: infinite indeterminacy is a function of the fact that the poem cannot be more than what it is, does not say more than it says, is finite. If the word can *mean* either "canvases" or "webs," it only *is toiles*. The existence of the word is irremediably determinate. Rather than choosing among interpretive indeterminacies, we are trying to situate its determinate existence.

Écart, déplacement, décalage

Let us recall some of Macherey's theses: (1) What the work does not say makes it what it is. (2) The necessity of the work is founded upon the multiplicity of its meanings. (3) Elaborating the work, the activity of critical interrogation institutes a certain distance, or rift, between the object and the object of knowledge, delimiting a measurable space and measuring, within it, the distance between several meanings. Consider de Man's reduction of "Obsession" to hermeneutic transparency—a gesture that is highly uncharacteristic, given his characteristic vigilance on this point. To stabilize his claim that "we all perfectly and quickly understand 'Obsession,'" de Man has to stabilize the meaning of the word *toiles* by referring to a previous draft, thus stabilizing the figure itself and the "possibility of representation" it asserts. Unlike the earlier draft, the work *does not say* "où peint," securing the reference to an artist's canvas. De Man interprets *what the poem says* through *something other than the poem*, rather than working from *what the poem does not say* toward the complex discrepancy that it *is*. By annihilating the negativity of what the poem does not say through reference to a draft that says *something else*, de Man translates it into mere intelligibility, failing to grasp the resistance of the final tercet to his translation. The opening quatrains and first tercet of "Obsession" may indeed be characterized by "figural stability"—we readily grasp the gothic chill linking woods and cathedrals, the subjective anguish exteriorized in the tumults of the sea, or the yearning for absolute negation extrapolated from the desire for a starless sky. *But* (*mais*) the problem presented by the final tercet is that its metaphor does not produce a stable figure: one cannot compose an image of *where* these vanished beings live ("où vivent"), of *where* their familiar gazes reside as they are encountered "bursting from my eye."

To measure the distance between several meanings, rather than either forcing an interpretive choice or forcing an interpretive synthesis, is to *locate* the dislocation their reticence imposes upon the poem. One registers the resistance of *toiles* to figural interpretation not merely to emphasize interpretive indeterminacy, but rather to indicate the force of determinacy itself. The being-there of *des toiles*, at the end of the first line of the final tercet, is riven between the ease with which it fits into rhyming with *ces étoiles* and the complex figural ambiguity it installs in apposition to absent stars. It is *positioned* by the grammar of the sonnet, at the end of a line beginning with a conjunctive qualification (*mais*), pushing apposition toward opposition. At the crux of "form" and "content," we begin to see the word *in* its location, *at* the intersection of the poem's apostrophes, its strident antihumanist negations, and its compensatory gestures of mediation, suggesting the dislocated site ("où vivent") of the uncanny. This "real complexity," which cannot be attributed to the controlling intention of an author or mitigated by the interpretive decision of a critic, consists neither in the form of the poem, nor in its content, nor in the synthesis of these into its poetic meaning, but rather in the tension between the way figuration is at once located and dislocated, the manner in which this tension, this resistance woven into its texture, *makes* the poem what it is through what, in its finitude, it does not say. This is the level at which the determinacy of poetic existence could be situated.

The Setting of the Romantic Sun

So far I have tried to elaborate what Macherey calls the "determinate silence" of Baudelaire's poem. But for Macherey, there is another crucial dimension of the determinacy of the literary work: its resistance to an ideological field from which it emerges, and which it transforms. For Macherey, the weaving of words into the new reality of a literary work creates a "distance that separates the work from the ideology," and this distance, he argues, "is encountered in its very letter" (149). How does the composition of the metaphor we have been investigating transform an ideological field from which it distances the poem?

The ideological problem at issue bears upon the function of the poetic imagination—specifically, the putative power of the imagination to figure its own limits. In the Romantic tradition Baudelaire extends and delimits, the word *ténèbres* is a major signifier of such figuration. For example, Hugo's great sequence, "Au bord de l'infini," begins with the sentence "J'avais devant les yeux les ténèbres."[10] The edge of infinity begins with darkness, with shadows, with spiritual doubt, and these *are there* before the speaker's eyes. Imagelessness is presented as image. Translating quite literally to retain the position of the pronouns:

> J'avais devant les yeux les ténèbres. L'abîme
> Qui n'a pas de rivage et qui n'a pas de cime
> Était là, morne, immense; et rien n'y remuait.
> Je me sentais perdu dans l'infini muet.
> Au fond, à travers l'ombre, impénétrable voile,
> On apercevait Dieu comme un sombre étoile.

> I had before my eyes the darkness. The abyss
> Which had no shore and which had no summit
> Was there, bleak, immense; and nothing stirred therein.
> I felt myself lost in infinite muteness.
> At bottom, through shadow, impenetrable veil,
> One descried God like a somber star.

Here, "les ténèbres" flows easily into "l'abîme. In the Romantic imagination, and often in Baudelaire's, the term is potentially exchangeable for a series of signifiers—*abîme, gouffre, l'ombre, muet*, and so on—all of which in one way or another portend the spiritual crisis of the retraction of God evoked by Hugo. Yet in "Obsession," we find "les ténèbres" *differentiated* from this chain of equivalences—from "le vide, et le noir, et le nu"—by the qualification of *mais*, and it is at precisely this moment of differentiation that the word becomes the tenor of a metaphor transforming it into *something else*. The figuration of the limits of the imagination, the figuration of a concession to these limits, is itself delimited by the failure of the figure to compose an image. Hugo's speaker has "les ténèbres" before his eyes, but when "les ténèbres" are figured as "des toiles," the torn sign into which this shadowy darkness is incorporated transforms it into something other than what is there before me. If I register the split referent of *des toiles*, then what I have before my eyes is not an image but a material signifier. Determining *les ténèbres* through its indeterminacy, *toiles* becomes the site of the signifier at which the figuration by the Romantic imagination of its own limits is captured and woven into a formal complexity exceeding the parameters of imagination per se. Such complexity requires *analysis, exposition* in order to exist: it exists only as an object of knowledge. And if such analysis does not make it exist, does not separate the literary work from the field of creative intention and receptive intuition, then the poem falls back out of its complexity, into the very ideology it has in fact transformed.

The exemplary reading of *Les fleurs du mal* through the ideological relay between creative intention and receptive intuition is that of Jean-Pierre Richard in *Poésie et profondeur*. To be clear, I say "exemplary" in part because Richard's phenomenological essay, "Profondeur de Baudelaire," is among the finest interpretations of *Les fleurs du mal* I have encountered, as subtle and as philosophically rich as it is beautifully written. But how does Richard proceed? He traces relations among images and "sensible schemes" in Baudelaire's oeuvre in order to limn the mysteries of analogy between spirit and reality that it explores. The hidden jewel, the glimmering of light through mist, interior shadows held in tension with heliotropism, the lustre of the sea, the transparent yet obdurate substance of a pane of glass (la vitre), the expressive flows of blood and fire and tears, the relation between putrefaction and the spiritualization of matter: all of these Richard draws from the poems as elements of "le monde baudelairien," which is also "le drame intérieur de Baudelaire" and, of course, "la mystique baudelarienne"—a shifting terrain of sensations that must be entered into and lived through the receptive imagination of the reader.[11] Relations among these images, textures of sensation, and logics of elemental mediation are drawn out of the context of the poems in which they are presented and recomposed in the seductive lucidity of Richard's prose, such that "la sorcellerie évocatoire" by which Baudelaire defined poetic writing becomes Richard's own method. As Richard acknowledges, this evocative sorcery "rests entirely upon a linguistic optimism" (160). "To each of these landscapes," he says of Baudelaire's sensory worlds, "corresponds a rhetoric," and this correspondence "would have been impossible if between language, mind, and reality, there did not exist, a priori, certain internal relations, certain analogies of structure." "Verbal architecture," Richard continues, "must rejoin a sensible architecture if one would pass seamlessly from a phrase to a reality and a reality to a phrase" (159). For Richard, this is "a consequence of the universal law of analogy between words and things" that is affirmed by both his critical method and Baudelaire's supposed doctrine of correspondences. What we have tried to show by elaborating a pivotal line in "Obsession" is that, on the contrary, Baudelaire's poetry arrives at its most complex determinations when it resists this law of analogy, when its figurative levels resist the synthesis of imagination, and when—regardless of Baudelaire's intentions—it disarticulates the evocative sorcery of words like *ténèbres* and *toiles*. For Richard, the interior hollow of conscience is "the space of ecstasy and vertigo which constitutes the locus of Baudelarian *spirituality*," but Richard will attempt to show how this hollow, or cavity (*creux*), is "replenished and humanized" by the "activity of the imagination" (95).[12] This exactly formulates the humanist ideology relayed through "the activity of the imagination" from the compositional activity of the poet to the receptive experience of the reader. And such humanism will always try to recuperate the sickness of Baudelaire's flowers by watering them with good intentions. When we produce an analysis of poetic determination rather than of the poetic imagination, we read not in terms of creation, intention, or technique and not in terms of "content" or "form" (which may always be subsumed back into the relay between technique and intention), but at the specific level of poetic existence rather than its expressive cause. The analysis of poetic determination grasps the resonance of poetic signs in a manner circumventing the power of imagination by showing that the nonidentity of the sign both to what it says and what it does not say is the field of determinacy that makes the poem what it is.

We can approach the stakes of this method, in the case of "Obsession," by considering *des toiles* as what Deleuze calls an "involuntary sign."[13] Again, the final tercet of the poem seems to be "about" such signs—the registration of gazes that "burst from my eye." Perhaps it is about madness, which is exactly what Deleuze is discussing when he refers to "involuntary signs that resist the sovereign organization of language and cannot be mastered in words and phrases, but rout the logos and involve us in another realm" (173). Perhaps the final tercet of "Obsession" attempts a *representation* of madness, or could be read as such: the speaker plunging, from his preference for a starless night and his pursuit of absolute vacancy, into a disturbing encounter with "those vanished beings" whose familiar gazes inhabit the very absence of determination he had sought, showing its emptiness to be replete with teeming, shadowy traces of undead life. Yet the *way* in which this putative representation transpires renders it irreducible to representation, and renders dubious the scene of representation itself. This is only appropriate, since madness cannot be represented; it is precisely that which evades and cancels powers of representation. The tercet can be grasped as an *instance* of madness, of obsession, only insofar as it is *not* a representation thereof but is rather the site of the advent of an involuntary sign that skews and disorders the metaphorical rendering of the limit of Romantic imagination, *ténèbres*. It is the resonance of this sign, *des toiles*, within and throughout the ideological field it transforms that renders it involuntary: though he is certainly capable of the intentional deployment of ambiguous signs, we gain nothing by speculating that Baudelaire set out, in this line, to displace the imaginary rendering of a major Romantic signifier. It is the capacity of involuntary signs to circumvent the productive and receptive power of imagination that renders them signs of a possible or inchoate madness, and here the delirium is that of the poem itself, rather than a psychological state represented by its author or "imagined" by its reader.[14] Just as it cannot be represented, madness is unimaginable.

Such analysis brings into focus "the materiality of the signifier," insofar as it disarticulates the referential dimension of the sign by articulating its divisions and measuring the consequences of its rifts for the understanding of its specificity. Through the kind of exposition we are practicing, what the sign does not say makes its curious obduracy appear. When we do not make it appear, this material obduracy is like the "forgotten canvas" of "A Carrion" (91), or perhaps "the green waters of Lethe" flowing in veins where blood should be (221). It is like the worms, "black companions without ears and eyes" (211), remorselessly traversing the ruins of Baudelaire's "happy corpse," or it is like a "cracked bell" insofar as its enfeebled voice is akin to that of a soldier "forgotten at the edge of a lake of blood, under a heap of corpses / And who dies, unmoving, with great pains" (215). The signifier is unmoving, yet it writhes under the weight of its companions. The more meticulous our efforts to uncover its sense, the more they point back to the stasis of its body: they help us recall *that* the signifier itself has been forgotten, rather than uncovering its hidden meaning. And this also means that the materiality of the signifier is not "like" anything but its material presentation: if we have tried to show how it resists figuration, this also includes the figuration *of* this resistance we have just been suggesting. Yet something else is forgotten even *by* appeals to the materiality of the signifier: its *existence*, the manner in which its discrepant sense not only resists figuration but also exceeds the physical fact of its inscription, is irreducible to its material presentation or its grammatical site, since it also occasions a determinate delirium of implications.

Of course, it is Paul de Man himself who points us to the material existence of the signifier while criticizing the "aesthetic ideology" of thematic critics like Jean-Pierre Richard,[15] which renders figural phenomena accessible to the synthesis of the imagination through the adequation of poetic language to correspondences between words and things. So if Macherey's *A Theory of Literary Production* offers the tools for a similar if less famous critique of aesthetic ideology, working more in an Althusserian than Derridean register, what is the difference between Macherey and de Man? Perhaps what separates them is primarily a matter of emphasis: where de Man presses home the incommensurability of grammar and rhetoric to figural reading, he stresses the disruptive power of figural language, and it is the indeterminacy of referential signification that foregrounds, for him, the materiality of the signifier. For Macherey, on the other hand, it is the silence of the work and the insistence of what it does not say that foregrounds the *determinacy* of work itself, that "makes it what is it" and that bears the trace of the work's own transformation of an ideological field. This may actually be, first and foremost, a *rhetorical* difference—which would be to read it from the side of de Man. But we could also say it is a *political* difference, since Macherey wants to understand materialist criticism as form of Marxist practice in the cultural field. I would split the difference: unlike certain Marxist critics of deconstruction, I see no reason why its methods should not offer crucial resources to Marxist cultural criticism.

Consider Walter Benjamin's hugely influential readings of Baudelaire. The elaboration of motifs presents a series of figures of the commodity. For example, Benjamin tells us in "Central Park" that "the stars in Baudelaire represent a picture puzzle of the commodity. They are the ever the same in great masses."[16] But insofar as the stars figure this picture puzzle, they are inadequate to its puzzling quality, and the stars are wished away in "Obsession" for precisely this reason: their light speaks a language we already know. Like commodities, they are "the ever the same in great masses," but unlike the commodity form analyzed by Marx, they do not seem to contain sufficient mysteries and are banished in pursuit of pure indetermination. Perhaps the puzzle of the commodity lives where we are not looking for it, and perhaps it is not legible as a *picture* puzzle, but rather in the ruse of a signifier that never locks into representation, or in the unfolding of a metaphor whose vehicle captures its tenor in the discrepancies of what it does not say, rather than conveying it toward the coherence of an image. If, like Benjamin, we proceed to read the prostitute as the figural incarnation of the commodity, or if we argue that "the shock experience which the passer-by has in the crowd corresponds to the isolated 'experiences' of the worker at his machine,"[17] we recuperate the instability of modernity through the stability of representation. That is, we reify that instability as stable correspondence, figure, image. For Benjamin, Baudelaire's line from "À une passante"—"A flash . . . then the night!—Fugitive beauty"—*figures* modernity as the fleetingness of fugitive figuration. The line "Mais les ténèbres sont elles-mêmes des toiles," on the other hand, resists the reification of the figure it does not quite convey, while presenting itself as the very model ("sont elles-même") of metaphor itself. This model is undermined as it is instantiated. My point is that we should question whether there can be anything like a *figure* of the commodity, or whether we might do better to limn the contours of the problem of reification where it is not represented. Perhaps *representations* of the commodity are a poor locus for thinking through the ideological force of reification, since figural sense often requires reification rather than teaching us to undo it. Marx deploys many metaphors, but he also analytically dismantles and theoretically re-elaborates social hieroglyphs in a manner suggesting that the critique of aesthetic ideology—the critique of reified figuration—is an indispensable element not only of literary criticism but also the critique of capital.

It is curious that close reading should have become associated with "formalism," because attention to "form" does not account for the prodigious indeterminacy of sense opened by meticulous attention to the contextual specificity of signs. But nor does the prodigious *attention* to indeterminacy taken up under the banner of deconstruction necessarily account for the *determinacy* of the literary work that is the effect of its finitude, its inability to transcend its reticent inscription by saying either *one thing* or *everything*. Perhaps appeals to "form" are a way of forgetting *both* the materiality of the sign and the excess of its sense over its materiality: we idealize form, we render it material, or we render it receptive (as in Kant). The specific dimension of poetic existence, limned by attention to poetic determination, involves a strange dialectic—one that repels not only the reduction to form, content, or matter but also their integral combination. When Macherey speaks, in a manner both strange and familiar, of interrogating the distances opened by the dislocations of literary production, I think this is what he has in mind. The dialectic of literary production—the production of a tautology—involves resisting the synthesis of the poem into form, into the unity of its levels of articulation. It disarticulates this unity in order to display its suspension, rather than sublating this suspension into a further movement. Is it a discrepancy between senses of the term *aufheben* that is thus at issue? Suspension or sublation: we have to choose. And rather than suspending *this* decision, we do choose. The dialectic of poetic determination suspends the poem in the element of discrepancy through which it exists. To grasp the being-there of the poem, to situate its existence, we have to sustain this suspension even as we elucidate the parameters of its tension. That would enable us to elaborate the work while leaving it as it is.

Appendix

LXXIX OBSESSION

Grands bois, vous m'effrayez comme des cathédrales;
Vous hurlez comme l'orgue; et dans nos cœurs maudits,
Chambres d'éternel deuil où vibrent de vieux râles,
Répondent les échos de vos *De profundis*.

Je te hais, Océan! tes bonds et tes tumultes,
Mon esprit les retrouve en lui; ce rire amer
De l'homme vaincu, plein de sanglots et d'insultes,
Je l'entends dans le rire énorme de la mer.

Comme tu me plairais, ô nuit! sans ces étoiles
Dont la lumière parle un langage connu!
Car je cherche le vide, et le noir, et le nu!

Mais les ténèbres sont elles-mêmes des toiles
Où vivent, jaillissant de mon œil par milliers,
Des êtres disparus aux regards familiers.

LXXIX OBSESSION

Deep woods, you frighten me like cathedrals;
You howl like the organ; and in our damned hearts,
Chambers of eternal mourning where old death rattles vibrate,
Respond the echoes of your *De profundis*.
I hate you, Ocean! your swells and your tumults,
My mind finds them in itself; this bitter laughter
Of the vanquished man, full of sobs and insults,
I hear in the enormous laughter of the sea.
How you would please me, o night! without these stars
Whose light speaks a language we know!
For I seek the void, and the black, and the bare!
But the shadows are themselves canvases
Where live, bursting from my eye by thousands,
Those vanished beings with familiar gazes.

Notes

1. Paul de Man, "Anthropomorphism and Trope in the Lyric," in *The Rhetoric of Romanticism* (New York: Columbia University Press, 1984), 239–62.

2. Pierre Macherey, *Pour une théorie de la production littéraire* (Paris: ENS Éditions, 2014), 46. Cited hereafter in the text. All translations from this edition are my own.

3. Charles Baudelaire, "Obsession," in *The Flowers of Evil*, trans. Nathan Brown (Zagreb: MaMa, 2021), 224. Cited hereafter in the text. The French text of this dual-language edition follows that of Charles Baudelaire, *Oeuvres complètes*, ed. Claude Pichois (Paris: Gallimard, 1975). See appendix for the full text of the poem with my translation.

4. Joanne Kyger, *The Tapestry and the Web* (San Francisco: Four Seasons Foundation, 1965), 19.

5. Gilles Deleuze, *Proust and Signs*, trans. Richard Howard (Minneapolis: University of Minnesota Press, 2000), 182.

6. Charles Baudelaire, *Les Fleurs du Mal*, trans. Richard Howard (Boston: David R. Godine, 1982), 77.

7. Elissa Marder, *Dead Time: Temporal Disorders in the Wake of Modernity (Baudelaire and Flaubert)* (Stanford, CA: Stanford University Press, 2001), 32.

8. Claude Pichois, "Notes et variantes," in Baudelaire, *Oeuvres complètes*, 981.

9. For Baudelaire's usage of *toiles* and *toile*, see Robert T. Cargo, *Concordance to Baudelaire's "Les Fleurs du Mal"* (Chapel Hill: University of North Carolina Press, 1965), 313.

10. Victor Hugo, *Oeuvres poétiques* II, ed. Pierre Albouy (Paris: Gallimard, 1967), 721. My translation.

11. Jean-Pierre Richard, *Poésie et profondeur* (Paris: Éditions du Seuil, 1955), 116, 93, 114. My translation.

12. Richard writes: "Ce creux, on verra comment l'activité de l'imagination parvint en effet chez Baudelaire à le remplir et à l'humaniser" (95).

13. Deleuze, *Proust and Signs*, 173.

14. The recondite circuits of madness require the indirections of psychoanalytic interpretation for their decoding, but in the case of poetic signs the unconscious of the author or the lyric speaker is not what is at issue. Rather, our task is to situate the signifier *within* the composition of the work, rather than elsewhere. Lacan works with poetic signs in exactly this way, analyzing the grammatical priority of metonymy in the construction of metaphor and thus emphasizing the grammatical *situation* of the signifier, its "positional articulation," as the ground of metaphorical expression, or tracking the signifier *peur* (fear), as its sense is transformed across the opening scene of Racine's *Athaliah*. Lacan does not interpret the unconscious of literary characters or authors, but rather analyzes the agency of the signifier at the level of its *position*. He deploys analysis of poetic language to emphasize that "language is a system of positional coherence, and . . . this system reproduces itself within itself with an extraordinary, and frightful, fecundity." Jacques Lacan, *Seminar: Book III*, trans. Russell Grigg, ed. Jacques-Alain Miller (New York: Norton, 1993), 226–27, 262–70.

15. In "Hypogram and Inscription," de Man includes Richard in a list of "thematic critics" along with Georges Poulet and (to a degree, he says) Maurice

Blanchot. Paul de Man, "Hypogram and Inscription," in *The Resistance to Theory*, ed. Wlad Godzich (Minneapolis: Minnesota University Press, 1986), 33.

16. Walter Benjamin, "Central Park," trans. Edmund Jephcott and Howard Eiland, in *The Writer of Modern Life: Essays on Charles Baudelaire*, ed. Michael W. Jennings (Cambridge, MA: Harvard University Press, 2006), 137.

17. Benjamin, "Some Motifs in Baudelaire," trans. Harry Zohn, in *The Writer of Modern Life*, 192.

What Is Materialist Analysis?

Pierre Macherey's Spinozist Epistemology

✦

Nick Nesbitt

Pierre Macherey's *A Theory of Literary Production* might seem, to all appearances, a mere work of literary criticism, familiar in its genre, modest in its intentions, a study in which, after a somewhat lengthy methodological introduction, Macherey proceeds to offer a number of "materialist" analyses of works ranging from Lenin's comments on Tolstoy to Jules Verne, Jorge Luis Borges, and Defoe's *Robinson Crusoe*. Such a view, however, would profoundly misrepresent the enormous scope and compass of the book's epistemological implications. Instead, I wish to argue in what follows that the achievement of *A Theory of Literary Production* is far more sweeping than the analysis of a handful of classic novels; Macherey, in this, his first book, in point of fact puts forward a generic protocol for the *properly materialist* analysis of textual, symbolic objects of all types, a fully and compellingly original analytical practice for the critique of discourse as such.

   To fully attend to the radicality of this gesture requires delineating the precise nature of Macherey's "materialism." Initially, it will surprise none of his readers that materialism in Macherey's understanding receives a comprehensively Spinozist inflection. While Macherey only mentions Spinoza nine times in the entire book, and then only in passing, Warren Montag has shown the degree to which Spinoza's epistemology—inflected through a series of intensive exchanges with Macherey's then-teacher Louis Althusser from 1961 onward—underwrites and founds an encompassing philosophico-critical project.[1] Indeed, it is now clear, given the trajectory of Macherey's research, that from his first, precocious contribution to *Reading Capital* in 1965, through his explosive and highly influential critique of Hegel's misreadings of Spinoza in *Hegel or Spinoza* (1979), and culminating in his extraordinarily meticulous, systematic, and original interpretation of Spinoza's *Ethics* across five volumes and over a thousand pages, Macherey has synthetically redeployed Spinoza to articulate a comprehensive theory of materialist analysis, one that fully takes into account and builds upon the classic Althusserian critiques of empiricism, hermeneutics, totality, and negative-Hegelian dialectics.

In what follows, after retracing the key assertions of Macherey's materialist methodology in *A Theory of Literary Production*, I expand this reading
both backward, to return to Macherey's underappreciated contribution to
Reading Capital, and forward, to argue that his 1965 analysis of the opening pages of *Capital* should rightfully be read in light of Macherey's later
elaboration of a Spinozist epistemology of a "non-Hegelian," "materialist
dialectic" both in the astounding final pages of *Hegel or Spinoza* as well as in
his five-volume interpretation of the *Ethics*.[2]

Textual Production in a Materialist Mode

A Theory of Literary Production initiates its materialist critique via a threefold
proscription: against empiricism, against hermeneutics, against expressive
totality. Each of these protocols resonates in consonance with Althusser's
famous critical introduction to *Reading Capital* published the year before.
Each of these proscriptions can in turn be traced to the subterranean influence of Spinoza on the thought of Althusser and his students, an influence to
be explicated and further elaborated in Macherey's later works.
    Against empiricism. If the study of literature traditionally attends to
an empirically accessible domain or field, Macherey rejects this "necessarily insufficient" orientation to argue instead that critical analysis, properly
understood, entails in every case the novel *construction* of its object of analysis: "Rational investigation bears directly upon objects that have no prior
existence, but are instead *produced.*"[3] This is the materialist lesson Althusser
had drawn from Marx's crucial 1857 methodological introduction to the
Grundrisse notebooks, where Marx rejects Adam Smith's empiricist, representational method to assert instead a properly materialist, *productionist*
epistemology.[4] If Smith famously asserts the universally observable nature
of human economic comportment as a "propensity to truck, barter, and
exchange," such an assertion constitutes the abstract, merely conceptual *representation* and generalization of an empirically observable series.[5] Against
the inadequacy of Smith's method of mere empiricist representation, flawed
in its derivation of general knowledge from immediate, sensuous impressions,
Marx—and Althusser and Macherey in his wake—asserts the autonomy of
conceptual production, the *reproduction* (as opposed to representation) of the
real object as what Marx calls a "thought-concrete" (*Gedankenkonkretum*).[6]
    Macherey redeploys this fundamental assertion of *Reading Capital* in the
opening pages of *A Theory of Literary Production*. Never the mere exposition or translation of a latent, hidden meaning, adequate knowledge of a
text requires the incipient production of an analytical discourse, an object
necessarily distinct from that initial text itself (6). This analysis will furthermore have as its content not the description of an authorial intention but the
presentation of the "laws of production" of the text in question, the synthetic

elaboration of the conditions of its situated necessity: "To know the conditions of a process: this is the true program of a theoretical investigation" (8,
10, translation modified). Such an inquiry will refuse the mere description of
a product (for transmission, for consumption); instead, it will formulate the
universal and necessary "laws of literary production," a general knowledge
of textual fabrication that is distinctly Spinozist in its affirmation of necessity, of an adequate knowledge of the common, universal notions of textual
production, before, ideally, further articulating the singular essence of any
given discursive object (13).[7]

Against textual hermeneutics. From the critique of empiricism necessarily
follows a refusal of any hermeneutic that would seek to reveal the hidden
truth lying latent within a text: "It is not enough to unfold the line of the
text to discover the message inscribed there, for this inscription would be
that of an empirical fact" (85, translation modified). Textual interpretation—
understood as the revelation of an immanent meaning (*sens*), as the true,
concealed content of a text that would take form in critical discourse—
inherently relies on an ideology of *depth*. Immanent critique constitutes, in
this view, an empiricism of the factic text in its putative self-sufficiency; in its
place, Macherey calls for adequate knowledge to be derived from the text,
but as its analytic supplement: neither translation of an immanent content
nor comprehension in light of a normative act of judgment indexified to an
objectified truth, instead, "analysis can hope to articulate the *necessity* determining the textual object" (87).

Macherey associates such a procedure with a weakened form of analysis.
If in so-called structural analysis (Macherey's example is Roland Barthes)
there occurs a certain minimal fabrication of "the object of an analysis," this
nonetheless remains an empirically derived, immanent criticism, one that
understands the text as the utilitarian carrier of an encoded message, "its
value lying in the specific information that it transmits" (158, translation
modified). This critical rendering of a message encrypted within the depths of
the text requires a mere act of translation to render its truth visible, *decoded*
into the language of structuralism, *reduced* into the form of a totalized structure of meaning "deposited in the interior of the work" (159, translation
modified). Montag has argued that in place of this structuralist hermeneutic,
the materialism of the textual object that Macherey calls for, on the model
of Spinoza's critique in the *Tractatus Theologico-Politicus*, considers "writing, as a part of nature in its materiality, as irreducible to anything outside of
itself, no longer secondary in relation to that which it represents or expresses,
a repetition of something posited as primary."[8] This materialism of the textual object, rejecting the hermeneutics of depth, attends to the pure textual
surface in its fully present materiality: "The work hides nothing, it holds no
secret: it is fully legible, offered to view, given up" (111, translation modified).

The literary work is thus fundamentally incomplete, contradictory, and
devoid of a coherent totality whose immanent meaning could be simply

decoded and translated via the revelatory logos of the critical operation. Macherey rejects any notion of the consistent unity of a text, affirming instead its necessary "incompleteness and informity" (88, translation modified). Analysis, in this view, consists not in revelation but in the production, as thought-concrete (Marx's *Gedankenkonkretum*), of the structure in its internal *décalage*, this uneven textual development "corresponding" to the work without constituting its mere reflection (89). Criticism devoted to the work's specious totality remains in this view mere interpretation, the rendition of a principle that would conjure the coherence of any such totality, the nominal identity of its unity, the reason underwriting its harmony (170).

On the Inadequacy of the Structuralist Combinatory

These critiques of empiricism, hermeneutics, and totality necessarily culminate in Macherey's comprehensive rejection of the notion of structure as totality. In *A Theory of Literary Production*, Macherey systematically deploys the critique of Claude Lévi-Strauss's structuralism that had been patiently elaborated in Althusser's seminar and subsequent exchanges between the two since 1961. Warren Montag has described in painstaking, revelatory detail the complex articulations of this critique, in which, most notably, it is Macherey, Althusser's astonishingly precocious student, who identifies the contradictions in the master's presentation of the concept of structure in *Reading Capital*.[9]

Elements of this critique of structuralism were first elaborated in Althusser's 1962–63 seminar on structuralism (in which Macherey participated), and subsequently developed in an exchange of letters between Althusser and Macherey at the moment of the publication of the *Reading Capital* seminar in 1965; again in 1966, in Althusser's 1963 essay "On the Materialist Dialectic: On the Unevenness of Origins," collected in *For Marx*; and again in "On Feuerbach" from 1967. As Montag shows, this discussion, marked by Althusser's self-contradictions, flashes of insight, backtracking, and self-censorship, never amounts to a coherent, totalized presentation of its object. After tracing an unpredictably inflected "prehistory" of structuralism, from Edmund Husserl and Wilhelm Dilthey through Georges Canguilhem, Tran Duc Thao, and Jacques Derrida, Montag focuses in particular on Althusser's twofold rejection of Lévi-Strauss's structuralist method, as simultaneously comprising a *transcendental idealism* and *empiricist functionalism*.

For Lévi-Strauss, Althusser argues in the 1962 seminar, the universal ban on incest identified by structural anthropology functions as a transhistorical, transcendental category that grounds human identity in its singular manifestations across time and space, determining the various possible kinship combinations (thus its description as a "combinatory"), in which the system of all possible kinship structures remains ultimately grounded by "the structure of the human mind."[10] Through the multiple historical variations of the implementation of this combinatory, humans produce social forms in exhaustive variation, but in accord with a limiting structural determination of which they are unaware. This amounts to the imputation on Lévi-Strauss's part of a social unconscious, one that remains, in Althusser's biting critique, "still a form of subjectivism that endows 'society' with the form of existence of a subject having intentions and objectives."[11] This unconscious structure, hidden beneath the manifest content of social comportments, requires Lévi-Strauss to decode hermeneutically its form of constraint as the identity of infinite variation across time.

Structural anthropology thus manages to articulate a *transcendental idealism*—the hidden nature of which requires hermeneutical elaboration—to which Lévi-Strauss appends in uneasy tension an even less satisfactory *empiricist functionalism*. The latter, wholly inadequate, functionalist explanation of the role of kinship becomes necessary for Lévi-Strauss, Althusser observes, insofar as the transcendental structural combinatory can only identify the admissibility of any given kinship combination within the compass of an ungrounded series of possible combinations. What the combinatory remains unable to explain is the causal *necessity* governing any specific instantiation, "why," in Althusser's summary rejection, "it is that this reality and no other has become and therefore is real."[12] To address this problem, Lévi-Strauss merely appends to the combinatory model a weak functionalism, referring the variety of empirical kinship systems to the putative survival needs of any given empirical group.[13]

In contrast to the Spinozist imperative to explain ends always by their necessary *causes*, kinship structures are thus for Lévi-Strauss to be comprehended and justified by the *ends* they serve. Althusser summarily rejects such an imaginary explanation of the unconscious structuration of society as the mere imputation of a spurious intentionality to a subject: in this case, neither God nor Man, but instead Structure.[14] The problem structural anthropology remains unable to address is precisely that to which Spinoza's epistemological undertaking addresses its labors: to know adequately what constitutes the necessity governing any singular essence, without recourse to a transcendental formalism of the combinatory.

To adequately grasp the necessity governing a text thus constitutes the challenge Pierre Macherey puts to a rightly conceived theory of literary production. Althusser was never able to fully articulate a theory of structural causality, but instead only managed to address his own theoretical hesitations and inconsistencies regarding the concept through the mere suppression of problematic passages in the second, 1968 edition of *Reading Capital*, passages that Macherey had initially brought to Althusser's attention in their correspondence of 1965–66.[15] In contrast, *A Theory of Literary Production* articulates a systematic critique of the concept of structure: rather than merely rejecting the term outright, Macherey distinguishes inadequate conceptions of structure—dependent upon notions of coherency, totality, functionalism, depth, and hermeneutic translation—from its more adequate conceptualization.

This more adequate understanding of structure is for Macherey to be indexified to (1) the Spinozist distinction between the work as an object of theoretical (structural) knowledge and that same work understood empirically, under the attribute of its material extension (as a tangible book one takes in hand to read); (2) the necessary affirmation of structure qualified as the infinite incompletion of any set;[16] (3) adequate understanding of such a notion of structure without recourse to a hermeneutics of revelation, affirming instead the immanent materiality of the text in its manifest articulations; and consequently, (4) an unremitting faithfulness to writing, taken in its immediate, necessary *materiality*, irreducible to any inherent, hidden meaning or intention.

Such are the propositions Macherey deploys in his discussion of structure in *A Theory of Literary Production*. If the concept of structure allows for comprehension of the "type of necessity from which the work derives," this necessity can refer neither to a unity derived from the putative productive intention of an author nor the formalist unification of the work via a transcendental theory of totality.[17] Structure is not to be discovered, latent within the hidden depths of the work, but is instead constituted in the very absence of a coherent totality of meaning, in the productive *décalage* and "real complexity" of the constructed thought object (114). Analysis—truly adequate, *materialist analysis* of an object of knowledge—can in this view only refer to "the constitution of a structure," the interpretive act of structuration (*structurer*) as the demonstrative deployment of elements, a process that constitutes, paradoxically, the object of knowledge in its infinite incompletion, as an "absence" (of the whole) (168). Such an absence will attend to this incoherence, to the gaps and contradictions of a text, as what Althusser had famously termed in *Reading Capital* a "symptomatic [*symptomale*] reading."[18]

Toward a Materialist Analysis of Form

In his 2006 afterword to the fortieth anniversary edition of *A Theory of Literary Production*, Macherey distills the question that, in hindsight, compelled the book's original intervention in 1966: "How was it possible to be simultaneously a materialist and a formalist?" (362). To this point, I have largely attended to this question, addressing the book's critiques of empiricism, hermeneutics, and totality, culminating in Macherey's critical diremption of inadequate from adequate notions of structure, while leaving what is for me the key, unaddressed problem of materialism itself in suspense. Now, it will not perhaps be immediately apparent that to undertake a materialist analysis of textual production in fact *poses* a problem. Indeed, the precise nature of *the object of a materialist analysis*, that of the nature of the *matter* to which any materialism must address itself, does not, in fact, constitute a problem explicitly registered in *A Theory of Literary Production* (nor, for that matter, anywhere else in Macherey's extensive corpus), which often speaks of material and matter but, aside from this quite explicit question posed in the 2006 afterword, never of materialism itself as an epistemological practice.[19]

It can seem immediately, intuitively obvious that Macherey, in accord with Althusser and his fellow Althusserian Étienne Balibar, practices a "materialist" form of analysis (in a materialist way, as the title of the 1998 Verso collection of Macherey's essays puts it), and that, moreover, this materialism is in some way consonant with the materialisms of those thinkers Macherey has repeatedly addressed, those whom Althusser called "the only materialist tradition": Lucretius, Spinoza, and Marx.[20] To be sure, Althusser famously asserted that in the texts composing *Reading Capital*, if "we were never structuralists," this is because "we were Spinozists," and in fact he further specifies that this entailed rejecting the "relation of adequacy between mind and thing, in the Aristotelian tradition."[21] In the absence of a more explicit critique of the concept of materialist analysis, however (and this is even more the case for Althusser himself), we are left to construct such a concept from the diverse (Spinozist, Marxian) materials of Macherey's many analyses addressed to other, related problems.[22]

More specifically, how are we to conceive a properly materialist analysis, given the various Althusserian proscriptions described above against empiricism, idealism, functionalism, the hermeneutics of depth, and totality, critiques that, as we have seen, Macherey wholly subscribes to and even further clarifies in *A Theory of Literary Production*? Though we will see that this is true as well for Macherey, the symptomatic status of the *object* of materialist analysis is particularly striking in Althusser's contributions to *Reading Capital*. Witness for example the (unacknowledged) problems raised by Althusser's well-known distinction, in the introductory essay of *Reading Capital*, between the thought-concrete (Marx's *Gedankenkonkretum*) and the so-called real object (41). Citing Marx's famous methodological assertion in the 1857 introduction to the *Grundrisse* that "thought appropriates the concrete, reproduces [*reproduziert*] it as the concrete in the mind [*geistig Konkretes*]," Althusser takes this assertion as epistemologically foundational for his project of a novel philosophical reading of *Capital* (as we have seen, Macherey will go on to deploy this same epistemological distinction in turn in *A Theory of Literary Production*).

At this crucial stage of his argument, Althusser has in section 10 of his essay elaborated a powerful critique of empiricism (as the revelation of the essential part of the "real," its "invisible kernel"), all the while constantly referring to a never-defined "real" object that stands in distinction to the thought-object: "the *structure* of the real *object*"; "the knowledge of that

real object itself as a real part of the real object to be known"; "the reality of the real object"; a truth putatively "inscribed in the structure of the
real object"; "the real structure of the real object" (36–38). Admittedly, the
object of this obsessive, relentless repetition of the undefined term "real" is
precisely indicated by Althusser: it is none other than "the [empiricist] play
on words . . . which involves the concept 'real,' rendering explicit the obfus-
cations of empiricism" (39). Althusser's diagnosis, for all the power of its
demonstration, nonetheless never addresses the evident underdetermination
of the notion of the "real"; in fact, his compulsive repetition of the qualifier
"real," rather than accruing clarity, merely resonates its hollow reiteration.
Empiricism, enfeebled in Althusser's diagnosis by its very unknowing play
on the word "real," stands revealed as an epistemological practice in which
"knowledge never arises except as a relation inside its real object between the
really distinct parts of that real object" (39). For all the true insight gained
into the limitations of an empiricist orientation, the reader is nonetheless left
perplexed before this delirious, obsessive repetition of the qualifier "real." If
the inadequacy of empiricist analysis is patent, we are left to wonder what
might constitute a more adequate, materialist articulation of the nature of
this "real" object of analysis than that which Althusser provides.

The powerful insight Althusser draws from his diagnosis of empiricism
identifies the latter's unknowing statement of an epistemological truth it has
disavowed: "When empiricism designates the essence as the object of knowledge, it admits something important and denegates it in the same instant:
it admits that the object of knowledge is not identical to the real object"
(40). This insight, the disavowed truth Althusser the analyst articulates from
the unknowing discourse of empiricism, thus serves as the bridge into the
next section of his argument (section 11), on Marx's correct and explicit
(conscious) distinction between the constructed object of thought (*Gedankenkonkretum*) and the "real" object.

Despite the clarity of this distinction (which, again, Macherey will reaffirm
and further clarify in *A Theory of Literary Production*), we are no closer to
an understanding of the nature of the Marxian real, which is instead ever
more obsessively invoked in mere incantation in this initial culmination of
Althusser's analysis. Against Hegelian idealism, a variant of the just-diagnosed
"confusion" of empiricism, "Marx defends," says Althusser, "the distinction
between the real object (the real-concrete or the real totality, . . . and the
object of knowledge . . . as a thought-object, absolutely distinct from the real
object, the real-concrete, the real totality" (41). What, then, is this Marxian
"real" Althusser seeks to conjure through such indeterminate invocation?[23]

The problem I am pointing to is not so much that Althusser here, in a
passage retained in all the various editions of *Reading Capital*, problematically asserts the finite, closed nature of the real as totality, precisely, that is,
the same point of confusion that Macherey would identify—in their 1965–
66 correspondence—in other, similarly problematic passages, paragraphs

that Althusser would not clarify but merely suppress in the 1968 edition of *Reading Capital*.[24] Rather, this fixated repetition of the indeterminate qualifier "real" in these pages points not only to a symptomatic theoretical malaise on the part of Althusser, but more generally, in what we could call the Althusserian-Spinozist materialism of Althusser, Balibar, and Macherey, to a (seemingly) problematic silence on the nature of the "real object" of materialist analysis on the part of these thinkers. I say seemingly because, properly understood, what appears as a problem in the form I'm presenting here bears in fact so obvious a (Spinozist) solution that it never seems to have required from these three thinkers an explicit articulation.

For Althusser in *Reading Capital*, the obsessive repetition of the qualifier "real" points already, within the materiality of this key text of Althusserian "structuralism," to a theoretical disquiet, announcing as if in proleptic, incantatory terms his future explicit and tortuously reasoned renunciation of "theoreticism" and a corresponding "Spinozism" in the post-1968 turn to a workerist "class struggle in theory."[25] This is to say that Althusser's punctual, ritual invocation of an indeterminate "real" arguably identifies a more general tendency of Marxian epistemology per se, a normative compulsion to refer to a material order of the "real," to a dimension of being that in its solicitation would inexplicably (in the absence of all reasoned demonstration) distinguish historical materialism from the various forms of idealism.

If any Marxist thought worthy of the name must certainly remain concomitant to the lived experience of injustice and suffering under capitalism, as a motive imperative driving the critique of political economy, it is nonetheless among the essential lessons of Althusser's own critique of empiricism, to say nothing of Marx himself or Spinoza before him, that the experience of injustice and suffering, in its transhistorical commonality to all human experience, is as such inherently unsuited to the determination of an adequate critique of the historically concrete nature of capitalism.[26] Put more simply, in the absence of substantial interrogation of the epistemological *object* of materialist analysis, this general tendency of Marxian critique to invoke an indeterminate materialist real, commonly voiced in passing as a mere materialist shibboleth, reaches a symptomatic pitch in Althusser's introduction to *Reading Capital*.

Reading Capital as a Theory of Literary Production

In the wake of his key contribution to *Reading Capital* (to which I will return below), Macherey has in his published work returned only once to the analysis of Marx's magnum opus, in the talk he gave on July 13, 1967, at Cérisy-la-Salle during the conference "Le centenaire du *Capital*."[27] Macherey's discussion of the object of analysis in *Capital* in both these texts (as is the case in *A Theory of Literary Production*) closely follows the series of imperatives first presented in *Reading Capital* and reiterated in *Theory*: Macherey argues that Marx's epistemological procedure in *Capital* constitutes the refusal of empiricism, idealism, hermeneutics, communication, genesis, and transcendental notions of totality.

To read *Capital* adequately, "to escape from the empiricist myth of reading," requires, Macherey reiterates, a "theoretical reading, constructing at each step its novelty, elaborating its principles. Reading so conceived is a theoretical practice: it produces in effect an effect [*en effet un effet*] of knowledge."[28] The result of such a reading of *Capital* will be an adequate understanding of the "systematic" nature of Marx's work, an "organization that depends upon the laws of theoretical rigor." That said—and this crucial point with which we are already familiar from *Theory* will prove key to Macherey's Spinozist reading of the "positive" dialectical form of *Capital*— the rigorous theoretical organization of *Capital* that Macherey identifies in this talk, as he had in his earlier chapter from *Reading Capital*, by no means implies that *Capital* forms a coherent, noncontradictory whole; on the contrary, *Capital*, like the literary works that constituted the object of *Theory*, is subject to "a strict incompletion [*inachèvement*]," an incompletion that calls upon its reader to "develop the logic proper to" *Capital*.[29]

As Althusser had before him in the passages of *Reading Capital* discussed above, Macherey reiterates the constructed, nonempiricist nature of the object of thought.[30] Macherey furthermore rigorously adheres to Althusser's primary distinction between the object of analysis (Marx's *Gedankenkonkretum*) and an (indeterminate) reference to a "real," presumably materialist, order. It is in this sense then that Macherey will assert that "the real [*le réel*] subsists outside of thought and preexists it. This difference between the real and the thought [*le pensé*] must be understood so as to avoid expression in a new form of empiricism that would conclude that thought is the emanation or mechanical reproduction of the real" (55).

While this last point constitutes a further reiteration of the now-familiar antiempiricism of *Theory* and *Reading Capital*, Macherey suddenly injects a properly Spinozist extension to this critique. Not only must an adequate reading of *Capital* reject all empiricism, but it must further refuse all forms of the neo-Cartesian distinction between thought and a material order of extension: "Nor can it [scientific discourse] constitute a dualism in which thought is exterior to the real, such that it would be necessary to think the coexistence of two independent orders." At the same time, it (scientific discourse) must bear some clear distinction from the material order. If "science is the science of the real," it involves no mere "transposition" or elaboration of a reflective, "allegorical object." Science involves "the institution of another form of reality. It is the production of a new real that is the thought real [*le réel pensé*]. . . . The thought real is not the real considered from another point of view, the interpreted real; *it is the real transformed*" (64, my emphasis).[31]

The point is difficult and subtle, and will arguably not receive adequate elaboration until Macherey's subsequent interpretations of Spinozist doctrine beginning with *Hegel or Spinoza*. While Macherey here reiterates Spinoza's distinction between the real and the idea of the real, the terms of Macherey's rejection of Cartesian dualism already point forward to his further discussion of Spinoza's concept of the attributes in *Hegel or Spinoza*, along with its further development and interpretation in his systematic and powerful critique of so-called parallelism and the proper understanding of the famous proposition 7 of *Ethics* II, "The order and connection of ideas is the same thing as the order and connection of things" (*Ordo et connexio idearum idem est, ac ordo, et connexio rerum*).

That said, for all the complex development and analysis this distinction between the object of thought (as thought-concrete) and the real object receives in Althusser and Macherey's reflection in this period, I wish to draw attention to the point that in the texts from which I have just quoted (and this could be shown to be the case as well for Balibar's 1967 Cérisy talk), there exists a remarkable imbalance between the degree of attention devoted to the elaboration of (Marx's) thought-object, while the so-called real object remains in each case entirely indeterminate.

The problem I am indicating is patent: if on the one hand any conceivable Marxist analysis must necessarily be in some meaningful sense "materialist," what can constitute the material *object* of a "materialist" analysis in the face of the Althusserian critiques of the following categories?

1) **Empiricism.** The "material" order that determines an adequate material analysis can be neither flatly tangible nor more generally sensuous. It is true that attention to the broadly sensuous not only allows for a "materialism" of the tactile but can account as well for the "materiality" of the text: that of spoken text (as in psychoanalytic discourse) in its audibility; that of letters not *tangible* (except as Braille) but instead eminently, materially *visible* on the printed page, or as pictorial texts (painting, cinema). That said, an adequate materialist analysis, following Spinoza's critique of the imaginary, first genre of knowledge, cannot remain exclusively subject to the sensuous order of the action of bodies on one another, but must attend instead to the demonstration of a necessary causal order at the level of the second (general) and third (singular, eternal) genres of knowledge.[32]

2) **Idealism.** Conversely, it is by definition inadmissible for an adequate materialism to revert to a mere idealism of the thought-object. A Marxian materialist critique cannot refer univocally to the "materialism" of the *Gedankenkonkretum* it constructs as an intervention in the infinite chain of the ideas of ideas but, as Marxian, must as well be indexified to some "real" object that

the former can be said to adequately "produce" (independently, without reflection or representation) in the order of thought.

3) **Hermeneutics.** No more than it can be said to inhere in sensuous perception, the object of materialism cannot be located in a hidden structure, kernel, or objective unconscious of that object to be revealed by analysis. The object of knowledge and the "real" object are to be rigorously distinguished; here again, the absolute Spinozist distinction between the attributes can be said to ground this fundamental Althusserian position.

Materialism in a Spinozist Way

Thus, while neither Althusser nor Macherey develops an explicit notion of the object of materialist analysis, both the proper formulation and the quite obvious but never stated Spinozist solution to this problem lie, I wish to argue, immediately at hand in the texts of high "Althusserianism" of 1965–67.[33] In essence, this is to claim that Althusser's famous general proposition in *Reading Capital* on the subterranean Spinozism of philosophy (Spinoza's "radical revolution was the object of a massive historical repression. . . . The history of philosophy's repressed Spinozism thus unfolded as a subterranean history" [250]) holds true for Althusserian epistemology itself, in which Spinozist thought functions as an occasionally acknowledged but never adequately explicated theoretical foundation.

In the wake of their combined Spinozist critiques of the subject-object logic of empiricism, of expressive totality, and of the functionalist combinatory of structuralism, Althusser, Macherey, and Balibar to my knowledge demonstrate no need to interrogate or define the object of materialist analysis. In contrast to the imprecision of many Hegelian readers of *Capital*, however, I argue that in the Spinozist epistemology that avowedly underlies their various analyses of *Capital, there is in fact no substantial distinction to be made between the "object" of materialist analysis and that of analysis itself.*[34] It is immediately obvious why the epistemological problem I spelled out above, which is problematic even at times for Marx and for negative dialectical readers of *Capital* up to the present, is for Althusser and Macherey quite simply a false, nonexistent problem, which rightly never even arises or needs be addressed by these intimate readers of Spinoza, once, that is, one accepts axiomatically the Spinozist ontology.

The problem of an object that materialist analysis would represent is a false problem, once one accepts instead that substance is indivisible, that the infinite attributes constitute, immediately, the expression of substance and its infinite modes as the determinations of those attributes, and that, above all, the order of ideas is one and the same thing as the order of things ("Ordo, et connexio idearum idem est, ac ordo, et connexio rerum"). To conceive of materialist analysis in terms of a substantial distinction and representational correlation between analysis and its object is, from a Spinozist perspective, inadmissible; it is to reintroduce precisely the Cartesian dualism of substances (between extension and the intellect) that Spinoza systematically critiques.

Judging by his powerful (private) critiques of Althusser's presentation of the concept of structural causality in the first edition of *Reading Capital*, Macherey seems to have developed a reading of Spinoza even more rigorous and systematic than Althusser's by 1965 at the latest, a reading that clearly determines the theoretical propositions of *A Theory of Literary Production*.[35] It is only in his writings since *Hegel or Spinoza*, however, that Macherey has fully explicated the interpretation of Spinoza that can retrospectively be said to determine the epistemology of the Althusserian texts of 1965–67. In *Hegel or Spinoza*, and above all in the second volume of his explication of the *Ethics*, Macherey reads Spinoza's demonstration of the identity of the formal structure or order of the attributes to constitute the singular essence of a substantialist materialism.

Rejecting point by point the Hegelian misreading of Spinoza in *Hegel or Spinoza*, Macherey affirms that, for Spinoza, the following propositions hold true:

1) The (infinite) attributes of substance cannot consist in a linear and countable or ordinal sequence (i.e., the attribute of thought, plus the attribute of extension, plus all the other infinite attributes). "The unity of substance is thus not an arithmetic unity . . . , an empty form of the One. . . . It is this infinitely diverse reality that comprises all its attributes and that expresses itself in their infinity. . . . One can no more count substance than one can count its attributes, at least if one renounces the point of view of imagination. . . . To say that there is a single substance is to speak from the imagination that can only consider the absolute negatively, from nothingness, that is, from the part of the possible, which it envelops."[36]

2) That the attributes do not coexist in ordinal relation implies in turn that they do not consist of elements defining one another in negative relation. "If all the attributes together belong to substance, constituting its being (*E* IP10S), they do not coexist within it as parts that would adjust to each other to finally compose the total system. If this were so, the attributes would define themselves in relation to each other through their reciprocal lack" (100).

3) This further implies that substance itself cannot be divided up into its various (infinite) attributes, but is instead indivisible. "To think the infinite, whether it be in the attribute (in a kind) or in substance (absolutely), is to exclude any notion of divisibility; substance is

> entirely complete in each of its attributes (because it is identical to
> them), just as, moreover, all extension is in each drop of water or
> all thought is in each idea. . . . The infinite is not a number; this is
> why it evades all division. Indivisible substance is not the sum of
> all its attributes" (100).

From these propositions Macherey then concludes that the relation of the
attributes is one of unitary (rather than comparative, negative) identity: "As
an attribute of substance, thought is *identical* to everything and therefore has
nothing above it, but the sequence through which it is realized poses, at the
same time, its absolute equality with all other forms in which substance is
also expressed, and these are infinite in number" (74).

The so-called parallelism of the attributes (a term that Spinoza never uses
in any of his writings, and which Macherey attributes to Leibniz), then, is
quite simply "inadmissible." This must be the case, Macherey argues, if one
reads the wording of proposition II7 attentively: in the statement "*Ordo et
connexio idearum idem est, ac ordo, et connexio rerum*," Spinoza identifies
the order and connection of ideas as not the same as the order of physical
bodies in extension (the other attribute to which humans have access), but
rather the same as that of *things (rerum)*, of all things without distinction,
including, of course, ideas themselves: "The word *things* [*res*] absolutely does
not, in a restrictive way, designate the modes of the attribute of extension,
but the modes of all the attributes, whatever they are, *including thought
itself. . . . This is one and the same order, one and the same connection*" (106,
emphasis in original).

Macherey goes on, in his subsequent explication of *Ethics* II, to further
develop this critique of the notion of "parallelism" in distinction to the more
adequate understanding of the relation of the order of the attributes as a
complex unity.[37] Macherey first repeats his assertion from *Hegel or Spinoza*
summarized above to the effect that *Ethics* II P7 must refer to the *identity* of
the order of ideas and the order of things, further specifying this assertion,
based first on grammatical and then apodictic determinations.

Grammatically, in the phrase "Ordo et connexio idearum idem est, ac
ordo, et connexio rerum," the masculine/neutral adjective *idem* cannot be
argued to apply to the feminine *connexio*. The phrase "is the same as" (*idem
est ac*) therefore cannot be said to apply to a ("parallel") relation *between*
two "independent sets [*ensembles*]," but instead qualifies a single order as
identical to itself. From this, Macherey concludes that the proper translation
of Spinoza's proposition should be "The order and connection of ideas *is the
same thing as* the order and connection of things."[38]

This assertion finds its immediate confirmation in the demonstration of
proposition 7, which points to its axiomatic basis in the initial axiom 4 of *de
Deo*, the meaning of which is eminently clear: ideas are subject to a single,
identical order that holds for all things.[39] In sum, Macherey concludes,

> Proposition 7 of *de Mente* does not affirm the extrinsic identity
> between two systems of order and connection facing each other, one
> of which would be the order of ideas and the other that of things
> bestowing on these ideas their objects, these things being themselves
> identified unilaterally as bodies. Instead, proposition 7 proposes that
> the order and connection inheres in its proper, intrinsic constitution
> to that to which all things in general are governed [*soumises*], and
> from which nothing distinguishes it. (73)

For Spinoza, in Macherey's reading, the order of causality of ideas is literally
"the same thing" as the order and causality of all things, including ideas;
there is, in other words, only one order and causality of things, which can be
apprehended through an infinite number of attributes (though humans only
have access to two, thought and extension).[40] To argue otherwise in the sense
of a "parallelism," Macherey insists, would be to reinstate a Cartesian dualism of thought and extension taken as distinct substances: "The 'parallelist'
reading of proposition 7 reinscribes the Spinozist doctrine in a dualist perspective, explaining all of nature through the relation of extended substance
and thought substance."[41]

On Telling Stories

In contrast to Macherey's minute attention to the letter of Spinoza's text and
relative inattention to articulating an autonomous materialist epistemology,
Althusser offers little concrete analysis of Spinoza's text, but instead proposes
at various moments a number of laconic, even enigmatic, one-line definitions of materialism. It is thus possible to orchestrate, in counterpoint to
Macherey's attention to Spinoza's demonstrations, the suggestive promise of
Althusser's allusive materialism. It would take a volume in itself to address
Althusser's various reiterations and returns to the related problems of historical and dialectical materialism, of the materialist turns in Marx's philosophy,
of the relation of materials of production to the capitalist mode of production, and the like. The "aleatory materialism" of Althusser's final period poses
similarly complex problems of interpretation beyond the scope of this essay,
which we might sum up in saying that in turning to Lucretius and Dem-
ocritus in his now-famous 1982 essay, Althusser distances himself on crucial
points from the Spinozist materialism of the 1960s and 70s with which I am
here concerned, and even more decisively from Macherey's arguably more
rigorous, literal readings of the Spinozist text since 1979.[42]

Leaving aside the circularity of the definition Althusser offers in lecture 3
of *Philosophy and the Spontaneous Philosophy of the Scientists* (the "materialist character" of science is characterized, as to its object, by "an external
object with a material existence") along with other definitions that merely

equate materialism with an adequate scientific practice,[43] in *The Future Lasts Forever*, Althusser offers the following definition of materialism: "'Not to indulge in storytelling' still remains for me the one and only definition of materialism."[44] Though Althusser makes no mention of Spinoza in this passage, "to resort to mere storytelling" neatly encapsulates the principal assertion of Spinoza's appendix to *Ethics* I: that reasoning inadequately from effects to causes is the basis of imaginary, ideological thinking. Materialism, in contrast, would thus implicitly seek always to argue from the adequate understanding of causes to the effects they produce.

In his 1985 text *"The Only Materialist Tradition,"* Althusser proposes another enigmatic yet even more auspicious definition of materialism: "Nominalism is not the royal road to materialism but *the only possible materialism*."[45] Here again, it lies far beyond the scope of this article to distinguish Althusser's flat assertion that nominalism is "the only possible materialism" from the innumerable accreted historical senses of nominalism, from the diverse critiques of universals and abstract objects as well as corresponding assertions of the reality of particular objects and of concrete objects. Instead, I will merely summarize the Spinozist construct Althusser's assertion is meant to encapsulate.

In the third section of *"The Only Materialist Tradition,"* in which this defi-nition of materialism appears, Althusser—in the course of a broad reflection on the centrality of Spinoza to his thinking—turns to his interpretation of Spinoza's third genre (*genus*) of knowledge, the "intuitive science [*scientiam intiutivam*]" that Spinoza characterizes as "the adequate knowledge of the essence of things [*adaequatam cognitionem essentiae rerum*]" (*E* IIP40S2). In Althusser's usage in this passage, the term "nominalisms" (in the plural) is adopted to refer precisely to such singular essences of things, things com-prehended as "singularities." Such singularities are to be distinguished from Spinoza's second genre of mere common or abstract universal notions (*notio-nes communes*), such as motion and rest taken as universal characteristics of all bodies in extension; these are explicitly, for Althusser, "generic and not 'general' constants." In Althusser's reading, Spinoza's invention of an ade-quate materialist ("nominalist") knowledge is thus held to encompass his discovery of "generic constants or invariants . . . which arise in the existence of singular 'cases.'" Such constants are to be distinguished from the univer-sal generality of "laws," which would fall under Spinoza's second genre of knowledge. Equally, it is their genericity as constants of any singular case that allows for what Althusser revealingly calls in clinical terms their "treatment," as distinct from any empirical or experimental verification.[46]

If a *law* would constitute an abstract or general universal, the *constant* arising in a given instance (a symptom in the analysand or patient, for example) allows for the adequate analysis and treatment of that case in its "nominalist" singularity: no universal treatment is proper for the singularity of every case, yet the analyst must construct an adequate knowledge of its causes and not be misled by mere surface impressions (the manifest content of the dream, say, or the visibility of bodily symptoms) to be inadequately attributed to imaginary causes. Such attention to *constants*, moreover, holds in Althusser's view for any singular being, for example a people (the Jews, in Spinoza's analysis in the *Tractatus Theologico-Politicus*) or what Althusser calls a "social singularity" (the critique of the capitalist social form in Marx, or political revolution for Lenin) (8).

Following this elaboration, along with a brief excursus on the *TTP* and Spinoza's "philosophical strategy" of "taking over the chief stronghold of the adversary" (10), Althusser then concludes his presentation with the affirmation of Spinoza's materialist "nominalism" quoted above. The attribute "nominalist" thus redeploys the critique of transcendentals that Althusser and Macherey had articulated in their parsing of Lévi-Strauss's structuralism in the 1960s: "Without ever sketching a transcendental genesis of meaning, truth, or the conditions of possibility of every truth, . . . [Spinoza] established himself within the factuality of a simple claim: 'We have a true idea'" (10–11). The "nominalist" materialist thus passes beyond the universal generality of common notions, of transcendental guarantees (such as Lévi-Strauss's kinship order or discourse in Gilles Deleuze's problematic definition of structuralism) to articulate instead the generic necessity of any singular essence.[47]

This final step then brings Althusser to define, in eminently clear and distinct terms, the fundamental Spinozist proposition that should be seen retrospectively to constitute the essential—yet unarticulated—order of Althusser and Macherey's epistemology in their works from 1965–67: "This *factual nominalism* was rediscovered—and with what genius!—in the famous distinction . . . between the *ideatum* and the *idea*, between the thing and its concept, between the dog that barks and the concept of the dog, which does not bark, between the circle that is round, and the idea of the circle, which is not round, and so on" (11).

What Althusser names his "nominalist" materialism in his late, 1985 text might indeed be more properly termed an *axiomatic, substantialist materialism*. For the proposition that the order of ideas and of things is the same thing is indeed an axiomatic proposition: its ground lies not in the apodictic, synthetic demonstration of proposition 7 in *Ethics* II, but instead in the initial axiomatic foundation of Spinoza's entire system. In fact, as mentioned above, the famous proposition 7 explicitly refers the reader back to *Ethics* I, axiom 4, and together, axioms 4, 5, and 6 of *Ethics* I constitute, Macherey demonstrates, the fundamental epistemological order of an inherent, necessary identity between the two orders or attributes of thought and extension.

While axioms 3–5 of *Ethics* I affirm the necessary structure of causality under both the attributes of extension and the intellect, it is axiom 6 that draws these together to affirm that the true idea "must be in conformity with its ideate [*debet cum suo ideato convenire*]" (IAx6). Macherey's interpretation of this key axiom bears citing in whole, as it is this statement that arguably should be taken to summarize the entire epistemological apparatus of Althusser's and Macherey's thought:

> This axiom [I6] takes up in a new perspective the general teaching [*enseignement*] from the initial definitions and axioms [of *Ethics* I]: as the thing is, so it is conceived, as well as the inverse: as the thing is conceived, in so far as this is a true knowledge, so it is, necessarily. For every idea in the intellect, in so far as it is true, that is to say, . . . well formed—since all ideas are true in the intellect that understands them, and at the same moment relates them to the ideate to which they are in a relation of conformity—there necessarily corresponds a content given in reality.[48]

This radical monism founds for Macherey a substance-based materialism, in which the "real"—an indeterminate, reflexively deployed category in Althusser's contribution to *Reading Capital* (41)—stands plainly revealed in Macherey's explication as neither mere sensuous materiality (empiricist, imagination-based materialism) nor transcendentally finite totality (idealism); the real is to be understood as substance itself, the infinite dynamic of the *causa sui* as "the process within which substance determines itself through the 'essences' that constitute it."[49] This substance-based materialism affirms that

> thought reality and extended reality coincide in the absolute being of substance, where they are only distinguished by the intellect. . . . There is just as much materiality, no more nor less, in reality envisaged from the perspective [*angle*] of the mental as when envisaged from the perspective of the bodily. . . . Mental reality is a reality unto itself [*une réalité à part entière*], whose elements, ideas, are materially existing things, no less consistent, in their own order, than those that materially compose extended nature. (Macherey, *Introduction à l'Éthique de Spinoza, la deuxième partie,* 5)

Conclusion: Reading *Capital* in a Materialist Way

When Macherey writes *A Theory of Literary Production* in 1966, he does so in the wake of his brief but quite brilliant reading of the first five pages of Marx's *Capital* in his contribution to *Reading Capital*.[50] As he writes of Spinoza, it is clear that for Macherey himself, theory cannot stand on its own as an autonomous and general protocol, but must instead follow (as it does in *A Theory of Literary Production*) in the wake of a determinate materialist analysis such as that he initially produces on Marx's *Capital*.

Keeping this in mind, I wish briefly to indicate in conclusion a few of the implications Macherey's Spinozist materialism continues to hold for a reading of Marx's *Capital* itself. To be sure, *Reading Capital* long ago brought to bear upon Marx's masterwork, both explicitly and silently, a multitude of the varied implications of the Spinozist critique; it must be said, however, that in its wake, Spinozist readings of *Capital* remain exceedingly rare. In light of Macherey's subsequent extensive and infinitesimal articulation of a Spinozist, materialist protocol for textual critique, a great many other implications of Spinozism nonetheless to my mind remain to be developed in contemporary readings of *Capital*, a field that remains, for all its insight and vibrancy, overwhelmingly determined by a negative dialectical and even Hegelian horizon. Let me briefly indicate just three of these possible paths for reading *Capital* in a Spinozist way:

1. In his 1965 contribution to *Reading Capital*, Macherey already discerns in *Capital* what he will subsequently, in *Hegel or Spinoza*, name a "positive [Spinozist] dialectic." In this long-overlooked yet insightful treatment of Marx's initial exposition of his concepts, Macherey argues that the movement of Marx's demonstration is governed by a number of logical "intermediaries," mediations that allow for a rigorous, apodictic demonstration of the initial characteristics of the value-form in a demonstration that develops *synthetically* rather than via dialectical *aufhebung*.

Macherey argues in particular for the fundamental heterogeneity of concepts such as wealth, use value, and value, a heterogeneity that itself constitutes "one of the fundamental conditions of scientific rigor" (188). The relations between what Marx calls the various "factors" of the commodity and the movement of Marx's exposition occasion no procedure of dialectical *aufhebung*, Macherey argues, but Marx's demonstration instead proceeds in a series of synthetic "ruptures" or leaps from one order to the next following the analytical exhaustion of each concept.

It is only in 1979, however, that Macherey will explicitly theorize this dialectic without negation in the closing pages of *Hegel or Spinoza*.[51] Macherey there identifies in Spinoza a dialectic without subject, teleology, or negation. This invocation of a positive, Spinozist dialectic puts in its place the logical subject and its function of grounding all true propositions: "What Spinoza refuses to think is the dialectic in a subject, which is exactly what Hegel does. [Spinoza] poses the problem of a dialectic of substance, that is, a materialist dialectic that does not presuppose its completion in its initial conditions through the means of a necessarily ideal teleology."[52] In this manner, Spinoza limits the principle of contradiction and its grounding in the subject to existences and not essences. As such, Macherey concludes, Spinoza's "theory of the subject" pertains above all to the constitution of bodies in extension (175). This limitation, moreover, holds for all bodies as such, not merely the human body, which nonetheless constitutes Spinoza's privileged example.

A Spinozist limitation of negative dialectic to existences can therefore serve to ground a materialist analysis of the (actually existing) body of capital, an analysis that starkly contrasts with all Hegelian idealism (*Capital* is no mere reorientation of the Hegelian dialectic placed "on its feet"), an analysis in which contradiction is strictly limited to the phenomenal features of the social forms constituting the body of capital in its existence (in the form of actual contradictions, between given forces and means of production, in the struggle over the working day or the violent imposition of primitive accumulation, and the like), while the *essential* nature of this social form (including the crucial confrontational relation between capital and the proletarian owners of labor power) will be adequately known by the intellect only as a thought-concrete without negation.[53] In this view, human social relations bear no inner, essential drive toward their culmination in capitalism, as the imaginary doctrines of liberalism and neoliberalism would have us believe. Instead, as Marx first argued in his presentation of so-called primitive accumulation, and Ellen Wood has further insisted, the historical body of capitalism is composed through a fundamental and renewed *system of constraint* based upon the methodical dispossession of the means of production and reproduction of the working class, to form a proletariat in the precise sense Marx gives the term, through the existential, juridical, and regulated compulsion of human bodies to compose themselves, in real subsumption, as subjects of the valorization of value under capitalism.[54]

2. A positive dialectic, such as Macherey already discerns in the opening pages of *Capital* in 1965 and subsequently articulates in *Hegel or Spinoza*, requires for its adequate conceptualization the *synthetic* mode of presentation that Spinoza upholds (*more geometrico*) against the Cartesian defense and deployment of an *analytic* analysis. While Althusser famously defends Marx's 1857 epistemological distinction between the thought-concrete (*Gedankenkonkretum*) and the "real" in Spinozist terms, a Spinozist *synthetic mode of presentation* arguably determines *Capital* to an even greater and unsuspected degree, and furthermore comes to displace the initial Hegelian negative dialectical formulations of the *Grundrisse* in the actual drafts of *Capital* after 1861.

The Spinozist, positive dialectic that Macherey identifies in the most theoretically developed arguments in *Capital*[55] implies that Marx's deployment of a "positive" dialectic throughout his manuscripts tends to displace the less adequate, negative, contradiction-based Hegelian dialectical structure still visible in the earlier drafts of *Capital*.[56] A contradiction-based dialectic is in this view inherently inadequate for the comprehension of the essential nature of capital, and moreover tends, in traditional, Left Ricardian readings of Marx (on the model of Alexandre Kojève) to represent this nature in the humanist form of subject-based, Hegelian conflicts—the struggle between proletariat and capitalist, between forces and relations of production, or that of a productive, conscious human subject whose intentionality transforms and humanizes nature.[57] Such a negative dialectic describes the development of the whole and its *aufhebung* in a process guaranteed by the rationality of the subject, whether human, logical, or absolute.

As Macherey first indicated in *Reading Capital*, Marx's *Gedankenkonkretum*—the unfinished work-in-progress we know as the three volumes of *Capital*—contains a fundamental, if largely invisible, synthetic mode of presentation of its claims.[58] The identification of various moments of a synthetic demonstration in Marx's argument remains crucial for more adequate construction of theoretical protocols for the reading of *Capital*. Take, for example, Marx's demonstration that slave-based labor is unambiguously incapable of creating surplus value. If we accept Marx's founding axiomatic affirmations—that capitalism is properly characterized in the abstract by the general accumulation of commodities, that abstract labor is the unique substance of value, that commodities necessarily have a dual form, and that labor power is the unique commodity capable of producing surplus value—we must conclude that slave labor is unambiguously incapable of creating surplus value, for all its real imbrication in the historical development of capital, no matter how great a contribution it demonstrably made to the accumulation of wealth and capture of profit, of use values, in the history of capitalism and that of human history *tout court*.

This is a theoretical point completely lost in the historicist literature on slavery and capitalism from Eric Williams to the present.[59] Slave labor, like the living labor of mules and the productive force of wind or water power, is, in Marx's analysis, only capable of transmitting preexisting value to the commodities it produces, creating no new, surplus value in the process.[60] As a general social form, capital contains a great number of forms of labor, governed by various modes of coercion, forms of remuneration and reproduction, and the like. Only one of those, however—wage labor in which the proletarian sells the commodity that is her property, her labor power—is, in Marx's analysis, capable of creating surplus value.

3. *Capital* should be read in light of the Spinozist epistemology of the three forms of knowledge: (1) imaginary; (2) via general or common notions; and as Althusser reminds us, (3) in light of eternity, as "the adequate knowledge of a complex object by the adequate knowledge of its complexity."[61] Each of these modes of understanding has in turn its element of truth and necessity, though only the third is fully adequate to the comprehension of its object.

An example of Marx's deployment of the *imaginary* occurs, for example, in his famous image of the "language of commodities": "Everything our analysis of the value of commodities previously told us is repeated by the linen itself, as soon as it enters into association with another commodity, the coat. Only *it reveals its thoughts in a language with which it alone is familiar, the language of commodities*. In order to tell us that labour creates its own value in its abstract quality of being human labour, it says that the coat, in so far as it counts as its equal, i.e. is value, consists of the same labour as it does itself."[62] Marx here supplements the synthetic analysis of the structure of capital as a social form (the object of chapter 1 prior to the appearance of this passage) with an imaginary figure, that of two animated commodities,

a length of linen and a coat, in an image that bears its own measure of truth
and even necessity. Marx seems to be telling his reader that the abstraction
that is value must be thought not only as concept but also vividly imagined,
in the form of an animated manifestation in the concrete materiality that is
the human symbolic order. This dreamlike dimension of Marx's critique is
indeed one necessary aspect of the object of Marx's materialist analysis. Fredric Jameson has in this sense identified the more general repetition of what he
terms "figural demonstration" as central to the stylistic apparatus of *Capital*,
a rhetorical process to which Marx repeatedly resorts in the attempt to represent to his reader the immaterial, real substance of surplus value, abstract
labor (in the above example), or in another example Jameson develops, in
the sense of the figuration of "separation" that occurs in Marx's analysis of
primitive accumulation.[63]

A second order of demonstration inherent in *Capital* is its presentation of
a structure of general notions or categories, as what Marx calls the "value-
form," an order that, grasped in the complexity of its general articulation,
constitutes the "structure" of capital in the Spinozist sense of the synchronic
that Althusser indicates.[64] This structure forms a general, universal exposition of the laws of the tendencies of capitalist valorization, accumulation,
and reproduction. Jean Laplanche and Jean-Bertrand Pontalis, invoking at
once Lévi-Strauss and Lacan, articulate this materialist concept of the object
of analysis that is the symbolic order with elegant simplicity: "The reality of
a symbolic order structuring interhuman reality" constitutes in this view a
"symbolic system": for Lévi-Strauss, kinship, language, and "economic relations"; for Lacan, the structure of the unconscious; and for Marx, I would
add, the social form of commodity production and valorization.[65]

Finally, Macherey's thought demonstrates—with no contradiction in terms
whatsoever—that an adequately materialist analysis requires above all that
we learn to read *Capital* from the perspective of the eternity of the singular
nature of its object. Such a reading might take many forms; for this reader of
Capital, it seems essential to take into account, for example, the full development of Marx's founding epistemological distinction between the production
of surplus value as a total mass and its subsequent distribution among many
individual capitals in the manifest form of profit via competition, such as Fred
Moseley has systematically argued. While Marx famously defines abstract
labor as the *substance* of surplus value ("The labor that forms the substance
of value is equal human labour, the expenditure of identical human labour-
power"), we might further say with Moseley that *surplus value, as distinct
from material wealth, itself forms the general substance of capital.*[66]

In this view, Marx abstracts from the temporal existence of production
and the phenomenology of individual laborers and capitalists, to present, at
every level of the increasing degrees of concretion that characterize his analysis in *Capital*, a *monetary analysis* that might rightly be characterized via
the eternity of the concept (in the sense that Spinoza speaks of the adequate

concept of the triangle[67]): "Money," Moseley writes, "is derived in the very first chapter (Section 3) of Volume I, as the *necessary form of appearance of abstract labor*, and from then on Marx's theory is about quantities of money that represent, and thus are determined by, quantities of labor time."[68]

This in turn entails—as Moseley demonstrates in detail across Marx's innumerable manuscripts—that *Capital* is constructed at two levels of determination: first, an initial determination of the production of a total mass of surplus volume (its "substance"), and subsequently, in analytical terms, via the determination of the distribution of that mass of value among competing individual capitals.[69] Marx's presentation, repeatedly invoking individual processes and factors of production, is admittedly confusing on this point; Moseley convincingly argues, however, that "Marx's theory in Volume I is about the total capital and the total surplus-value produced in the economy as a whole, [even though] the theory is [necessarily] illustrated in terms of an individual capital and even a single, solitary worker. . . . Individual capitals are not analysed as separate and distinct real capitals, but rather as representatives and 'aliquot parts' of the total social capital."[70] As Marx himself writes, "In capitalist production [i.e., in Volume I], *each capital is assumed to be a unit, an aliquot part of the total* capital."[71] Here again, following Moseley's analysis, we see the necessary inherence of all three forms of knowledge in the adequate presentation of Marx's object, even including in his apodictic, synthetic analysis the imaginary figure of the "single, solitary worker."

These few concluding suggestions, of course, here constitute no more than the intimation of a multitude of questions Macherey's materialist critique raises for the ongoing project of an adequate reading of Marx's *Capital*. They remain to be developed in Spinozist readings of *Capital* to come.

Attention to the capacious brilliance of Pierre Macherey's *A Theory of Literary Production* necessarily draws the reader onward to interrogate the general nature of materialist critique, such as Macherey has developed that notion across the broad expanse of a life of philosophical analysis. No mere didactic exposition of the Spinozist system, the writings of Pierre Macherey as a whole construct for contemporary thought the adequate notion of a veritably materialist analysis of the conceptual system of knowledge, both in its immediate forms of appearance as a symbolic system and in the eternity of its singular concepts. Such, one might rightfully conclude, is the nature of Macherey's theoretical project: to grasp the eternal *in a materialist way*.

Notes

1. Warren Montag, *Althusser and His Contemporaries* (Durham, NC: Duke University Press 2013); Montag, "Editor's Introduction," in Pierre Macherey, *In a Materialist Way: Selected Essays* (New York: Verso, 1998). The research and work on this study was supported by the Czech Science Foundation (GAČR) within the project (GA 19-20319S) "From Bolzano to Badiou."

2. Louis Althusser, Étienne Balibar, Roger Establet, Pierre Macherey, and Jacques Rancière, *Reading Capital: The Complete Edition*, trans. Ben Brewster and David Fernbach (New York: Verso, 2015), 175–213. Pierre Macherey, *Hegel or Spinoza*, trans. Susan M. Ruddick (Minneapolis: University of Minnesota Press, 2011), 213; *Introduction à l'Ethique de Spinoza*, 5 vols. (Paris: Presses Universitaires de France, 1997–2001).

3. Pierre Macherey, *A Theory of Literary Production*, trans. Geoffrey Wall (New York: Routledge, 2006), 6, translation modified, my emphasis. Henceforth cited in the text.

4. "Marx defends the distinction between the real object (the real-concrete or the real totality, which 'retains its autonomous existence outside the head (*Kopf*) just as before,' and the object of knowledge, a product of the thought which produces it in itself as a thought-concrete (*Gedankenkonkretum*), as a thought-totality (*Gedankentotalität*), i.e., as a thought-object, absolutely distinct from the real-object, the real-concrete." *Reading Capital*, 41. See also Karl Marx, *Grundrisse* (New York: Penguin, 1973), 101. For an outstanding recent explication of Marx's methodology as presented in the 1857 introduction, see Juan Iñigo Carrera, "Method: From *Grundrisse* to *Capital*," in *In Marx's Laboratory: Critical Interpretations of the Grundrisse*, ed. Ricardo Bellofiore, Guido Starosta, and Peter D. Thomas (Chicago: Haymarket, 2014), 43–70.

5. Adam Smith, *The Wealth of Nations* (New York: Penguin, 1974), 11.

6. *Reading Capital*, 41. "However far back we ascend, into the past of a branch of knowledge, we are never dealing with a 'pure' sensuous intuition or mere 'representation,' but with an *always-already* complex raw material, a structure of 'intuition' or 'representation' which combines together in a peculiar '*Verbindung*' sensuous, technical, and ideological elements; that therefore knowledge never, as empiricism desperately demands it should, confronts a *pure object* which is then identical to the *real object* of which knowledge aimed to produce precisely . . . the knowledge." *Reading Capital*, 43, emphasis in original. Similarly, in "On the Materialist Dialectic," Althusser writes, in terms that directly invoke the epistemology of Jean Cavaillès and Gaston Bachelard, that "a science never works on an existence whose essence is pure immediacy and singularity ('sensations' of 'individuals'). . . . A science always works on existing concepts." Louis Althusser, "On the Materialist Dialectic," in *For Marx*, trans. Ben Brewster (New York: Verso, 2005,) 184.

7. Spinoza's critique of empiricism is absolute: "Insofar as the human mind imagines an external body, to that extent it does not have an adequate knowledge of it" (*Quatenus mens humana corpus externum imaginatur aetenus adaequatam ejus cognitionem non habet*), and again, the corollary to proposition 29, "Whenever the human mind perceives things after the common order of nature, it does not have an adequate knowledge of itself, nor of its body, nor of external bodies, but only a confused and fragmentary knowledge" (*Mens humana quoties ex communi naturae ordine res percipit nec sui ipsius nec sui corporis nec corporum externorum adaequatam habet cognitionem*). Spinoza, *Ethics*, in *Complete Works*, trans. Samuel Shirley (Indianapolis: Hackett, 2002), EIIP26C and EIIP29C. Translation modified. The following abbreviations are used to refer to the *Ethics*: I–V = Part of the *Ethics*; A = Axiom; P = Proposition; D = Definition; C = Corollary; S = Scholium; App = Appendix.

8. Warren Montag, *Bodies, Masses, Power: Spinoza and His Contemporaries* (New York: Verso, 1999), 5.

9. Warren Montag, *Althusser and His Contemporaries: Philosophy's Perpetual War* (Durham, NC: Duke University Press, 2013), chs. 3–5.

10. Lévi-Strauss, cited in Montag, *Althusser and His Contemporaries*, 68.

11. Cited in Montag, *Althusser and His Contemporaries*, 69.

12. Cited in Montag, *Althusser and His Contemporaries*, 68.

13. Montag, *Althusser and His Contemporaries*, 69.

14. In the famous appendix to *Ethics* I (a key text, moreover, for Althusser's appropriation of Spinoza), Spinoza's example of such faulty reasoning from empirical effect backward to an imaginary cause is that of a tile falling from a roof, which, in striking a passerby, is (necessarily but inadequately) attributed to a vindictive deity by the imagination of the observer of this empirical event. "Nature," Spinoza trenchantly retorts, "has no end prescribed to it [*naturam finem nullum sibi praefixum habere*] and all final causes are but figments of the human imagination. . . . The doctrine of final causes turns Nature completely upside down, for it regards as an effect that which is in fact a cause, and vice versa." Spinoza, *Ethics* I, App., translation modified. See also Macherey's insightfully detailed explication of this passage in the final section of his analysis of *Ethics* I in *Introduction à l'Éthique de Spinoza. La première partie: La nature des choses* (Paris: Presses Universitaires de France, 1998), 205–70.

15. Montag, *Althusser and His Contemporaries*, ch. 5.

16. In *Hegel or Spinoza*, Macherey cites Gilles Deleuze's lapidary formulation of this key proposition of a Spinozist materialist dialectic: "Nature as the production of the diverse can only be an infinite sum, that is, a sum that does not totalize its own elements." Macherey, *Hegel or Spinoza*, trans. Susan M. Ruddick (Minneapolis: University of Minnesota Press, 2011), 195, quoted in Montag, *Althusser and His Contemporaries*, 187. Althusser will in fact take on (without explicit attribution) Macherey's critique of the notion of totality in the 1976 *Essays in Self-Criticism*, where he writes that "Spinoza served us as a (sometimes direct, sometimes very indirect) reference: in his effort to grasp . . . a Whole without closure, which is only the active relation between its parts." Quoted in Vittorio Morfino, *Plural Temporality: Transindividuality and the Aleatory between Spinoza and Althusser* (Chicago: Haymarket, 2015), 93n11.

17. Macherey, *A Theory of Literary Production*, 45, 55, translation modified.

18. See *Reading Capital*, 26. See also Robert J. C. Young, "Rereading the Symptomatic Reading," in *The Concept in Crisis: Reading Capital Today*, ed. Nick Nesbitt (Durham, NC: Duke University Press, 2017), 35–48.

19. The exceptions are two brief mentions of the title of Lenin's *Materialism and Empirio-criticism* (*A Theory of Literary Production*, 118, 134), and one in passing of "historical materialism" (172), none of which initiate critical reflection on the concept.

20. See Louis Althusser, "The Only Materialist Tradition, Part I: Spinoza," in *The New Spinoza*, ed. *Warren Montag and Ted Stolze* (Minneapolis: University of Minnesota Press, 1997), 3–20. Macherey notes the crucial influence of Lucretius in Spinoza's elaboration of the appendix to *Ethics* I. Macherey, *In a Materialist Way*, 238.

21. Althusser, *Essays in Self-Criticism* (London: NLB, 1976 [1972]), 132, 137, quoted in Morfino, *Plural Temporality*, 2, 4.

22. In *La philosophie de Marx* ([Paris: La Découverte, 2014], 98), Étienne Balibar observes in passing that in the 1845 *Theses on Feuerbach*, "Marx's materialism has nothing to do with a reference to matter [but is instead] a strange 'materialism without matter.'" Alberto Toscano has extrapolated on Balibar's suggestive comment in relation to Sohn-Rethel and I. I. Rubin's analysis of the value form, proposing that Marx's subsequent analysis of the capitalist social form of value constitutes precisely such a materialism, one in which, as Marx famously comments in *Capital*, "not an atom of matter enters into the objectivity of commodities as values." Alberto Toscano, "Materialism without Matter: Abstraction, Absence, and Social Form," *Textual Practice* 28, no. 7 (2014): 1221–40. See Karl Marx, *Capital* (New York: Penguin, 1976), 138.

23. Étienne Balibar analyzes Althusser's presentation of this problem in somewhat different terms than I am proposing in "Althusser's Object," *Social Text* 39 (Summer 1994): 157–88, esp. 162–64.

24. Montag, *Althusser and His Contemporaries*, ch. 5.

25. Althusser, *Éléments d'autocritique* (Paris: Hachette, 1974).

26. It should be added that, though neither Althusser nor Macherey explicitly states so, their shared critique of empiricism in *Reading Capital* and *A Theory of Literary Production* necessarily finds its ground and fully adequate demonstration in Spinoza's critique of the first, imaginary genre of knowledge, both in the appendix to Part I and the demonstrations of propositions 21–31 in *Ethics* II, *De mente*.

27. Macherey, "Lire *Le Capital*," in *Le centenaire du "Capital"* (Paris: Hermann, 2012). Macherey's July 13 talk was followed immediately by that of Étienne Balibar, titled "La Science du 'Capital,'" both of which are immediately followed in the published version of the proceedings by some thirty pages of rich and often polemical discussion with the other members of the colloquium. Thanks to Étienne Balibar for calling my attention to this volume. I discuss Macherey's contribution to *Reading Capital* after these chronologically subsequent works because in my view it constitutes already in 1965 a precocious, initial iteration of the "positive" dialectic without negation of the negation that he will call for in the final chapter of *Hegel ou Spinoza* in 1979.

28. *Le centenaire du "Capital,"* 54.

29. *Le centenaire du "Capital,"* 55. "We can even say," Macherey continues, "that the enterprise of a total or 'totalizing' reading is ideological in its essence: it lies at the root [*au principe*] of all revisionisms, which are absolute by vocation. . . . A scientific text can only be taken up on the condition of being continued: a closed, repetitive reading is itself an ideological reading" (57, 61). Macherey continues in this vein to reiterate various subsidiary themes from *Theory*, here applied to the reading of *Capital*, including the critique of all *commentary*, and the mere aesthetic delectation of texts (60).

30. "Scientific discourse has been produced as a new reality. . . . Knowledge is a reflection only of itself." *Le centenaire du "Capital,"* 61.

31. Macherey is categorical in his elaboration of this point in the ensuing discussion: "A science is defined by an object that is constructed according to a definition—not [empirically] by an object given by reality [*la réalité*]—and by

functional rules. . . . The object of *Capital* is an object constructed theoretically, and this is precisely why *Capital* is not a formal system. If we were to read it as a closed system, this would constitute an interpretive reading, a repetition and reprisal of a completed system. . . . Marx did not record [in *Capital*] the theoretical results spontaneously issued from a historical 'experience' " (92, 93).

32. The Spinozist critique of empiricist materialism thus stands at odds with Adrian Johnston's articulation of a post-Lacanian, post-Althusserian materialism: "My project implicitly brings back into the picture the Baconian roots of the sciences. This amounts to an insistence that the 'new method' of empirical experimentation (crucial to Galileo as well as Bacon) cannot be historically revised away at the behest of an agenda to reduce scientificity to nothing more than pure mathematical-style formalization alone." In essence, Johnston is here questioning the fundamentally formalist trajectory of French historical epistemology from Alexandre Koyré and Jean Cavaillès to Lacan, the Cahiers pour l'Analyse collective, and Alain Badiou's subsequent "materialist dialectic" since his *Being and Event* (1987). Adrian Johnston, *Prolegomena to Any Future Materialism, vol. 1, The Outcome of French Philosophy* (Evanston, IL: Northwestern University Press, 2012), 6. On the Cahiers pour l'Analyse, see Peter Hallward and Knox Peden, eds., *Concept and Form*, vols. 2 and 2 (New York: Verso, 2012).

33. Under this category I would include not only the published volumes *For Marx, Reading Capital, A Theory of Literary Production*, and Macherey and Balibar's contributions to the Cérisy colloquium "*Le centennaire du Capital*," but also the various exchanges of the Groupe Spinoza and related texts such as Althusser's 1966 "Sur Lévi-Strauss" in Louis Althusser, *Écrits philosophiques et politiques*, vol. 2, ed. François Matheron (Stock/IMEC, 1994). On the Groupe Spinoza, Alain Badiou has reflected: "The Groupe Spinoza was a group composed by Althusser, with some friends of Althusser, all reading *Capital* practically, engaged in the project to write a sort of synthesis of our epistemological convictions. The idea was to produce a fundamental book concerning theory: concerning what theory is, what constitutes an epistemological rupture and so on; to propose something like an educational book concerning all these sorts of themes. All that was destroyed by 1968 and, after that, by very strong political differences and struggles." Alain Badiou, "The Althusserian Definition of 'Theory,' " in *The Concept in Crisis: Reading Capital Today*, ed. Nick Nesbitt (Durham, NC: Duke University Press, 2017), 25.

34. As Althusser famously wrote in the 1972 *Essays in Self-Criticism*, "If we were never structuralists, we can now explain why: . . . we were guilty of an equally powerful and compromising passion: *we were Spinozists.*" Quoted in Morfino, *Plural Temporality*, 2. Vittorio Morfino points to the decisive influence Spinoza brought to bear on Althusser's 1965 reading of *Capital*: "The reference to Spinoza . . . is fundamental with respect to three decisive questions in the Althusserian re-reading of Marxism: the process of knowledge, structural causality, and ideology." Morfino, *Plural Temporality*, 2–3. For an outstanding, often critical and always informative recent example of the ongoing effort to read *Capital* as a palimpsest of Hegel's *Logic*, see Fred Moseley and Tony Smith, eds., *Marx's "Capital" and Hegel's "Logic": A Reexamination*, (Chicago: Haymarket, 2015).

35. Montag, *Althusser and His Contemporaries*, ch. 5.

36. *Hegel or Spinoza*, 99, 104.

37. Macherey, *Introduction à l'Éthique de Spinoza, la deuxième partie: La réalité mentale* (Paris: Presses Universitaires de France, 1997), 71–81. I insist on this development in Macherey's 1997 volume, which as of this writing is, like the other four volumes in the series, unavailable in English translation. Not only does it constitute the most developed explication of Macherey's substantialist, Spinozist materialism, but, moreover, the 400-plus pages of this crucial second volume of his explication are currently out of print even in the French original. All translations from this volume are mine.

38. Macherey, *Introduction à l'Éthique de Spinoza* II, 71.

39. Macherey, *Introduction à l'Éthique de Spinoza* II, 72.

40. Jason Read, "The Order and Connection of Ideas: Theoretical Practice in Macherey's Turn to Spinoza," *Rethinking Marxism* 19, no. 4 (2007): 511. The present analysis in general draws upon Read's limpid analysis of Althusser's and Macherey's related readings of Spinoza, to interrogate in its light the epistemological object of a Spinozist materialism.

41. "For this [parallelist] reading to be possible would require that, in the enunciation of the proposition, not only would the neutral singular *idem* [thing] have to be replaced by the masculine plural *iidem sunt*, but also that the term *corporum* [bodies] be implicitly substituted for the term *rerum*." Macherey, *Introduction à l'Ethique de Spinoza* II, 72. Spinoza's explication of this proposition unequivocally corresponds to Macherey's reading: "And so, whether we conceive Nature under the attribute of Extension or under the attribute of Thought or under any other attribute, we find one and the same order, or one and the same connection of causes—that is, the same things following one another." Spinoza, *Ethics* II P7S. Cf. Macherey, *Hegel or Spinoza*, 106; Read, "The Order and Connection of Ideas," 507–8.

42. One striking example of this incongruity is Althusser's assertion in "The Underground Current of the Materialism of the Encounter" (1982) that "for Spinoza, the object of philosophy is the void." This is not simply a "paradoxical thesis," as Althusser observes; it is quite simply antithetical to Spinoza's explicit and extensive critique of the concept of the void in Book I of the *Ethics*. The free-floating associations of Althusser's argument culminate weakly in the metaphorical (rather than ontological) conclusion that Spinoza asserted "*the void that is philosophy itself*." Louis Althusser, *Philosophy of the Encounter: Later Writings, 1978–1987* (New York: Verso, 2006), 178, italics in original. In fact, Macherey shows that Spinoza, reaffirming Descartes's critique, decisively rejects the atomism of the Ancients as fully inadequate, imaginary representation, to explicitly affirm instead that "'matter is everywhere the same' [*materia ubique eadem est*] in its substantial principle." Macherey, *Introduction à l'Ethique de Spinoza. La première partie: La nature des choses* (Paris: Presses Universitaires de France, 1998), 124. "Corporeal substance," Spinoza writes unambiguously, "can be conceived only as infinite, one, and indivisible" (*Ethics* I P15S). Macherey consequently reads these passages in proposition 15 of Book I and its Scholium as "the affirmation of a plenitude [of substance] leaving no place for void, absence, or negativity. . . . Substance is thought reality in the intense intimacy of its self-relation . . . such that nothing else, not even nothingness . . . can disturb its infinite positivity. . . . To conceive of extension as constituted of distinct parts is to deny its infinity." In contrast to the Ancients' imaginary depiction of atoms in a void, "only the intellect," Macherey concludes,

"is apt [*en mesure*] to understand that the materiality of extended substance is given at once as an indivisible totality." Macherey, *Introduction à l'Ethique de Spinoza I*, 128, 129. Althusser's related, imagistic redeployment of the thesis of the parallelism of the attributes in "Materialism of the Encounter"—which Althusser claims "fall in the empty space of their determination" (Althusser, *Philosophy of the Encounter*,177)—repeats the philosophical commonplace of so-called parallelism that Macherey will subject to such extensive and compelling critique in both *Hegel or Spinoza* (ch. 3) and his analysis of proposition 7 of *Ethics* II.

43. Louis Althusser, *Philosophy and the Spontaneous Philosophy of the Scientists* (New York: Verso, 1990), 135. In *Reading Capital*, following Lenin, Althusser affirms that "in the expression 'historical materialism,' 'materialism' means no more than science, and the expression is strictly synonymous with that of "science of history" (360). Althusser will reiterate this definition, for example in "Lenin and Philosophy": "Historical materialism thus means: science of history," and again, in modified form, in "Lenin before Hegel," where he refers to "the materialist thesis of the material existence and of the objectivity of scientific knowledge." Louis Althusser, *Lenin and Philosophy and Other Essays* (New York: Monthly Review Press, 2001), 23, 83.

44. Louis Althusser, *The Future Lasts Forever: A Memoir*, trans. Richard Veasey (New York: New Press, 1993), 221.

45. Louis Althusser, "The Only Materialist Tradition, Part I: Spinoza," in *The New Spinoza*, ed. Warren Montag and Ted Stolze (Minneapolis: University of Minnesota Press, 1997), 10.

46. The constants diagnosed in any singularity "do not constitute the object of a will to *verification* in an abstract renewable experimental *dispositive*, as in physics or chemistry, but whose repetitive insistence permits us to mark the form of singularity in presence and, therefore, its treatment." Althusser, "The Only Materialist Tradition," 8.

47. On Althusser and Macherey's critique of Deleuze's famous text, see Montag, *Althusser and His Contemporaries*, 96–100.

48. Macherey, *Introduction à l'Ethique de Spinoza I*, 61, my translation.

49. Macherey, "Lire *Le Capital*," in *Le centenaire du "Capital"*), 91. Were this identity of the real with substance not sufficiently clear, Macherey even glosses in passing in *Hegel or Spinoza*—again without even bothering to draw attention to what should be perfectly obvious from a properly Spinozist perspective—the equivalence of the "real" with substance itself: Spinoza "eliminates from his conception of the real, from substance, any idea of a hierarchical subordination of elements." Macherey, *Hegel or Spinoza*, 74.

50. Pierre Macherey, "On the Process of Exposition of Capital," in Althusser, *Reading Capital*, 175–213; see also Nick Nesbitt, "Value as Symptom," in *The Concept in Crisis*, 243–49.

51. It should be recalled that in French usage, the notion of dialectic refers quite generally to "the set of means deployed in discussion to demonstrate or refute" (*Le Robert*) prior to its more specific indication of the sublation of contradiction, as in Hegel or Adorno.

52. *Hegel or Spinoza*, 170.

53. "In response to [Hegel's] finalist conception that abstractly summarizes an infinite sequence of determinations in the fiction of a unique intention, we must

substitute an integrally causal explanation, one that does not take into account anything but the external relations of bodies." Macherey, *Hegel or Spinoza*, 177.

54. "Each part of the [Spinozist] body," Macherey writes, "belongs to this global form that is the body taken in its entirety, not according to its own essence, but in light of this external liaison, *whose transitive necessity is one of constraint, which holds together all the elements. . . .* The reason for this harmony is not found in an obscure predetermination of singular essences that inclines them to converge all together toward a unique essence (an ideal nature) but in *the transitive relationship of determination that constrains them, provisionally, to associate.*" *Hegel or Spinoza*, 177, my emphasis. See Ellen Meiksins Wood, *The Origins of Capitalism* (New York: Verso 2002 [1999]). On Marx's various definitions of the proletariat, see Nick Nesbitt, *The Price of Slavery: Capitalism and Revolution in the Caribbean* (Charlottesville: University of Virginia Press, 2022).

55. Chapter 1 of volume 1, precisely the passage Macherey analyzes in *Reading Capital*, is undoubtedly the section that Marx rewrote more than any other, from the closing pages of the *Grundrisse* through the various drafts and editions, to Marx's final 1881 notes on his further intended revisions to volume I. On the latter, see Michael Heinrich, *An Introduction to the Three Volumes of Karl Marx's "Capital,"* trans. Alexander Locascio (New York: Monthly Review Press, 2012), 92–93; and, especially, Heinrich's extraordinarily detailed, line by line explication of the synthetic logic governing Marx's demonstrations in the first seven chapters of *Capital* in Michael Heinrich, *How to Read Marx's Capital: Commentary and Explanations on the Beginning Chapters*, trans., Alexander Locascio (New York, Monthly Review Press, 2021).

56. Jacques Bidet, *Exploring Marx's Capital* (Chicago: Haymarket, 2005), 132–95.

57. See Alexandre Kojève, *Introduction à la lecture de Hegel* (Paris: Gallimard, 1980). Among the key theoretical distinctions Marx analyzes in the opening pages of *Capital* (in pure abstraction from prices, capital, and the human owners of commodities themselves) is that between the production of wealth (in the form of use values), exchange value, and value itself (*Reading Capital*, 188–93). These fundamental categorial determinations not only delineate Marx's decisive break with Ricardian value theory (Marx was not a Left Ricardian) but remained as well a distinction generally overlooked by the productivist orientation of traditional, Leninist Marxism. On the concept of Left Ricardianism—that is, the failure clearly to distinguish wealth from value and the consequent promotion of the redistribution of that wealth rather than the overcoming of the capitalist mode of production—see Patrick Murray, "The Illusion of the Economic: The Trinity Formula and the 'Religion of Everyday Life,' " in Martha Campbell and Geert Reuten, eds., *The Culmination of Capital: Essays on Volume III of Marx's Capital* (New York: Palgrave 2002), 250–52.

58. Jacques Bidet has insightfully identified crucial moments of what I am calling after Macherey a positive dialectic in *Capital*. Implicitly developing Macherey's precocious, Althusserian identification of various nondialectical conceptual leaps in the opening pages of *Capital*, Bidet points to the crucial movement from the concept of the commodity to that of capital in Marx's exposition (from part 1 to part 2, chs. 4–6)—a passage "devoid of dialectical continuity, genesis, deduction, or transition—between the presentation, that is to say, of C-M-C and that

of M-C-M." Bidet describes this as an "isolated intervention" at this crucial axial moment of Marx's argument, one in which contradiction (the apparent impossibility that the exchange of equal values can nonetheless produce surplus value) is not a matter of essence, but ideological existence, a merely apparent contradiction that in fact shrivels away in the face of Marx's synthetic presentation of the concept of surplus value and valorization in chapter 6. Jacques Bidet, "The Sale and Purchase of Labour-Power," in *Exploring Marx's Capital*, 160–62.

59. Eric Williams, *Capitalism and Slavery* (Chapel Hill: University of North Carolina Press, 1994). I develop this argument in detail in *The Price of Slavery*.

60. See Dale Tomich, "Introduction to the Second Edition: The Capitalist World-Economy as a Small Island," in *Slavery in the Circuit of Sugar: Martinique and the World Economy 1830–1848* (Albany: SUNY Press, 2016); Charles Post, *The American Road to Capitalism* (Chicago: Haymarket, 2012). These two volumes are—in my view, and quite surprisingly so, given the limpid clarity of Marx's (admittedly dispersed) analysis—the only theoretically coherent conceptualizations of the relation of slavery and capitalism in the vast literature on the topic since Marx, whom both Tomich and Post echo and develop, i.e., that plantation slavery forms an integral and essential component in global capitalism since the eighteenth century, but that within that complex articulation, slaves, viewed analytically as constant capital, do not create, but merely relay, surplus value.

61. *Reading Capital*, 255.

62. Marx, *Capital*, 143, my emphasis.

63. Fredric Jameson, *Representing Capital: A Reading of Volume One* (New York: Verso 2014) 31, 81–93.

64. Marx, *Capital*, vol. 1, ch. 1.3, "The Value-Form"; *Reading Capital*, 255.

65. Jean Laplanche and Jean-Bertrand Pontalis, *Vocabulaire de la psychanalyse* (Paris: Presses Universitaires de France, 1967), 475. The encompassing nature of the symbolic, both exceeding and preceding the interpellation of the subject, was reaffirmed by Slavoj Žižek in the context of his initial critique of Althusser: "The 'real abstraction' is unthinkable in the frame of the fundamental Althusserian distinction between the 'real object' and the 'object of knowledge' in so far as it introduces a third element which subverts the very field of this distinction: the form of the thought previous and external to the thought—in short: the symbolic order." Quoted in Alberto Toscano, "The Open Secret of Real Abstraction," *Rethinking Marxism* 20, no. 2 (2008): 279. The point here is not Žižek's oblique critique of Althusser, but rather his fundamental reassertion of the Lacanian notion of the symbolic order as the objective field in which Marxian critique and subjectivity itself unfold.

66. Marx, *Capital*, 129. "The most essential common property of all capitals [i.e., its 'substance'] . . . is the production of surplus-value." Fred Moseley, *Money and Totality: A Macro-Monetary Interpretation of Marx's Logic in Capital and the End of the "Transformation Problem"* (Chicago: Haymarket, 2017), 43.

67. "From the nature of a triangle it follows from eternity to eternity that its three angles are equal to two right angles." Spinoza, *Ethics* I P17S. It should be noted in the context of this argument, that to indicate the movement of *Capital from the abstract to the concrete* is to grasp the "concrete" not as the abandonment of an abstract conceptual order for that of an empiricist, sensuous concretion but to invoke instead the meaning of "concrete" closest to the Latin

concrescere, indicating the cohesion or growing together of parts into a complex mass, compound, or composite (always remaining in the attribute of thought). Compare Bidet, *Exploring Marx's Capital*, 174.

68. Moseley, *Money and Totality*, 9.

69. "The total amount of surplus-value must be determined prior to its division into individual parts." Marx, quoted in Moseley, *Money and Totality*, 46.

70. Moseley, *Money and Totality*, 45–46.

71. Quoted in Moseley, *Money and Totality*, 46, Moseley's insertion.

Blackness: N'est Pas?

✦

David Marriott

Exergue

Fanon: "Le Noir n'est pas un homme."[1] And this other text, by Pierre Macherey, from an essay on Althusser and Fanon: Is not the racially interpellated subject "the spokesperson or the echo of a remark of which *he is not*, himself, the author, and which does not come out of his mouth in a spontaneous fashion, but which has been dictated by another voice, a voice that remains silent?"[2]

We have yet to understand the being that is not, whereby it is the echo of a silence that cannot be communicated except through gaps—ruptures—in language; to recover the moment of its silence, before it can be established in the realm of being, before it is bleached white by ontology or representation. We must try to hear, within this silence, the yet to be understood experience of blackness, in order to pose the question of its being anew, before its reading can crystallize around the question of what it is or, as Fanon conceives of it, is not, and the question of whether blackness should ever be considered a conventional form of humanism. To describe this experience of nonbeing, this echoing that turns ontology on its head, as a voice speaking without authorship, without origin, and as though a voice overheard is to know that blackness cannot be uttered without at once being echoed by a voice that is not: n'est pas.

This is doubtless more than a question of reading. To explore it we must renounce the usual methods of psychoanalysis or philosophy, and we must never allow ourselves to be guided by what we may know of being (whether as an unasked question or as an unknowingness somehow unaccounted for or disavowed). None of the concepts of phenomenology, even and especially in the implicit sense of intentionality, consciousness, or affect, must be allowed to exert an organizing role. What is imperative is the gesture that attends to the undecidability of what blackness is, and not the "science" that reads it as invariably a question of force, power, ideology, and violence (and I would add to that identity, desire, and faith). What is originary—in Fanon's phrasing of this "is not"—is the caesura that establishes the distance between

humanism and the difficulty of defining blackness as personhood in general;
perhaps this is why Fanon prefers terms such as "persona" or "mask"; as for
the hold exerted by ontology upon the being of the black in order to wrest
from it its truth as nonreason, criminality, pathology, or excess, one might
say that undecidability characterizes these debates insofar as the meaning of
blackness derives from this caesura from the start. We must therefore speak
of this initial *n'est pas* without assuming the possibility of a judgment, or a
right to distinction; we must speak of blackness as neither type nor emblem,
neither law nor resemblance, and we must leave in abeyance everything that
could figure it as a definitive conclusion, or as a literal truth; we must speak
of this *n'est pas*, of this silence set, of this void instituted between humanism
and the limits of the human, without ever relying on the fantasy of "speaking" or "representing" what blackness is or claims to be.

Then, and then only, will we be able to understand why blackness poses
a question that has yet to be formulated, and for which similarly there is
still no answer. In fact, I would suggest that the one thing which will keep us
from understanding the status of blackness is inherent to blackness itself. To
explain why, let me briefly turn to the ambiguous ways in which blackness
has been read by philosophy, or a certain philosophy—a reading that is, in a
very originary and very violent way, unable to pose, let alone answer, what it
is that makes blackness both black *and* undecidable. Here silence and speech,
being and nonbeing are inextricably involved: inseparable since they are not
yet distinguished but are nevertheless misrecognized each as the other, the
one in relation to the other, in the undecidable exchange that separates them
and that allows neither knowledge nor testimony to prevail.

I

Not everyone becomes a subject in the same way. There is nothing unique
or obscure in this point of view; rather it has become something of a truism
to say that the subject is always inscribed, implicated by what it assays; or,
to be a subject is to be subjected by what is thereby engraved (by ideology
or discourse). This apparently commonsense point is what motivates Pierre
Macherey's critique of Althusser and his notion of interpellation. Where,
Macherey claims, in the classical scene of interpellation, the question posed
by the enigmatic call (*appel*) of ideology is understood by all because, on the
level of language, *each is spoken by his or her place in language*, and each is
sequestered by what is sayable; in other words, in society, each is subject to
the Other's language, and to speak is to be constituted by a subjection, which
at best might justify Althusser's claim, as Macherey presents it, that in being
hailed (by a "hey you!") we all turn around (*retourner*) in exactly the same
way. But what this scene perhaps overlooks is how we are so very differently
determined by the situations we find ourselves in. In Macherey's account of

the person of color, for example, he poses three challenges to the Althusserian formula:

1. For the subject who is *made to be* black there is "the feeling of not being a subject like the others, but a subject with something added, or perhaps we should say something missing"; accordingly, this subject "is not [*n'est pas*], like the one of whom Althusser speaks, a turned subject [*un sujet retourné*], but a doubled subject, who is divided between an *I* and this *more (or less) which cannot be recognized or connoted as such* (14, 18).
2. Whereas the Althusserian formula of subjection "draws its efficacy from its purely verbal character: it is projected from behind, from a source systematically concealed from sight," the subject of color "is constituted as such in the order of the visible, in plain sight, so to speak, and this changes everything"; it is an actual encounter "between two intersecting gazes" (14, 15).
3. As such, one does not become a subject of color "except by entering into a relation [*rapport*] with others," a situation that, because it unfolds in plain sight, "brings consciousness into the foreground and presupposes no reference to an unconscious [in contrast to Althusser, who famously compares ideology to the unconscious]" (15, 16).

In all three instances, Macherey thinks that Althusser is right to say that the positioning of the subject by ideology is not delusory or imposed, but he thinks that this does not justify Althusser's move to a notion of interpellation that "isolates the one who receives it, suspending the relations that he or she might entertain with other people," merely because we are all considered to be subjected in exactly the same way (16).[3] In other words, each is refracted differently in the other's language according to the qualities of its otherness; the *retourné* barely suffices as an account of social differences. In both cases 1 and 2, Macherey thinks that the iconic "Tiens, un nègre!" (Look, a nigger!") episode from Frantz Fanon's 1952 text, *Black Skin, White Masks,* offers a differing account of subjectivation, and that his extrapolation of it brings it much closer "to the data of lived experience": more especially in case 2, Macherey's notion of an actual encounter "in plain sight" is supposed to show that there is no turning-around scenario for the black subject, but rather a traumatizing encounter with a "gaze that fixes him" (15); case 3, which Macherey thinks comes closest to Fanon's supposed turn to a phenomenology of lived experience, is more troublesome and is described as follows:

What first strikes us in this exposition is how it underscores the cumulative nature of the process by which is installed—in the mind of someone who, here, says "I"—the feeling of not being a subject like the others, but a subject with something added, or perhaps we should

say something missing, since the addition in question is color, a characteristic with negative connotations, the absence of colorlessness:
we begin with an observation, tied to the intervention of an external
stimulus, an onlooker's gaze on his body and his skin, an observation
that exhibits an objective status from the outset; there then develops,
in the mind of the one undergoing this test, a growing psychic tension leading from amusement, which is a form of acceptance, to the
feeling that something unacceptable is happening, something strictly
unbearable, at least under normal conditions. (14)

Whatever the virtues of Macherey's general construal of Althusser's theory
(we will return to that question in a moment), it seems fairly clear that he
has not at all grasped Fanon's main argument in *Black Skin, White Masks*
concerning *le vécu du Noir*. This may be because, just as Althusser's account
of ideology has to be understood, I am suggesting, on the basis of the universality of the "linguistic or symbolic order," so Fanon's own thinking of
the subject who is made *nègre*, which is also indebted to a radical rereading
of Sartre, also has to be understood on the basis of his earlier treatment of
an apparently quite different account of *subjectivation* to which Macherey
rather surprisingly never refers in these contexts, that of the moment when
Fanon says ideology speaks through the black subject, namely the *feeling* of
being on one's guard before any actual racist encounter, and one, moreover,
that he takes as proof of how one has already been unconsciously determined
by the ideology of negrophobia. "How can we explain, for example, that a
black guy who has passed his baccalaureate and arrives at the Sorbonne to
study for his degree in philosophy is already on his guard before there is the
sign of any conflict?" (123). What Fanon puts forward here is in fact very
similar to Althusser: the encounter with "Tiens, un nègre!" is unbearable not
because it is actually lived but because it is already the result of a truly enigmatic interpellation in which the signifier (and not the sign or the gaze) acts
as the unconscious confirmation and reminder that one is already racially
subjected. Thus, what is traumatizing is not the word that paints an image
of the real and that serves to discipline the subject into racial difference, but
the identification that makes the signifier into an unconsciously internal referential effect that blackens (via a kind of hallucinated perception) language,
being, world. The former acts as a confirmation, so to speak, that one was
already subjected by the latter, meaning that its enigmatic meaning is already
there, in me. And just as the *tiens* is all the more intensely received because its
meaning is doubly impenetrable, its meaning (without being disclosed) is the
discovery of an affect that is neither *in* language nor *outside* it.

In *Black Skin, White Masks*, this earlier treatment occurs in the discussion of Hegel's account of being in the famously obscure opening section of
chapter 5, "The Lived Experience of the Black Man" (which comes just after
the iconic "tiens" episode).

> There is in fact a "being for other," as described by Hegel, but any
> ontology is made impossible in a colonized and acculturated society.
> Apparently, those who have written on the subject have not taken this
> sufficiently into consideration. In the weltanschauung of a colonized
> people, there is an impurity or a flaw that prohibits any ontological
> explanation. (89–90)

Fanon has shown that Hegel's account of being for others (*für andere, être-pour-autrui*) depends on a view of self-consciousness centered on recognition, but which requires that every ontology is made unattainable in the colony, for "there is an impurity, a flaw, that prohibits any ontological explanation." What is this impurity that places me *outside* of myself but that is also a means of self-knowing? And how is one to account for this flaw that speaks from the side of the real (that is, the place where what is communicated is absent, prohibited)? This account of ontology as centered on prohibition is, according to Macherey, complicated by Fanon's own treatment of "the limit that speculation on the subject of being qua being encounters," that is to say, when it encounters a being that is also "being qua not-being [*être en tant qu'on n'est pas*], which is not the same thing at all" (16), but even that more complex account, in Macherey's view, presupposes a being that "teems with the unthought and the unsaid" (and of which Sartre's notion of a *néant de son propre être*, mentioned in *Black Skin, White Masks* and of course in many other places by Fanon, and explicitly linked by him to a desire not to be, is a telling example). Macherey uses this account to underscore the point that racial difference has no universal equivalent. But Fanon's critique of ontology—of which the "tiens" episode is a key illustration—suggests that there is a difference *within* the very category of difference that cannot be represented by or reproduced *as* difference even if we thenceforth read it as what results directly from the discovery of racial difference. Fanon's extremely subtle point is that blackness does not have a language of its own, or what it reproduces, what it utters, is a ventriloquy (in the proper sense of the term) that *speaks by itself*: in other words, contrary to the notion of interpellation, blackness has no articulation, for even its difference is borrowed; the result is a language whose idiom is that of a *n'est pas*. The *n'est pas*, certainly, is a very paradoxical object: without figure, without oppositional term, without remainder. In short, it is *what has always been said* but also what interrupts *being-said*: it is essentially what remains in place by being out of place, like a corpse that *corpses*.[4] In *Black Skin, White Masks*, the problem of this *n'est pas*—the problem of situating the nonbeing of the black—is ontological rather than ideological, then, not because it starts from the problem of how people are subjectivated by their interpellation, but how certain subjects have to assume a being that is not in order to be recognized as subjects.[5] In brief, nonbeing is not the same for everyone, and in fact, the being that is made not to be (*n'est pas*) is not entirely a question of ontology (and so is different from Sartre's *néant* or *rien*). The placement of this *n'est pas* within a theory of ideology is therefore designed to solve a theoretical problem. That problem is not simply that of an unsaid (in Macherey's language), but refers to the effects of a prohibition that is maintained in being and is reproduced as a nonbeing that blackens. It is a problem that Fanon, in his early work, primarily engages via Sartre—not to say Freud and Hegel—and which has to be understood on the basis of his treatment of the moment at which the black understands that it is also *nègre*, or perhaps was always already *nègre*, a moment that Fanon puts forward as belated, namely *nachträglich*. Or, the discovery of one's racial difference is always a belated discovery.

In *Black Skin, White Masks*, Fanon suggests that the drift of Sartre's demonstration—in *Being and Nothingness, Black Orpheus*, and a host of other texts—in fact underscores why ontology, and therefore phenomenology, is unable to think this black deficiency of being, its impurity, and precisely at the point where its prohibition introduces a more menacing untimeliness (and of which it could be said that blackness is *nachträglich* to even Freud's notion of *Nachträglichkeit*) and in a way that complicates how Sartre understands the relation between consciousness and being: "For once this friend, this born Hegelian, had forgotten that consciousness needs to get lost in the night of the absolute, the only condition for attaining self-consciousness. To counter rationalism he recalled the negative side, but he forgot that this negativity draws its value from a virtually substantial absoluity [*absoluité*]. Consciousness committed to experience knows nothing, has to know nothing, of the essence and determination of its being" (112–13). What I want to argue here is that what makes blackness both absolute and virtual is also what makes it incomprehensible to both reason and ontology as traditionally understood (by which I mean: the white rhetoric of universality). Let us briefly consider why. In *Being and Nothingness*, first published in 1943, Sartre argues that as soon as we admit that for being to appear there has to be a corresponding state of consciousness, or that being in-itself (*an-sich*) or rather within-itself (*in-sich*) does not appear on its own, we must also accept that the being that appears presupposes something that is nonpresent and nonevident, and that is its actual ontic foundation.[6] So if being is only as appearing (as in phenomenology) *for* somebody, which is to say for a subject, that appearance must therefore be ontically grounded in something that is outside itself before it can be determined for a subject. The priority of being over appearance is thus deduced not from the side of the object—which for Sartre is transcendent to our experiences of it—but from a subject (or self-) consciousness that is characterized as being entirely apparent to itself, and which is nothing more than its intentionality. Whatever the phenomenological precision of this argument, or whatever it means to have a self-consciousness, for Sartre self-consciousness has no content in or through itself; all content must be given it from the outside. More, it is a "non-substantial absolute," once again, and this should not come as a surprise, because "it exists only to the degree to which it appears," and "it is total emptiness (since the entire world is outside it . . .)."[7] Since, then, self-consciousness is empty, insubstantial, a nonbeing, a *néant*, that is ontically, transitively dependent on being, it is always in an intentional relation to what carrries it, namely, the *en-soi* that is identical to and completely filled by itself, and which has no emptiness or internal division. Rhetorically, there is no attempt here to go from the language of ontology to that of racial difference. And yet, in those texts in which the question of racial difference is explicit, Sartre seems to present racial self-awareness as either an escape from self-consciousness (which he describes as irreal) or as the embrace of race as a quasi-objective essence (which he describes as a deluded self-objectification). In both instances, the subject intentionally denies (or inauthentically refuses) its own being. However, as the quotation from Fanon suggests, what these two examples fail to grasp and what Sartre forgets (in his turn to phenomenology) is the extent to which the subject who refuses to be black is never able to escape the negrophobic effect of that refusal on his or her psyche, so that the response to interpellation is not the feigned escaping or embrace of difference but the sudden disclosedness (what Heidegger calls *Erschlossenheit*) of an *en-soi* that is paradoxically full of its own nonbeing and is overwhelmed by all the *négatités* that come with it: shame, despair, and guilt, that is to say, all those feelings that leave a residue and cannot simply be negated at the level of consciousness. This is what Fanon means when he says that the black subject remains haunted by a virtually substantial absoluity, for it is made to empty itself of everything absolute or transcendental. In a word, blackness cannot know itself eidetically as spirit. In going on to say, after reaffirming that consciousness is dependent on being, that the black has no actuality of being but also no possibility as being, Fanon is making the appearance of this *n'est pas* into a fundamental challenge to ontology. Blackness becomes an absoluity that can only affirm itself as a *n'est pas* (and consequently as a forbidden possibility), because its "*être été*" (being made-to-be) only appears insofar as it is not, and as something less than a *rien* but never quite a *néant*. But this nonbeing is not the subject's own. "This reconsideration of myself, this thematization, was not my idea," Fanon writes (92). As a matter of fact, the black is the subject who allows nonbeing to appear—it assumes it as its essence, and its way of being is being-made-to-be-the-*en-soi*-that-is-not (*n'est pas*); it is the *être été* that reproduces itself as a *n'est pas*: where, then, is its contradiction, where is its impurity?

To answer, we must, despite the epistemological paradox of the object, say that blackness is the expression of its perpetual effacement. Silence, or *retournement*, is denied us, not because our speech has no status, or we don't speak clearly or well, but because *all speech is on the side of a racial law*. To speak black or white is still to have a role imposed: either that of a shimmer or blemish added on, or that of an obligatory delusion that is also a failure to speak at all. Or else the speaker is hampered by what is said without being said, what is absent: the idiom of a law that simply communicates the *ban* (the affective politics) of negrophobia: in this case what is unconsciously said can only be expressed, so to speak, by its effect: the effect of a being that is excruciated. This is why any lapsus in speech is irreversible: a white idiom can only show a black delivery as impure, bad, comedic; as a failure to speak "properly," and will either be corrected or perfected by a judgment that is likened to a condemnation. Anyone preparing to speak "Parisian" (among other blacks) will, then, be conscious that each word articulates as a *n'est pas* that is always on the side of a racial law. But not being is not being nothing, and deficiency is not a negation but rather contains an affirmation of another sort in itself. A deficiency of being may be indistinguishable from the fault that empties it, but this deficiency does not exclude the power, the affect, of absolutity that is the fault line of its very structure (a point that is as hard to express as it is to grasp). In other words, what has been or can be produced as *nègre* also raises, in a very profound way, what counts as human subjection.

It can now be seen that what Sartre has forgotten is what it means to *be* a *nègre* independently of any intent or desire we may have. This apparently negative virtually substantial absolutity, then, would be in fact the positive condition of the impurity or flaw by which the black knows nothing (*n'est pas*) of the essences and determinations of its being. For our purposes here, the essential part of the analysis is that it implies that ontology has itself forgotten how being-for-others is structured by this *n'est pas*, and that its apparent simplicity and self-identity harbors a black alterity that means both that it has an absolutity (it is not simply an escape, as Sartre has it) *and* that that absolutity is not simply that of an intersubjective unsaid—that is, the anonymous voice of ideology speaking through the subject—but an enigmatic prohibition: in Fanon's reading, *the black is made to be nonbeing rather than an inauthentic failure to be*, the *être en tant qu'on n'est pas* is not just the presencing of a deficiency but involves something more like the flickering of a warning sign, an interdiction, an essential ban or exclusion, however evanescent or fleeting. And this being-made-to-be, which explicitly alludes to Sartre's "être été" in *Being and Nothingness*, appears to have a characteristic that could be described as the ideological response, in culture, to the very possibility of black desire.[8] (This could be linked to other figures in Fanon of a disallowed or forbidden path, such as the "prohibitions and barriers" in *The Wretched of the Earth* and the more general figure of zones and blockades).[9] The black is stuck, paralyzed before a prohibited path not because it is emptied of *être en-soi*, but because, contrary to Sartre, blackness cannot be made into a ground of being and so guarded, fenced off, as a new epistemic ground. Blackness, in other words, is not encountered on the way to being, like an obstacle, but rather in what lies beyond it: the deficiency by which it finds itself lacerated, severed, scattered (which is what passes for the black experience of the world). And this allows him further to play on the fact that in French, the word *être* is not just a transitive verb in the present tense but also can be used in the passive voice, which Macherey has not succeeded in grasping in his more simple account of ideology. This element of nonbeing in the analysis (and Fanon is certainly crediting Sartre with this insight, albeit one that also involves an element of blindness) would then bespeak an essential limit for how Fanon understands Sartre's phenomenology in its efforts to go to "intentionality" and would open onto what Fanon famously develops here and elsewhere as the evanescent structure of a *n'est pas*, which has to be thought of as more originary than either being or ideology. Although Fanon never to my knowledge makes the connection explicit, this complication of the Hegelian notion of the *pour-soi* is of a piece with his own ambivalent fascination with Sartre's notion of nausea. And the sense that even if, for Sartre, it is through the subject that nothing (the *néant*) comes into the world, the black subject cannot "be its own nothing," for the thing that makes it into nonbeing does not belong to it, and is not its own doing, for it does not seek to determine itself as nonbeing (and thus as a *néant de son proper être*) but discovers that its nonbeing is outside of itself, and so beyond authenticity or intentionality. In other words, it is not enough to be ontically black to be consciously so, but nor is it enough to be interpellated *as* black to be unconsciously black in one's drives and desire.

Returning to *Black Skin, White Masks* and leaving aside for now Fanon's initially enigmatic alignment in that text of blackness and ontology, of blackness and impossibility, let us try, the better to grasp what Macherey has wrong here, to understand the overall argumentative structure of Fanon's text (its reading of negrophobia as ideology). Fanon claims that negrophobia is endemic to the system and institutions of the colony and is itself grounded in a moment of inaugural violence that it cannot ever simply integrate or absorb. This claim is not simply an empirical or historical claim about actually existing systems or institutions (although the question of how the de facto violence of the colony becomes de jure, legitimated by a logic of racial sovereignty, is also at stake). This founding violence does indeed seem to have something of the character of the Althusserian version of interpellation, in that it is radically constitutive of the subject and thus marks a complete subjectivation whose interruptive, decisive character we have been associating with the temporality of the "tiens" episode. But to capture this violent structure—the performative power of negrophobia—it is telling that Fanon's discourse comes up against its limit: it has to move away from both the language of phenomenology and that of psychoanalysis, to grasp the meaning of what he calls the *n'est pas*. To give just one example; it occurs after the introduction of the "*schéma épidermique racial*": "I approached the other [*l'autre*] . . . and the other evanescent, hostile but not opaque, transparent, absent, disappeared. Nausea" (90, 92, translation modified).

On the basis of this claim, Fanon will argue that this founding, evanescent, or ungrounded violence does not simply disappear along with the (white) other who institutes it, but that the trace of it remains as a kind of nausea. To

the extent that what is thus instituted as *nègre* is not just a system of domination with its predictable outcomes (and Macherey concedes in all three types
of case that negrophobia is not repressive in this sense), then the decision not
to be *nègre*, in as much as this is ever a decision, always takes place in the
nauseating recollection, as it were, of that ungrounded foundational moment.
Insofar as we are dealing with a prohibition that is itself absent, evanescent,
decisions made in the name of freedom are then always in principle, however unknown in fact, imprisoned within the formal instituted framework of
a racial law (what Fanon calls "imposition") within which antiblackness is
judged and pronounced. Fanon gives this imprisoning a very strong characterization in terms of aporia, in that in this view *any* decision to not be black
to some extent attests to an interdiction at the level of being: the White Man
(*le Blanc*), he writes, "had no scruples about imprisoning me," which is the
reason why the I here not only is outside of itself (*être-là*) but experiences
itself as *the effect of a call that is nihilating* (92). Every time the subject hears
the word *nègre*, every time that it tries to affect a correctly subsumed white
example, according to a determinant judgment of what it *ought* (not) to be, it
experiences this nausea by which the ego *hemorrhages* into an experience of
aporia. This emptying out, this lessening: the terms converge on the concept
of effacement in ways that remain to be understood, and that will force us
to revise our understanding of Fanon's relation to Sartre, Marx, and Lacan.

Freedom, then (as opposed to resistance or complicity), always entails,
however minimally, this moment of nausea in which negrophobia uncovers
the vicissitudes of this *être-là*. Macherey would not deny this: indeed, this is
just where he thinks Fanon (as opposed to Althusser) is right, but he thinks
nothing in the structure as laid out so far justifies what he presents as Fanon's
refusal of the unconscious. After a further argument, which attempts to show
that negrophobia in general gives rise to a nausea that is certainly related
to that described by Sartre in the context we are exploring, Fanon lists and
discusses three aporias in the sense we have just given, and it is here that
we will be able to understand the general logic of the *être-là* that Macherey
is overlooking. Although all three of these aporias (which overlap to some
extent, or perhaps can be thought of as redescribing one and the same impossibility from three slightly different angles, in terms of what Fanon calls the
interdicted accomplishment of an infinite desuturation) are germane to the
questions here, and the nearest Fanon comes actually to saying what the
être-là is in the context of the third, it is actually in the first that the logic in
question is most readily understood.

The first aporia, "an object among other objects," reveals how blackness
is possessed by a cultural voice that is not its own: we can thus say that
the appearance of the *nègre* is consequent to the white disappearance of the
subject (its evanescence), and for there to have been a subject, there must
have been something other than the subject for its "being" to just disappear
from the world—what, in a different context, Fanon calls the *existentiale*

situation of vertigo and nausea. This much we have seen Macherey concede. On the other hand (this is what Macherey seems not to have grasped when he claims that for Fanon "one is never a subject pure and simple, or a subject in an absolute sense, but only ever a subject in a situation" [18]), the action or decision to not be a subject (or to be a subject condemned and judged as deficient) must nonetheless still have a relation to absoluity and thereby to a certain loss. Fanon describes the situation as follows:

> Locked in this suffocating reification, I appealed to the Other so that his liberating gaze, gliding over my body suddenly smoothed of rough edges, would give me back the lightness of being I thought I had lost, and taking me out of the world put me back in the world. But just as I get to the other slope I stumble, and the Other fixes me with his gaze, his gestures and attitude, the same way you fix a preparation with a dye. I lose my temper, demand an explanation. . . . Nothing doing. I explode. Here are the fragments put together by another me. (89)

The gaze that reifies or objectifies me must at one and the same time be the gaze that frees me from reification, and thus gives me back my world, yet without being one with or entirely consistent with the world, thus always to some extent contesting or suspending my access to the world. This means the *I* that aspires to the world can never simply or confidently be *known* to be in it, on the one hand because of the desire that defines the decision as such (in its contentment and wretchedness) and on the other because the *I*'s belonging to the world will again be subject to the same aporia as that of the object. This means, says Fanon, that in a sense blackness has to invent, or more properly, reinvent the world as though for the first time in its discovery of it as lost (and each case is, *ex hypothesi,* a loss that is *already known*). This moment (however fraught) of reinvention then repeats, in however minimal a way, the founding violence of the exclusion itself, as already described. In short, for blackness to be in the world, it must, in its self-awareness, be both liberated and excluded: it must preserve itself as fixed or suspended in order to reinvent itself in each case, or reinvent itself as a (white, slavish) affirmation in the free confirmation of its negrophobic principle. Each time it is fixed, each time it finds itself excluded by a white interpretation (narratives, values, reasoning), it also knows that only a white gaze can guarantee it absolutely. At least, if the gaze that guarantees it in no uncertain terms is also what censors or nihilates it, then to be repeatedly seen by it, which always happens in part and according to the necessary iterability of negrophobia, is to be returned to being not as tragedy but as a farce—but to that extent one will say of the black that he is purely free only if he doesn't confirm or refer to blackness or if, because he doesn't want to lose himself, if he suspends his decision, he stops at the undecidable but always violently resolved, that is to say, buried, dissimulated, repressed, blackness of his being. Here the *être-là* is what establishes the call by which the being of the black is destined—or, more tellingly, learns to *become the being of its disappearance* rather than the appearance of its being.

Macherey would perhaps say that this is just the kind of situation he is describing in his first case (i.e., the gaze as a logic of domination).[10] If that were so, then at the very least his criticism of Althusser would be unjustified because to that extent they would in fact be agreeing. But it seems as though they are not exactly saying the same thing: Macherey's description of "a specified subject, a normed subject, a subject for and under norms," which is supposed to capture the "(apparent) legitimacy" and the "(real) efficacy" of racist interpellation and, despite its claim to be essentially a correction of Althusser, in fact systematically minimizes the elements of complicity (already in the desire to be put back into the world), of violence and undecidability, that are showing up in Fanon's account (19).

Indeed, it seems that the question of decision—what it establishes or makes happen (in the sense of being the enigmatic point of a pathological inability to decide)—is the object of Fanon's second aporia. The point here (Fanon also formulates this argument in the wake of his polemical exchange with Sartre) is that for the black "to make myself known" (in the sense of being recognized, that is, as a consciousness that is aware of its freedom), there must be a recognition by others that "all I want is to be anonymous" (95, 96). In this sense, "anonymity" means a little more than not being noticed; it refers rather to a desire to be recognized as not *nègre* even though what is recognized as *nègre must* be a misrecognition, a situation in which the desire to go unrecognized by a misrecognition is always an *impossible* recognition. On the one hand, this involves a tension between being a subject pure and simple in the sense of being in a relation to others and the singularity of the situation that we have already laid out and which Fanon here redescribes as an undecidable "evanescence" between two contradictory but equally imperative injunctions (so a kind of double bind): to become white insofar as one is condemned as black but always in the awareness that one's whiteness is impossible, heterogeneous, and irreducible, and on the other hand, something that seems just as pernicious and that the least one can say it is not made immediately perspicuous: thus, to be black means: embrace one's deficiency, its impurity and necessary disappearance as one's most singular possession. Fanon says that blackness is the experience of that which, though heterogeneous to what it means to be human as well as what ought and yet cannot be human, has to give itself up to the impossible decision to be while refusing-embracing its nonbeing. Without this vicious circle, he says, apparently repeating an earlier point, the decision not to be black would not be a decision and would amount to a negrophobic imposition. Throughout all of this fraught characterization Fanon comes back to the assertion that "the proof was there, implacable. My blackness was there, dense and undeniable. And it tormented me, pursued me, made me uneasy, and exasperated me"

(96). The point is that if blackness is undeniable, to have a density of being, then it must exceed or suspend not merely the generality of what it means to be a subject, to which it nonetheless retains the relationship laid out in the first aporia, but also the idea that a decision to be is something that is never simply done or made by a subject, in the sense that there would first be a subject in its self-identity and relative self-sufficiency, and that it would subsequently come to make (or suffer) a loss of being on the basis of that subjecthood. In a way that is certainly still Sartrean in its inspiration if not its details, Fanon will argue that a thinking based on the subject is unable to account for blackness: even if one wanted to say that the subject was made black or that blackness happened to it, in Fanon's view the word and concept "subject" would severely block and limit that thought (just as earlier we were able to criticize Sartre's subjectivist account of self-certainty). As often around these matters, Fanon is quite vehement: "I was not mistaken. It was hatred; I was hated, detested, and despised, not by my next-door neighbor or a close cousin, but by an entire race (97–98). And "Victory was playing cat and mouse; it was thumbing its nose at me. As the saying goes: now you see me, now you don't. . . . And in one sense, if I had to define myself I would say I am the one who waits" (99, translation modified)

Undecidability, then, seems at the very least to involve an appearance that also involves one's disappearance ("Now you see me, now you don't") and a belated awareness that one is hated in one's very being. To that extent, and contrary to the Sartrean account we were reading earlier, if the white subject is entirely characterized by its transparent emptiness (since the entire world is outside it) and to some extent is the consequence of what happens or befalls it as a simple event or contingency, for the black subject, as Fanon puts it, the world is already *there* (*être-là*), aversive, hostile, even hateful, and what befalls it is expected. This aspect too, which Fanon is again suggesting must be present, however minimally, in any decision (not) to be black (the decision not to be *nègre*), suggests an opacity that, in a word, blackens ego, cogito, and bodily schema. Further (and this aspect of Fanon's discussion seems entirely absent from Macherey, though not from Sartre), this trial or ordeal of undecidability is not simply a transient moment (thought of as an impasse in a Hegelian sense). The undecidability that I am (or perhaps, given what we have just said, the "it" that is hated, or that is added, *the it that is me*), which is at once seen and unseen, and once it has happened produces nausea, this *it* remains marked by undecidability, and according to a pervasive logic of a necessary alterity in which what is *être-là* is never simply *there*, or more precisely, it is *not an il y a*. And it remains marked by undecidability in the mode of spectrality, which will be a crucial aspect of Fanon's thinking and make his theory of subjectivation slightly different again from Althusser's (and a fortiori Macherey's). The spectrality of black undecidability will remain with the question of what an assured self-certainty would mean for the being of the black (or even whether it ever has a real ground for questioning its appearing as black, for questioning what something is is not the same thing as saying that it is). Certainly, the real must lend itself to a figuration, to a concept, but for Sartre the actuality of the *en-soi* is not affected by this appearing. For Fanon, on the other hand, the figure and concept of blackness introduces a schism that alters being; it is not present in itself but refers to something that has been cut open and amputated; moreover, this hemorrhaging challenges not only the subject's consistency but its ontic presupposition as an existence. It is not so much a dependency on how being appears as a realization that blackness reveals the being of an appearing dependence. "I am a slave not to the 'idea' others have of me, but to my appearance," Fanon tells us (95). This is why it cannot be surmounted or sublated, but remains caught, lodged like a ghost in an undecidable decision that it either blindly follows or affirms as the law of its existence.

After some remarks about how this situation reached in the first two aporias (something in you more than you, undecidability of the decision [not] to be black as coming from somewhere other than the subject, whose arrival or refusal I do not master or control) might lead to an accusation of madness or neurosis (which again brings us back to Freud) and other remarks about a reluctance (if not an outright refusal) to align the sense of being "too late" said to be at work in these descriptions with the idea of racial difference, Fanon moves to his third aporia, which will explicitly bring us back to Freud but also suggest a way in which the Sartrean and Freudian versions of ontology cannot be separated as rapidly and cleanly as Macherey seems and needs to think in order to sustain his reading of Fanon's own interpellation.

The third aporia—"I wade in black irrationality, I am up to my neck in it, as a rational response to white irrationality"—at first seems little more than an inversion of the adage (from the Acts of the Apostles) that we must meet unreason with reason. The reason that is unreason is thus the reason why I have turned to irrationality. For Fanon, this inversion ruptures the kind of ecstatic irrationality at play in Léopold Senghor's aesthetic theory of negritude and, most importantly, affects the relationship between jouissance and knowledge. Just as he comes up against something unreasoned in being-for others, Fanon realizes that the turn to black irrationality is also a symptom of the desire to make himself known—but the knowledge of what it means to be black in a certain sense comes before knowledge and blocks it. And even if it were possible to counter racist scientific knowledge with black poetic knowledge, that decision would still take the form of the irruptive *être-nègre* that he is trying better to understand. Hence Fanon's irritated, frustrated response to Sartre's *Black Orpheus*, and the argument that blackness is in a transitive-transitory relation to historical knowledge, *as such*, and that it must always remain a finite moment of urgency and discovery, and that it cannot be the consequence or effect of a theoretical or historical knowledge, given that the latter is the outcome of a dialectic that precedes the distinction between reason and unreason, which *must* precede it. Having written on this elsewhere, I won't go into detail here.[11] But Fanon's response—"So they were countering my irrationality with rationality, my rationality with the 'true rationality'" (111)—recalls Fanon's discussion of *Being and Nothingness* that we described earlier: the call of ideology in Macherey's discussion of Althusser puts an end to any doubt the moment one is summoned; here speculation ceases and one's destiny is about to be decided. The difference here, however, has precisely to do with the quality of the urgency Fanon ascribes to racial thinking: eschatological as it may be in a certain sense, here the belief that race is a destiny does not seem to occur *at the end* of discussion or deliberation, nor even exactly *as an outcome* of such discussion and deliberation, but through its intrinsic negrophobia, to cut short deliberation and discussion, which are in principle irrelevant and which, however necessary they may be to the prospect of a reasoned response to blackness (and blackness is never simply a question of reason, says Fanon), are necessarily displaced by a phantasm whose existence is sui generis. And so it is not surprising that Fanon immediately invokes here not consciousness but indeed an "impulsiveness": negritude is the acting out of an "impulsive position," he writes, which is driven to see in blackness an *en-soi* that is complete or "immanent in itself," precisely because it refuses to see or know how it is itself unreasoned, driven by the desire not to be (114). But this desire to make blackness into a moment of decision (in the sense of discovery), to make it into an *is* rather than an *is not*, is always preceded (structurally and epistemologically, says Fanon) by the moment of negrophobic interpellation. This is why, as Fanon points out, the decision to present blackness as an *en-soi* is never a question of rationality (*verständlichkeit*) or negation, but rather the result of a subjectivation that is always and everywhere the imperfect, imcomplete imbrication of one's being. Or, as Fanon puts it, "Où me situer? Ou, si vous préférez: où me fourrer?" (Where do I fit in? Or, if you prefer: where should I put myself?; 91/93 translation modified)

II

Irony as the negative is the way; it is not the truth but the way.
—Kierkegaard, *The Concept of Irony*

This questioning is in fact a constant one in Fanon, first appearing in his published work as the famous final sentence of *Black Skin, White Masks*: "O my body, always make me a man who questions!" (206). The emphatic, exclamatory distinctions of Fanon's texts are often in tension with the precarious, even agonistic nature of what is being expressed, in as much as they concern the way blackness is *denegated*—more or less explicitly alluded to many times in Fanon's work, functioning as a kind of watchword or slogan but never once given a precise definition or a detailed reading. In *Towards*

the African Revolution (Pour la révolution africaine), published in 1964 but
based on articles from 1952–61, for example, the same kind of emphatic but
precarious assertion expresses a harsh irony: "It thus seems that the West
Indian, after the great white error, is now living in the great black mirage."[12]
In the second essay in the volume, "West Indians and Africans," first published in *Esprit* in 1955, Fanon suggests a possible connection between irony
and what he refers to as a "defense against neurosis," provoking him to state
that, in the West Indies, irony (and incidentally the reference to the great
black mirage returns us to the context of the third aporia and the racial-
cultural politics of negritude—irony is in fact used to question the somewhat
impassioned invocation of a negritude) is paradigmatic. In the essay, Fanon's
reading of negritude—which does not mention explicitly his own earlier
reading in *Black Skin, White Masks*, though he does invoke irony as a kind
of dissimulation—helps us see how the three aporias presented separately in
Black Skin, White Masks are related in the general thought of an irony that is
both psychoanalytic and historical (the resonance with Macherey's analysis
of the *unsaid* in *A Theory of Literary Production* is something to which we
will return): "Jankélévitch has shown that irony is one of the forms that good
conscience assumes. It is true that in the West Indies irony is a mechanism of
a defense against neurosis. A West Indian, in particular an intellectual who
is no longer on the level of irony, discovers his Negritude. Thus, while in
Europe irony protects against the existential anguish, in Martinique it protects against negritude" (19). The explicit invocation of irony as a defense
against anguish and neurosis is clear here, but the idea that irony also names
a dialectic of black history (in the Antilles, in Africa) may not be so obvious.
In the essay we find, "Until 1939 the West Indian lived, thought, dreamed
(we have shown this in *Black Skin, White Masks*) composed poems, wrote
novels exactly as a white man would have done," but "in 1945 he [the West
Indian] discovered himself to be not only black but a Negro [*Nègre*]," a discovery that came from the reading of Aimé Césaire's *Return to My Native
Land (Cahier d'un retour au pays natal)* (26, 25). And again, in 1939 the
West Indian "was continually recalling that he was not a Negro," but "from
1945 on, the West Indian in France was continually to recall that he *was* a
Negro" (24–25). What happens between 1939 and 1945? Fanon cites two
linked events: the publication, in 1939, of Césaire's *Return to My Native
Land*, and the forced deployment in 1943 of ten thousand racist Vichy sailors
in Martinique after the fall of France. According to Fanon, the confrontation
with white racism forced Martinicans to analyze their metaphysical fabula-
tions apropos of French imperialism, but it was Césaire's poetics, defined
specifically as a *négritude*, that permitted them to ask the question "Am I a
nègre?"—a question that acted rather like a parabasis in that it interrupted
and intruded upon the illusion of West Indian society and rhetoric, forcing
them to rethink the strictly ideological relation between "being neither white
nor Negro" (a class definition), and the function of such rhetoric when faced

with the event or decision of negrophobia. We are then in the presence of two sign systems imbricated within each other; in the first, history is not so much a defense against irony as the most ironic of discourses, and in the second, negritude is the means by which an antiblack black racism can be expressed and denoted. Which is to say that the desire to be, or not to be, *un nègre* is always the denegation of what one actually is and a defense against what one appears to be but is not. The irony here has a very specific meaning, which the reference to Vladimir Jankélévitch's *Irony* (*L'ironie;* 1936) makes more complicated than it might at first appear. What is it that makes negritude an ironic poetics? *Negritude* is essentially the convergence of different signifieds in a single signifier according to which blackness is both excessive and subtractive, both concept and unreason, both truth and pseudology. It is this specific element that, for my part, I call a *parabasis*: "Parabasis is the interruption of a discourse by a shift in the rhetorical register," writes Paul de Man. This shift is also linked to an interruptive "intrusion" (as such, the word not only gives us a different way of thinking about the "tiens" passages, but also about Fanon's reading of them).[13] The oscillation between error and mirage would suggest that the parabasis is permanent in the sense de Man gives it in his reading of Schlegel: that the interruption—the interdiction—takes place successively, infinitely, so that we could say *blackness is the permanent parabasis of an antiblack allegory*, and irony refers to its necessary undoing and what, historically, links it to an economy of aberration. This is the logic of both the metaphysical fantasy (of blackness), as an excess that is infinitely subtractive, and a dialectic that is structured by enmity. "I mean, for example, that the enemy of the Negro is often not the white man but a man of his own color" (17). What disrupts is, then, the disillusion that permanently blackens all irony. But there is no recuperation in terms of a historical dialectic, as we saw in Fanon's response to Sartre, for the great black hole is a mirage, and even irony cannot expose what it really is, for what it reveals is an enmity launched against one's own impossible reflection. And just as, when considered historically, blackness is a mirage, in the same way, when considered as irony, it reveals a negrophobia or—the same thing—a negritude that henceforth makes comprehensible an enmity of which irony, formed as a defense, is the most precarious, suspended, and interrupted of signs.

Simplifying greatly, it seems to me that whereas Macherey's sense of Althusserian interpellation seems to come primarily from an unequivocal, supposedly unironic account of being spoken, Fanon's reference to irony—or, if you prefer, black irony, which by its interruption and utter ambiguity gives one the impression that defense and enmity have changed names and even content, according to a metaphysics of intrusion—is where the said and the unsaid are, precisely, both allegories of the same (ghostly, traumatic) encounter with what is considered to be *nègre*. Let us consider these two oppositions.

First, in the West Indies, the decision to *be* is always troubled by a desire that, we know, both idealizes and repels blackness, and so is unwilling and unable to decide between them, and hence chooses neither. Irony offers an illusory escape from such indecision; whether this derives from a good conscience (Jankélévitch) or a bad conscience (Sartre), the refusal of apodictic certainty (the assertiveness of ideology) is not simply evasive, nor is it resistant. Fanon accuses the black ironist of being *defensive*; that is to say, the failure to decide between content (truth) and form (appearance), or between white (message) and black (medium) gives rise, historically, to an aporia that cannot decide between illusion and error. I do not believe, as a matter of fact, that blackness can proceed without a certain undecidability as to its object (as we know, nothing is more resolutely elusive and paradoxical than the language of racial authenticity); nor do I believe that *le vécu noir*, heir of a thousand anecdotes and fables, at once mythic, ideological, and stereotypic, can be divested of irony without risk of further illusion. Hence Fanon's criticism of the metaphors by which West Indians express their superiority to Africans, for example, and the vision that subsists through them: that of a feeling of racial inferiority hidden behind the *nègre* as signifier. It is this argument, itself ironical, that explains why blackness is inevitably experienced as a permanent parabasis (I am referring here to the word *intrusion* rather than, say, imposition, or interpellation, and the trope by which it is communicated: the metaphor that makes blackness appear as a black hole, and the various invocations of a paradoxically repelling attraction, as an asymptote that famously touches on its own negation, but in a way that is always liminal, indecisive, because it refuses to know what it already knows and will not verbalize the words, or the concepts, that would free it from such equivocation). Contrary to Jankélévitch, then, for whom irony reveals the truth behind illusion, perhaps it would be better to say that blackness is disclosed by a distance incapable of being traversed or negated. If, then (as Fanon consistently formulates it according to the logic of aporia), one were to try to answer the question "How is blackness possible?" then one would need to deconstruct this very opposition between irony and history, irony and truth.

The second, much more recent opposition, of a more Marxist aspect largely tributary to the Althusserian paradigm of science/ideology, is that of the *unsaid* of literature. Literature makes us aware of what it cannot say or is prevented from saying, an unsaid that both structures and fissures the semantic codes of the text (a limit that literature mouths silently); the unsaid is constructed as the limit of ideology, but it is through it that ideology speaks. At the very end of his introduction to *A Theory of Literary Production*, first published in 1966, Macherey gives a brief summing up of this "unsaid" structure, which establishes "that absence around which a real complexity is knit."[14] This absence is determinate but not determined. The unsaid is then seen as the absent (though coded) residue of what the work *cannot say* or necessarily leaves unsaid; it is (the real, historical) elision that "founds the speech of the work" (if we define that speech as a kind of "vanishing" without which it could not be heard), which precedes its meaning *as* history (if we set meaning in opposition to its *denegation*—a word Macherey borrows from Lacan but doesn't really define as such) (85, 86).[15] Just as the opposition between surface and depth implies a hermeneutic vision, so the unsaid/meaning opposition implies an ultimately dialectical vision (under cover of a logic of confrontation): there is a reduction of the unsaid to that of a symptom (the idea that each work is "haunted by the absence of repressed words which make their return") and of the symptom to history, where the unspoken "receives the means" of its "realization." Literature, the trace of the unsaid, because it is specifically this trace, then makes negatively explicit its historic function, which Macherey here describes as its production. It is the task of any Marxist reading to show how the work establishes, symptomatically performs, and ideologically assumes its history, in the same way that the *"unconscious of the work"* establishes repression (the way an abscess reveals an underlying disease), in order to lance the process of its suppuration (53). Hence, we arrive at the paradox of an unsaid that governs any reading as such, the entire pertinence of an indetermination (in relation to form, ideology, discourse, or history) that has no signified, yet through which everything happens or is produced as the "real" of the work.

I suggest that the unsaid is what haunts every literary production. How, then, can we read or interpret it, and how does it relate to the *situation* of blackness? To answer this question we need to inquire more closely into the relation between language and ideology. To do so, I take as my example Macherey's later reading of Fanon's *Black Skin, White Masks*. Accordingly, we will see how blackness is produced—sutured—by a theory of reading which concedes that the essence of ideology is the production of a universal structure but in ways that make blackness itself invisible, which is absurd.

Let us take first the opposition of the unsaid and meaning, of subjection (*l'assujettissement*) and interpellation. No doubt how we read includes a certain relation to how we, in turn, are irreducibly read. The Marxist structural analysis of ideology is wholly based on the conviction (and the dialectical proof) that we subsist by how we reproduce ideology: in short, to occupy the grammar by which we are recognized as subjects we *"must answer"* the call of ideology, for there is "no possibility of dodging it" or its logic of reproducibility: the effects of ideology can be varied without altering this underlying structure (12). That Macherey should then say of the black that the "operation of selection" also takes "the form of a relegation," as implacable as it is overdetermined, has exactly the same narrative (or, more precisely, structural) function as *l'assujettissement* does in Althusser (e.g., the way the subject "is called upon" is irreducible, since it is functionally necessary to the sequence by which the subject becomes elocutionary, or expressive of ideology) (13).

The error, however—and it is here that we must modify Macherey's reading of blackness—would be to forget the irony by which the black realizes its untruth; what this (forgetting, as we have just said) forgets is not what brings about the content or the signified of selection, the racist forms of understanding that are assumed to be already *there* (*être-là*), but the form, the signifier, or if we prefer, the permanent parabasis by which the subject is desutured and *as such is never symbolizable* (for blackness is always articulated around a position that has no here-there (*juste là*); its signified is a never-having-been-there (or is more akin to a kind of hallucination), as we have shown in Fanon and even more clearly in his reading of psychoanalysis. Further, Fanon attempts to bring to light—without reference to verisimilitude or allegory—an interplay between voice and signifier in which the black (or more exactly the black who is ideologically whitened) *does not need the "tiens" to be heard for it to have an effect*, for the place it is communicated *from* is already echoed by a drive *toward* it, a *n'est pas* that is located at the *other* end, as it were, of desire and reality, of subject and ideology; moreover this drive is *absent*—it necessarily slips away from any image or history of meaning, and even though it is full of malice and a certain defensiveness, this is an irony that has no symbolic code, genre, or disposition, whatever the material uses of ideology.

Hence we can no longer *see* blackness as the overdetermined effect of a structural situation. Blackness is not relegated but effaced; in the black, there is only whiteness, or more precisely, the black in its blackness is only a denegation of form—consequently, *there is no subject of blackness*. We can say metaphorically that the black is subjected not by what he is but by what he is *not*: neither host nor parasite, the *nègre* resolutely intrudes as an obscene intrusion; as such, blackness confuses distance and limit, not because of nausea or even autoimmunity, but because it is an abolition that is freely chosen (that is, a self-effacement that is always a forced choice). Doubtless, this is why its voicing is not primarily phenomenological (Macherey) nor *automatic* (Althusser), *but that which recedes*, as it were, from discourse, truth, and ideology. What is more ironic, more undecidable, more interruptive, than this structure by which blackness experiences itself as fixed in its effacement and declares itself free in its chosen unfreedom?

III

Now let us turn to the second opposition, that of irony and history, which is in effect the opposition of Fanonism and Marxist phenomenology. There is a kind of intermediate step here that will lead us to the parabasis we are trying to understand in the irony Fanon is invoking. Here too, we must refine our vision of what blackness is (or is not).

What enables Macherey to question Althusser is, as we have seen, the belief that the theory of ideology is blind to the functioning of difference. It is a blindness that is symptomatic, unsaid. And therefore, says Macherey, it has to be decrypted. The features of the unsaid are, of course, undeniably drawn from Althusser, or at least from his idea of a symptomatic reading (the belief that what is unsaid is both absent and what grounds the text in a *real histori-cal rationality*, i.e., a hermeneutics): like any discourse that claims to expose what is absent, how does one finally know that one has grasped the truth of ideology? What is its reference? How does it surreptitiously persist, con-stantly repeated by the work, without its meaning or signified being anything but what is *meant* by ideology? These propositions seem to be both excessive and insufficient: excessive because meaning is always returned to its referent, and the text thereby becomes the incarnation of an absolute reference; insuf-ficient because the operation of *conversion* or *decryption* is never explained in all its depth. A word on this last point.

We know that the unsaid of the work, what determines at once its task and its limits, is the ideology that takes place by never taking place *as such*: there is no text without repression, or literature begins as the sign or allegory of a displacement; but, in order to think this, critique must be able to make repres-sion representable, for why otherwise would we read it? A Marxist theory of reading must thus expressly become the structure, the code, by which the unsaid emerges as the resolution of its ideologically repressed reference. Now, the irony of blackness (the black irony of thought) has essentially nothing to do with reference or repression. Of course, it can include symptoms, but it does not need to be repressed for it to be unconscious. Fanon constantly talks about how blackness is the depositary of a cultural hatred that directly opens a black hole *within* the psyche, in ways that are necessarily unknown or ambiguous but no less real or traumatic for all that. Blackness is the signi-fier of a text that intrudes, but what intrudes has no determinable meaning beyond the intrusion itself, to the point where blackness is the experience of a paradox: *an unconscious affect that is itself not unconscious*. It is better to speak, more neutrally, of a form that lacks repression, or for whom repres-sion is lacking. Let us even add, perhaps, that without arrival—or at least without the appearance of arrival—intrusion does not function as a meaning (a signified that is unsaid), but is the effect of an entire culture. But even here we are not really going far enough, for what remains to be described is a van-ishing that is neither an event nor an occasion, and so cannot be dialectically overdetermined as something unsaid or simply interpellated.

Whence Fanon's view of a black *n'est pas*: a figure that does not lend itself to figuration—or even production; a figure that subsequently is not a *vernei-nung*; a figure that is not tropological but that reveals a dramatic antithetical turning point Fanon characterizes as a *contre coup* or ricochet, that is, an adversative signifier that throws one off balance, out of kilter, off guard. In the "Tiens, un nègre!" example, such a moment is foregrounded not by the various metaphors but by the exclamation mark that suggests the gaze can-not be grasped as readily or straightforwardly as Macherey suggests, that is, as an intruding sense or intention, but as a punctuation without content. By carrying this distinction to its conclusions, we are working toward why blackness requires a different language than ontology. It is, Fanon says, the paradoxical figure of what cannot be figured, and that is indeed without phrase or sentence, even though it can be uttered, or said, and in respect to which the word *black* is little more than an antilogy, whose signified opens onto a perpetual parabasis in which Fanon suggests we experience the impossible: "I made up my mind to laugh myself to tears, but that had become impossible."[16]

Such sentences make it obvious why the *n'est pas* is not the work of a repression. But they also make it quite clear why the *n'est pas* cannot, consequently, be conceived as an existential situation. To explain why, consider the following passage from *Black Skin, White Masks*: "One of the traits of the Antillean is his desire to dominate the other. He steers his course through the other. It is always a question of subject, and the object is totally ignored. I try to read admiration in the eyes of the other, and if, as luck would have it, the other sends back an unpleasant reflection, I run the mirror down: the other is a real idiot [*un imbécile*]" (186). And: "Each of them wants *to be*, wants to *flaunt himself*. Every act of an Antillean is dependent on the Other—not because the Other remains his final goal for the purpose of communing with him as described by Adler, but simply because it is the Other who asserts him in his need to enhance his status" (187 translation modified). So what is the Antillean's relation to the other? It is marked by one generic feature (which attaches it to an idiocy that is indeed foolish, which, not surprisingly perhaps, does not distinguish it from a complex rhetorical irony): the obligatory desire to be "full of myself" and to declare to the other that this "wish for fullness" is already, in itself, the sign of an insufficiency that is both litotic and rhetorical. If these sentences of Fanon's are deeply ironic, it is because they show how the black desire to *be* is already foolish because it cannot fulfill itself (and presumably because it is mediated, dependent), and for whom the other is of the same order as a reflection that renders not plenitude but its opposite, a self-image that is inclined to be suspicious (of itself) because the other is inattentive to my (fictitious) exemplary status) (187). These sentences, in their complex rhetorical inversions, seem to me, then, to present black identity as a kind of pseudonymous delusion, one marked by a rivalrous relation to another that, in this view, is in fact an ironical self-relation. What we must grasp here is not that such irony might *seem* foolish, but what it bespeaks is a claim to being that is radically displaced from being and that Fanon habitually describes as an antagonym.

This is not all. The black is a *comparaison* that itself has no status, in the sense given it through the pages of *Black Skin, White Masks*, with its image of a distrust that is *itself* negrophobic when viewed from a black perspective, which bespeaks an envy of the white *néant* that it lacks, such that it masks what is missing and cannot be ironized away. This insight has considerable consequence for Fanon's understanding of interpellation since it corresponds to a confusion—not so much of appearing with phenomena—but of the *néant* with cogito, as if the other that besets me (and who plunges me into a black hole) could be simply annulled, or again, dispensed with, along the lines of a chiasmic reversal. So when Fanon writes, "The question is always whether he [the other] is less intelligent than I, blacker than I, or less good than I" (186), what is being thematized ironically is also an example of foolish undecidability (and indeed, of mirage and error). Amid such uncertainty and gnomic inversion it is hard to tell desire from a kind of pathological narcissism that, in a further paradoxical twist, also communicates a form of mastery and satisfaction, but one that can only perform itself as a kind of ontological stupidity, as is further evidenced by the fact that it is so obviously haunted by what it is not, a *n'est pas* that Fanon draws attention to as an obligation that makes the decision to *be* both constrained and aporetic. Put another way, it is clear that, if blackness is *n'est pas*, a *non-étant* otherwise repressed by phenomenology, clinically it signifies not so much "*a being by which nothingness comes to things*" (the words are Sartre's) as a nothingness whose being is a thing and which reproduces itself as the imprint or turning point of a destitution that is also its most luxurious possession.[17] It follows that, for Fanon, blackness is not a dialectical struggle between an *en-soi* and cogito, but an aporetic struggle over the status of what is lacking, one that is linked not to how one is seen or how one imagines oneself being seen, but to *a disgrace of being* stupefied by irony.

Condemned, unconscious, prohibited—and yet performed: let us say that blackness cannot affirm, or choose, itself, for it is already chosen—by which I mean that it cannot pass from indecision to a transformation of what subordinates it; the paradoxical gravity, and fate, by which it is at once undecidably mad, foolish, and deluded; and, as is so often the case, bespeaks an almost religious love for what would destroy it, and that luxuriates in both the choice and the experience; and for want of this 'knowledge' should be seen as an inheritance based on culture and not on pathology (and consequently is never *just* a question of unconscious desire). The *n'est pas* certainly has some affinity with a symptomatic morphology, but it differs from it on one fundamental point (the predicates associated with these aporias imply a self-blinding irony that, once again, is never simply ideological): the *n'est pas* (whose form is derived from a logic of corpsing) cannot be resolved (*aufheben*) nor negated, for as Macherey shows perhaps in spite of himself, it speaks to the ways in which blackness is the depositary of culture, how it is excluded, not just selected; out of kilter, not just turned around; nihilated, not just subjected.

To return, in conclusion, to the concept of interpellation that I discussed at the beginning: in my opinion, it must consist today not in trying to see history within the unsaid of the text. In *Black Skin, White Masks* the unsaid is not the form of the text but that which can never be said, which I would prefer to call, at least in this essay, the permanent parabasis of a black allegory. The problem of what it means to be a subject can only be treated in relation to what I call an undecidable question; which, to continue the metaphor, can be summed up by saying that, if hitherto we have read black texts as stupidly referential (as identical to their situation), it would be better to read them as the place where blackness is suspended or interrupted (as a question of authenticity), whose irony, as Fanon describes it in reading Césaire, is nothing but an abyssal infinity—which envelops and absorbs nothing other than the black hole of its relation to both ontology and destruction.

Notes

An earlier version of this paper was presented at the seminar "Unthinking Affect: Blackness, Incapacity, Negativity," at the American Comparative Literature Association, 2019. My thanks to Tyrone Palmer and the other participants.

1. Frantz Fanon, *Peau noire, masques blancs* (Paris: Éditions du Seuil, 1995), 6. Frantz Fanon, *Black Skin, White Masks*, trans. Richard Philcox (New York: Grove Press, 2008). Page numbers in the text refer to the Philcox translation.

2. Pierre Macherey, "Figures of Interpellation in Althusser and Fanon," *Radical Philosophy* 173 (May/June 2012): 17, my emphasis. When Macherey, describing the effect of Althusser's iconic 1970 essay, "Ideology and ISA," tells us that it was "particularly disconcerting" to him, whose "enigma" he was "left to decrypt"— the decision to interrogate that enigma and its formulas (an odd phrase that conveys something systematic in relation to meaning) is what leads him to turn to Fanon, specifically *Black Skin, White Masks* and the sentence "Tiens, un nègre!": "It is interesting to compare them," he writes, and to contrast their "taking up [of] the problem of subjectivation [*subjectivation*]" (9). But what also remains enigmatic, or at least rhetorically unexplained, is how this return to the notion of *retournement*, whose limits are scrupulously reproduced, does not include Macherey's own use of the concept in *A Theory of Literary Production*, to capture the *difference* between art and ideology; or how art makes ideology *visible*, decipherable, by exposing its imaginary contours as in a broken mirror. This displaced genealogy would seem to suggest (contrary to Macherey) a *retourné* that is itself ambiguous, displaced, absent; there is even, in this subtle and odd reversal, a suspicion that blackness is the *inverted* image of this earlier attachment, and so the means by which the *retourné* makes visible the belief, posterior to Althusser, that ideology is a specular relation, and/or how art presents a real that is the (black?) reversal of ideology. The pattern is itself paradoxical, ironical, and too precise (which does not mean innocent) not to be deliberate.

3. Significantly, Macherey says that Althusser's notion of subjection allows Marxist literary theory to go beyond the "classical" reading of ideology, in which "*ideology is defined by what it is not*, by what it fails to be, or, to put it another way, by the distance it keeps from the real and its materiality" (9, my italics). This old traditional understanding of ideology, in brief, is disappointing for it can only see ideology as a *reflection* of, rather than effective agent of, social reproduction: in fact, Macherey insists that ideology is neither a representational nor reactive response to the real. This "*is* not"—its rhetoric or what it calls into question— will be of much concern to us in what follows given its ubiquity in both *A Theory of Literary Production* and this later essay on Althusser and Fanon.

4. For a detailed analysis of these terms and figures see my *Whither Fanon? Studies in the Blackness of Being* (Palo Alto, CA: Stanford University Press, 2018).

5. Moreover, what exists here as *n'est pas*, or its interruption, is essentially a vanishing point *within* meaning. This is why we perhaps should not name it as an ontology, or seek a meaning in it that amounts to a political ontology or—the same thing—a para-ontology. It is quite significant that these terms rely on ontological language to describe what blackness *is* (as a trope whose meaning is thenceforth beyond analogy or hermeneutics); see recent texts by Frank Wilderson, *Red, White & Black: Cinema and the Structure of U.S. Antagonisms* (Durham: Duke University Press, 2010); Sylvia Wynter, *On Being Human as Praxis* (Durham: Duke University Press, 2015); and Nahum Chandler, *X—The Problem of the Negro as a Problem for Thought* (New York: Fordham University Press, 2014).

6. Jean-Paul Sartre, *L'être et le néant: Essai d'ontologie phénoménologique* (Paris: Gallimard, 1943). All references are to the English translation: *Being and Nothingness*, trans. Hazel E. Barnes (New York: Philosophical Library, 1966).

7. Sartre, *Being and Nothingness*, 17.

8. Sartre, *Being and Nothingness*, 22n14.

9. Frantz Fanon, *The Wretched of the Earth*, trans. Richard Philcox (New York: Grove Press, 2004), 65.

10. After references to Sartre's *Reflections on the Jewish Question* (*Réflexions sur la question juive;* 1946), Macherey argues that Fanon's analysis remains existential, phenomenological—that it is constituted by a *situation*, "which is to say on the plane that is at once that of being for itself and that of being for the other, in a certain historical context" (17). It follows that a subject is only "ever a subject in a situation," and that is because the subject is always *overdetermined*: "Which is to say a subject specified according to the norms of the situation" (18). And it is because Althusser fails to ask or question "the criteria imposed by the situation" that he also fails to see how interpellation is both a process of *selection* and *relegation* (19). This is what we might call the true thrust of Macherey's *anti-Althusserian decryption*: subjection is not only a recruitment by which the subject learns to subject itself; it is also a prescription by which some are told that they are less than human, resisted as the very negation of agency and will.

11. See chapter 10, "The Abyssal," in my *Whither Fanon?*

12. Frantz Fanon, "West Indians and Africans," in *Towards the African Revolution*, trans. Haakon Chevalier (New York: Grove Press, 1967), 27.

13. Paul de Man, "The Concept of Irony," in *The Aesthetic Ideology*, ed. Andrzej Warminski (Minneapolis: University of Minnesota Press, 1996), 178.

14. Pierre Macherey, *A Theory of Literary Production*, trans. Geoffrey Wall (London: Routledge & Kegan Paul, 1978), 101.

15. See Jacques Lacan, "Response to Jean Hyppolite's Commentary on Freud's 'Verneinung' (1954)," trans. B. Fink, H. Fink, and R. Grigg, in *Écrits: The First Complete Edition in English* (New York: W. W. Norton, 2006), 308–33. For an elaboration of Fanon's relation to Lacan, see my *Lacan Noir* (London: Palgrave Macmillan, 2021).

16. Fanon, *Black Skin, White Masks*, 112; cited in Macherey, 14.

17. Sartre, *Being and Nothingness*, 57. Reading across from *A Theory of Literary Production* to *Black Skin, White Masks*, it is precisely absence that can be described as a situation of being overdetermined by, and an indeterminate relation to, a desire that reproduces itself as impossibility. As *ruinare*, the *n'est pas* is

not, or not only, a negation: we could also say that it subsists as an ontological impurity that is the trace of the other within us; consequently, there is no defense against it, for it is how blackness absents itself—whitens itself—that overdetermines its own negrophobic appearance as a passion that is violently envious, morally unjust.

What Do We Mean When We Speak of the Surface of a Text?

Reflections on Macherey's
A Theory of Literary Production

✦

Warren Montag

There is perhaps no greater testimony to the power of Pierre Macherey's *A Theory of Literary Production* than the criticisms it continues to attract fifty years after its initial publication in 1966. To be sure, the criticisms are not the same as those that immediately followed its publication more than fifty years ago, nor the criticisms it provoked when it appeared slightly more than ten years later, in English translation. Because its English-language readers saw Macherey's text as an application of Althusserianism (as they understood it) to literature, it incurred a charge similar to that leveled at *Reading Capital*: if Althusser was a structural Marxist, Macherey could be described as Marxist formalist. The mass of material published since then by Macherey and the texts by Althusser published after his death have made such readings unsustainable, although not simply by adding to our knowledge of the theoretical conjuncture in which they were written. More importantly, the later works have shifted the relation of the visible and the invisible, the legible and the illegible within *Reading Capital* and *Theory*. If it is true that Althusser and Macherey were engaged in a critique of structuralism, their objective was not simply to invalidate it. Instead, they sought to identify and describe the conflict that traversed it and, more importantly, to take sides with one of its parties against the other, or others. Accordingly, before we can follow Macherey's line of march through the field of structuralist notions of the literary text, we must first confront the obstacles that have obscured essential parts of his exposition.

Macherey's *A Theory of Literary Production* was introduced, before it appeared in English translation, by Terry Eagleton, who provided an account of the text that played a decisive role in determining how it was read and understood.[1] While generally sympathetic to Macherey's account of the *illusions,* or "fallacies" (as the term was rendered in English), that blocked the development of a theory of literary production, Eagleton found Macherey's critique of the notion of the hidden unity, whether thematic or formal, of literary works to be nothing less than a symptomatic lapse. According to Eagleton, Macherey had simply inverted the assumption of coherence, replacing system, structure, and order with disorder, discrepancy, and irregularity, and therefore the presence of order with its absence. Macherey, Eagleton argued, had failed to see that hidden in the depths is not an elaborate system too intricate to be seen in an initial reading but precisely the absence of the work's real content, which is thus not an absence at all in the strict sense but a distant presence, the work's historical referent, waiting to be traced to its hiding place.

More recently, the proponents of the tendency known as "surface reading" have identified Macherey not as a Marxist formalist but as a hermeneutic thinker for whom the readable surface of the text is little more than a ruse or diversion to be disregarded in the search for the truth the text seeks to conceal.[2] According to this argument, for Marxists such as Macherey, the text serves as a pretext to talk about what is outside of it: the ideology that represents the interests of the dominant class by masking itself as reality. The perspective of surface reading coincides at a key point with Eagleton's understanding of the notion of absence in *Theory*: both hold that Macherey, driven by the conviction that the truth and reality of a text lie outside of it, proposes a theory of reading as a movement from a deceptive surface to the depths, where disavowed truths are hidden. And there is no more effective hiding place than under an absence. Such a reading of Macherey, however, instantiates the very denial of the surface of his text that their reading ascribes to him: they fail to confront his consistent rejection of the "fallacy of depth," his repudiation of the notion of the hidden interior of a text, and his reiterated assertion that the text is irreducible to anything outside of itself. In fact, they have appropriated Macherey's own arguments, not to reveal the contradictory character of his text but to reduce it to a "hidden agenda" that must be rejected in toto. But surface readers have posed the question of the surface, and by doing so in relation to *Theory*, they have placed the notion of the surface of the text squarely in front of us, thereby making visible the fact that the word "surface" applied to literary and philosophical text serves to signify, more than anything else, a collective ignorance and incomprehension: we do not know, and more importantly do not know that we do not know, what we mean when we say "the surface of the literary work," above all when we argue that the idea of a textual depth is fallacy, illusion, or ruse. If there is no depth, no hidden dimension, what does it mean to speak of a surface?

We might begin to confront these problems by noting that "surface," the word as well as the concept, applied to texts, literary or otherwise, did not figure in any of the commentaries on or criticisms of Macherey's text at the moment of its appearance. The fact that Macherey could describe the literary work in its entirety as a "thin surface"[3] lacking any depth, was systematically overlooked by critics and partisans like. This is particularly noteworthy given the attention devoted to the concept of surface by a number of prominent French thinkers within a year or two of the publication of *Theory* in 1966, above all, Jacques Lacan, Louis Althusser, and Gilles Deleuze. Accordingly, if we want to grasp the surface of the literary work as a concept rather than a simple metaphor, a concept that, understood in its specificity, allows us to think about singular works, as well as about the institution of literature understood globally, in a new way, there may be no better place to begin such an inquiry than the concatenation of analyses and arguments devoted to the notion of surface as it develops in Macherey's text. *Theory* offers some of the essential elements of a definition of the surface of a text, but we will find and identify them only by following the precise written form of his arguments, even when they lead us beyond the limits of his text to other texts and other thinkers, from Althusser to Spinoza. In fact, it might be argued that his text offers a series of answers or responses to questions that are not only missing from *Theory* but have yet, even now, to be posed. To disentangle and separate out his answers, however, we must pose the absent questions that logically precede them. We seem to be caught in a circle, but one from which there is a way out and, more important, a way forward. Invoking Spinoza's assertion that "we have a true idea,"[4] we may begin by asking a single, but by no means simple, question: what is the meaning of what has been said up to this point, concerning the surface of a text? In what chains of synonymy can the word "surface," applied to a text, be found, and from what semantic fields have these words and chains of words been drawn?

First, the word itself. To understand Macherey's repeated recourse to *surface* (as well as the closely related *superficies*), we must acknowledge the fact that there is something unsettling and strange in his use of the term. In fact, Macherey is engaged in a strategic rehabilitation of a word whose metaphorical use in relation to texts was nearly always pejorative, inescapably associated with the imputation of superficiality, exteriority, and secondary. Further, as noted earlier, he was not alone in his attempt to push the semantic boundaries of "surface" with the aim of unbalancing its hierarchical opposition to the historically privileged notion of depth: to take only two of the most prominent of his contemporaries, both Deleuze and Lacan, in different ways, saw this opposition—particularly the priority of depth over surface—as one of the most formidable barriers to an adequate understanding of *langages* (in opposition to *langue*), discourses, and statements, and both sought to reclaim and use the notion of surface to shift the balance of power between the terms. Their importance for Macherey is not a matter of influence, his or theirs, but rather lies in the convergence of objectives and forces that for a time made them all objective allies and opened up a new way for thought.

In *The Logic of Sense* (1969), Deleuze situates his reading of Lewis Carroll as a thinker of "surface effects" in the reversal of the hierarchy of surface and depth that he argues is particularly visible in the fiction of such contemporaries as Alain Robbe-Grillet, Pierre Klossowski, and Michel Tournier. In particular, Tournier's *Friday, or, The Other Island* (*Vendredi ou les limbes du Pacifique*), a rewriting of Defoe's *Robinson Crusoe*, represents, for Deleuze, a call to renounce the depths in favor of the surface.[5] Tournier's novel, Deleuze argues, takes Robinson through three stages, each possessing its own experience of knowledge. The absence of the other on Robinson's island before Friday's arrival initially appears as an absence of what is necessary to the intelligibility of the world: the perspective of the other's knowledge, present but inaccessible to the knowing subject. Deleuze characterizes this form of knowledge as neurotic, a knowledge made possible only by what it lacks, a knowledge of the limits of knowledge. The second kind of knowledge confronts the lack of the lack, leaving the world deprived of the dimension of depth and therefore of meaning; everything that was earlier thought to be a copy of an inaccessible model becomes a simulacrum without an original, or a vestige of what has never existed. This is the derealized world of psychosis. But with the third kind of knowledge comes the realization that Robinson's salvation requires that he reject the valorization "of depth at the expense of surface," predicated on the notion that surface signifies "a minimum of depth" rather than a "vast dimension" to be known. Robinson must seek his salvation by "returning to the surface" to discover what is dispersed across it: singular events, free of any founding or final vertical authority.[6] He discovers the truth captured in Nietzsche's phrase: "The 'apparent' world is the only world: the 'true world' is just added to it by a lie" (*Die "scheinbare" Welt ist die einzige: die "wahre Welt" ist nur hinzugelogen*).[7]

For Lacan, psychoanalytic practice demonstrates the inadequacy of the notion that psychoanalysis could be understood as a "depth psychology," based on a conception of the unconscious as a repository of hidden impulses and meanings, arising either from bodily instincts or from an original intersubjectivity, according to which an alter ego is present, but inaccessible, to consciousness, requiring a hermeneutic procedure that treats the surface as an obstacle that must be removed to reveal the truth it serves to conceal. Drawing a line of demarcation within Ferdinand de Saussure's theory of the sign as stated in the *Course in General Linguistics*, Lacan shows that alongside the triune notion of signifier, signified, and referent conceived as a vertical hierarchy in which meaning derives from a reality outside of language, there exists a theory of pure horizontality in which what Saussure called the signified was not the idea or concept in the mind, outside of but present to language, but simply another signifier, part of a chain of intersecting chains of signifiers. What had been conceptualized as the depth beneath the surface, the vertical relation that alone made meaning possible, could be reconfigured as a nonorientable surface, that is, a closed band with a single surface. Lacan repeatedly invoked the images of the Mobius strip and the Klein bottle to capture the paradox of a depth that must be understood as a continuation of the surface. Further, he insisted not only on the horizontality of the process of signification (the signified is not outside of language, whether an idea or thing, but is always only another signifier in an endless chain), but also on the fact that the relation between consciousness and the unconscious cannot be understood as surface and depth.

A key component of Lacan's rejection of any notion of depth was his insistence on the primacy of the letter, the "material support that concrete discourse borrows from language,"[8] which as such is the most "superficial" of the elements involved in the production of meaning, that which functions only to the extent it represents or stands in for something more real than itself, an ideality by definition outside of and prior to the material. In opposition, Lacan insists that the letter "produces all the effects of truth in man without involving the spirit at all. It is none other than Freud who had this revelation, and he called his discovery the unconscious" (*produit tous ses effets de vérité dans l'homme, sans que l'esprit ait le moins du monde à s'en mêler. Cette révélation, c'est à Freud qu'elle s'est faite, et sa découverte, il l'a appelée l'inconscient*).[9] He thus eliminates the vertical hierarchy of surface and depth and spirit and letter in favor of the pure horizontality of material surfaces: the consciousness/unconscious opposition can no longer be understood as a relation of representation or expression of unconscious depth in surface consciousness, but must be envisaged rather as an oscillation perpetually enacted on the surface and barred from any recourse to a deeper reality.

While Macherey clearly shares the materialist orientation evident in Deleuze and Lacan, it is the study of literary discourse and literary works and the specific problems this study both encounters and engenders that determine his turn to the surface, with the aim not only of recovering it but of developing a concept adequate to it. He begins with the notion of literary discourse understood as a writer's act, a notion that suggests an authorial intention of which the work is the realization. Rather than dismiss the notion of an act that precedes the work as its cause and the source of its meaning, however, he displaces the author and the action that emanates from him in favor of the work itself understood as a surface whose cause is entirely coincident with it, existing neither prior to nor outside it: "Let us summarize: the writer's act is realized entirely at the level of a statement; it constitutes a discourse and is itself constituted by this discourse alone: it cannot be *referred* to anything external to it; all its truth or validity is crystallized in the thin surface of discourse" (*Reprenons: l'acte de l'écrivain se réalise tout entier au niveau d'un énoncé; il constitue un discours et est lui-même constitué par ce seul discours: il ne peut être référé à rien d'extérieur ; toute sa vérité, ou sa validité, se trouve cristallisée en cette surface mince du discours*).[10]

The sentence, which progressively leads the reader away from the search for a depth beneath the surface, begins by postulating a paradox. The speech act or act of enunciation does not take the form of a realization of an intention (whether subjective or objective, an idea or a form) external to it or a passage from the potential to the actual. Nothing exists of the enunciative act outside of or prior to it: its meaning is entirely consubstantial or coextensive with the act itself. The phrase *"il ne peut être référé à rien d'extérieur"* should not be understood simply to mean that the writer's act of enunciation cannot be "referred" or "related" to anything outside of itself. *Référer* suggests something like "traced back to"—that is, traced back to something more primary, a moment of origin or genesis in the absence of which the literary work could not exist. If it cannot be "referred" in this sense to anything outside of itself, as Macherey argues, then the work is nothing but surface without the depth in which its meaning and truth would remain enclosed until the act of interpretation lifted the cover. The surface is precisely that horizontality where meanings exist unconcealed and available. It is a space that offers no hiding places and holds nothing in reserve because there exists no point on or in it where meanings might be withheld from view: as surface, it is legible and visible in its entirety. But Macherey chooses to postpone the development of the disparate components of this sentence, immediately qualifying it as "unsatisfactory because it is empty and purely formal" (*insuffisante, d'abord parce qu'elle est vide, parfaitement formelle*).[11]

The sentence concerning the writer's act, however, even as it leads the reader away from the search for a repository of meaning or significance beyond, under or over the thin surface of discourse, remains insufficient and abstract not simply because of its "empty and purely formal," character, but in another sense that Macherey does not address. The history of the very concept of "surface," its meanings and functions, is a complex and overdetermined history that cannot be consigned to the past but, to follow Macherey's description, is crystallized in the surface in the particles and elements that constitute it. "Surface" appeared in French, before English, as a replacement for the Latin term of which it represents the translation: *superficies*. It is particularly important to note that even in classical Latin the word *super-facie*, or super/highest/outermost face, already exhibited a tension between the notion of face (or facet) as the character, nature, or form of a given thing or person presented to the viewer, that which allows us to grasp the composition and form of a thing, on the one hand, and the notion that being the outermost, "surface" or superficies is that behind which may exist other unseen properties or attributes whose nature, perhaps antithetical to that exhibited on the surface, is concealed by what is visible. From this second sense came the notion of the superficial, a conception of the surface as an externality discontinuous with what is internal, mere appearance, perhaps even a mask (*prosopon/*προσωπον or *persona*) that takes precedence over the real face, a kind of distillation or crystallization of a too disparate reality.

The effect of Macherey's sentence is to separate the two meanings of "superficies" or "surface": on the one hand, what we might call the materiality of surface, that is, its irreducibility to anything more real or true than itself, which thus allows it to crystallize into an object available to knowledge, and on the other, the concept of surface to which depth is added and which therefore constitutes a devaluation or degradation of surface as mere appearance or even as an active concealment of what lies hidden in the depths. To separate the first meaning from the second requires an appreciation of the force of the second in shaping the ways we think about language, discourse, and texts even now.

The conception of surface as degraded expression emerged out of the diverse currents of Platonism and neo-Platonism, in the form of the emanationist and expressivist notions of causality used to explain the creation of a material world out of an immaterial God. These notions were mobilized above all in the early stages of Christianity (beginning with Paul's introduction of the allegorical and typological readings of the Hebrew scriptures later institutionalized in Augustine's *De doctrina Christiana*), where the surface is defined by its distance from an originating cause; it is the uppermost or outermost layer and as such too far removed from the truth to be able to express it faithfully (φάντασμα rather than φαινόμενον). Surface is the face presented to the world, a facet (*facette: un petit visage*, or small face), the way in which a thing appears to the perceiver. This does not mean that the surface or facet is subjective; on the contrary, it represents the necessarily partial, diminished, and degraded relation of the outermost expression to the inner nature it is supposed to express. The Greek term, *prosopon* (προσωπον), is translated into Latin both as *facies* and *persona*, that is, as face, visage, or external appearance or form, but also as mask and, hence, disguise.

Macherey's assertion that scripture "could once have seemed to be the model of all books"[12] reminds us that the conception of scripture as a particular kind of text that would unveil its meaning only to readers who knew to interpret and not simply read it, conditions the way we think about literary works. His use of the past tense, "might at one time have appeared," refers to a decisive event in the history of reading practices, the threshold or break marked by the publication of Spinoza's *Tractatus Theologico-Politicus*, in particular chapter 7, "On the Interpretation of Scripture." Spinoza introduced an unprecedented protocol of reading by examining both the effects of the allegorical and typological readings of scripture and the assumptions underlying such readings. In particular, early Christian practices of scriptural interpretation appropriated many of the concepts and metaphors discussed above to justify precisely what Spinoza subjects to a critique: the imposition of meanings that are foreign and opposed to the actual words of the text, whether Hebrew or Greek, invoking the idea of the surface to declare its exteriority to the hidden dimension in which its truth resides. In this way, as Augustine argued, even the Hebrew language of the Old Testament could be understood as mere surface, a transitory, impermant, and inessential excrescence, perhaps even a form of concealment, which must not be confused with the meaning it conveys, a superseded mask or shell that once served to protect a truth the world is now prepared to receive.

Interpretation as it is practiced, according to Spinoza, is the act of deny-
ing or rejecting (*negare*) the text of the Holy Scripture (Spinoza sometimes
replaces the singular with the plural, "Scriptures") itself in its actual existence in order to replace it with some human invention. He points to the
importance of the motif of the inner and outer as one of the central organizing principles expressed in the Greek of the New Testament. The outer
surface becomes a veil (Κάλυμμα) whose function is to conceal (καλύπτω) a
mystery (μυστήριον), a secret (κρύπτην) or that which is hidden (κρυπτὸν).[13]
Paul in particular affirms the opposition between the inner man and outer
man as an expression of the primary opposition between the spirit (pneuma/
πνεῦμα, that is, breath, the principle of life and animation, a translation of
the Hebrew נשמה and rendered into Latin as *spiritus*) and the flesh. The latter, understood as excrescence, veil, facet, surface, is devalued: that which
pertains to the flesh decays daily, while spirit or breath, invisible, is perpetually renewed (1 Cor 4:16). Things seen are subjected to things unseen, the
temporary (πρόσκαιρα) to the eternal (αἰώνια) (1 Cor 4:18), and the spirit is
instructed to seek truth in "the deep things of God" (ἁ βάθη τοῦ Θεοῦ). Finally,
the declaration that ὁ Λόγος σὰρξ ἐγένετο, "the word became flesh," in order
"to dwell among us" (ἐσκήνωσεν ἐν ἡμῖν; John 1:14), visible in its very invis-
ibility and legible in the sense that the flesh of words and letters attracts us
only to take us beyond itself to the invisible things of the spirit.

Macherey's intervention, above all his mobilization of Spinoza's critique
of the existing modes of interpretation, allows us to see the emergence of a
certain notion of surface as face, facet, superficies as a means of devaluing
and degrading what amounts to the bodily, literal existence of discourse or
text, depriving it of substance, rendering it a derivative expression of something more real or true than itself. Near the end of his discussion of "Some
Concepts" (part 1 of *Theory*) he returns to the theme of the work's depth,
that which is hidden or masked by the surface. Of all the epistemological
obstacles to an adequate knowledge of what we can continue provisionally
to call literature, none exercises more power to compel our thought than that
of depth, the interior. Macherey refers to the hermeneutic approach, one that
seeks to interpret the work (and we should recall that the Latin verb *interpre-
tor* meant to translate as well as to perform the activity we now designate as
"interpretation")

> as a very curious repetition *that says more by saying less*: a purifying
> repetition at the end of which a meaning which had been up to that
> point hidden appears in its unadorned truth. The work is nothing
> more than the expression of this meaning, the envelope that contains
> it and that must be broken open for it to be seen. The interpreter car-
> ries out this liberating violence: he unmakes in order to remake the
> work *in the image of its meaning, making it* thus directly designate
> that of which it is the indirect expression. To interpret is thus also

to translate, to say in obvious terms what is contained and withheld
in an obscure and incomplete language. To translate and reduce: to
bring the work in its apparent diversity back to its unique (sole and
irreplaceable) signification.[14]

Let us note that the language of interpretation as described by Macherey
preserves the terminology and conceptual apparatus of biblical hermeneutics:
the true meaning of scripture is hidden, as if the work keeps it like a secret
or has buried it deep in the earth, its earth, like treasure, suggesting that the
work is filled with the dross whose sole purpose is to conceal the true meaning and that, at the moment of interpretation, which is also a revelation or
uncovering (apocalypsis/ἀποκάλυψις), must be displaced, removed, and set
aside. What is found on the surface of the text, according to this model, is
strictly speaking superfluous; it exists to conceal and is that which must be set
aside, peeled back, broken up like an outer crust or simply dissolved. There
is perhaps no better example of the imperative to pass beyond the text than
Paul's interpretation of Deuteronomy 25:4, "Do not muzzle the ox while it
is treading out the grain," which served as a model of reading for Augustine. For Paul (1 Cor 9:9), the commandment is written in a kind of code:
because God cannot be concerned with oxen, the true referent of this passage
must be his workers, those who preach his word. They, according to Paul's
translation, or rather decoding, of the passage, must be given sustenance by
those among whom they labor. Nothing remains of the actual words of the
commandment; they have been exchanged, to use Macherey's term, for the
meaning that they both allude to and dissimulate. This is above all a matter of value: the moment at which the true meaning of a phrase or work is
recovered is simultaneously the moment that the surface, having fulfilled its
purpose as a means of conveyance, is revealed to be worthless and perhaps
even harmful if its worthlessness is not understood. Such readings assume
not simply the opposition of appearance and essence but also that of inner
and outer, interior and exterior: beneath the planar space of the surface must
exist the depths of the work, the space where the true meaning awaits its
revelation.

It is important to note that for Macherey the conceptual oppositions of
interior/exterior and surface/depth cannot simply be rejected by means of
an act of critical will or a founding decision, including a critique that seeks
to unmask the theological remnants of secular thought. They are not mere
fallacies or illusions in the usual sense of the term, which will wither and
disappear in the face of rational critique, nor do there exist ready-made
concepts with which to replace them. They are obstacles endowed with an
institutional and material character, and as such their existence, as well as
the hegemony they exercise, is necessary, part of the terrain on which Macherey operates. His reference here is not to Althusser, as might be expected,
but to the work of Pierre Bourdieu and Alain Darbel on the museum as the

institutional correlate of the "love of art, " a supposedly free space open in principle to all, in which individuals moved by their decisions alone interact with works of art.[15] Bourdieu and Darbel show, in contrast, that the museum at its entrance and throughout its capacious interiors is minutely regulated by rituals and practices that enforce an unequal access to art and a profoundly hierarchical distribution of the supposedly intangible ability to "love" or merely appreciate art. Given the material and objective character of reading and interpreting literature, an activity endowed with an institutional existence, above all in schools and universities, rather than attempt to replace these categories, it will be enough to displace and unsettle precisely those assumptions that appear unquestionable: Macherey is fond of citing Althusser's expression *faire bouger les choses*, "to shake things up."[16] By drawing a line of demarcation not only between surface and depth but within the concept of surface itself, Macherey makes visible the necessity that governs the way we think about texts and in doing so begins, however slightly, to weaken its grip: "The work has no interior, no exterior: or rather its interior is like an exterior, displayed, burst open. It is thus given over to the eye that looks through it as if it had been skinned or, better, cut open. Opened up: to show itself this way is the work's closure" (*L'œuvre n'a pas d'intérieur, pas d'extérieur: ou plutôt, son intérieur est comme un extérieur, exhibé, éclaté. Ainsi elle est livrée à l'œil qui la fouille comme une dépouille, mieux comme un écorché. Le ventre ouvert: car c'est pour elle une fermeture de se montrer ainsi*).[17]

Here, in a single sentence, Macherey nullifies the opposition between interior and exterior, only to immediately recognize the impossibility of such a nullification, offering instead a redefinition of the interior that renders it "like an exterior." He proposes that we understand the interior as itself an exterior, that is, neither secret nor hidden but displayed, unconcealed because a book "hides nothing, neither contains nor keeps any secret" and is thus "readable in its entirety." But more than that, if the work is "an" exterior, it is one of many, as if what we once thought of as the distinction between exterior and interior were really a distinction between multiple exteriors, or a plurality of discontinuous surfaces. Such a heterogeneous surface cannot be understood as fixed or static: like the lithosphere consisting of a multiplicity of moving plates, constantly converging and diverging, the literary work is dynamic, in movement, its edges and borders constantly changing. In fact, we can say, following Macherey, that the "writer's act," the speech act, especially insofar as it is coextensive with the work, is not the creation or production of a closed and self-sufficient whole whose architectonic unity is hidden and must be recovered from its depths. It is not even the production of a continuous surface (like a Mobius strip), but an always fragile conjunction of a multiplicity of divergent surfaces.

But what is at stake in the assertion that the literary work should be regarded as pure surface? Macherey's arguments recall an often overlooked passage in Spinoza's *Tractatus Theologico-Politicus*: "The method of inter-preting Scripture is no different from the method of interpreting Nature, and is in fact in complete accord with it."[18] Words are things, writing and speak-ing are actions like any other; the written text, scripture, is not outside of nature or separate from it, but, like all that exists, a part of nature. Nature in this context signifies that which cannot be explained on the basis of what lies outside of it, in the final causes of God's will or as an expression of or emana-tion from something that transcends it. Nature must be understood on the basis of itself alone, "through a careful inquiry to derive from nature itself the certain data from which the definition of natural things can be deduced."[19] But, unlike Newton, whose discovery of an orderly, law-governed universe allowed him to affirm notions of providence and divine economy, Spinoza does not reconfigure transcendental teleology as an immanent teleology. On the contrary, in the appendix to *Ethics* I, Spinoza declares the notions of natural order and economy to be projections onto nature that prevent us from understanding those phenomena typically thought of as evil—plagues, wars, famines—as necessarily determined like everything in nature, and to see them instead as miraculous expressions of God's will, or on the contrary, interruptions or failures of a natural order.

Spinoza prevents us from exchanging the text for its truth, to use Mach-erey's phrase, by declaring that in reading scripture our sole concern must be the meaning or sense of its words and phrases, without regard to their truth. Meaning in this sense is a matter neither of reason nor of doctrine; it is determined strictly by what Spinoza calls "usage [*usus*]."[20] The meaning of a word cannot be assigned by an interpretation; a word possesses no mean-ings but those history and fortune have assigned to it in the actualized state of a given language at a given time. Spinoza is thus no more a proponent of the literal against the figurative than of truth against meaning; the only opposition that matters to him is that of the possible and the impossible, that is, of actually existing and nonexisting senses or uses, both literal and metaphorical, of specific words, an opposition necessarily internal to a given language.[21] From this perspective, allegorical and typological readings appear as attempts to "extort" (*extorquere*) or "torture" (*torquere*) scripture and thereby force from it the false statements interpreters need to support their doctrines.[22]

To diminish not only the power but the very possibility of interpretation as it has been practiced, Spinoza, near the beginning of chapter 7, introduces a phrase or, better, an equation whose strangeness has not been appreciated even today: "Scriptures, or the mind of the Holy Spirit [*Scripturas, sive Spir-itu Sancti Mentum*]"[23] The Latin conjunction *sive*, translated here as "or," suggests an equivalence or identity between the nouns it connects, as if to declare that the scriptures, in the plural and therefore in their very diversity, are not expressions or manifestations of the mind of the Holy Spirit, but rather that mind itself, which would thus have no existence outside of them.

The strategic function of Spinoza's equation is to rule out the possibility of overcoming or resolving the contradictions, discrepancies, undecidable ambiguities that are so clearly displayed both between and within the scriptures. They must instead be understood as necessarily pertaining to the mind of the Holy Spirit in its perfection: "By reality and perfection I mean the same thing" (*Ethics* II, definition 6). Just as the scriptures as they have been selected and assembled are the mind of the Holy Spirit and not a representation of it, so it is inconceivable that there exists something of which the Holy Spirit would be the expression, the truth of its truth. Readers who have added the dimension of depth as a means of converting the text into something other than itself by resolving its contradictions and discrepancies, do so because they regard what Spinoza has defined as the mind of the Holy Spirit as imperfect and flawed, in need of correction by means of both interpretation and translation. Spinoza instead instructs us to explain the immanence of the Holy Spirit in the scriptures as it is, without recourse to transcendental norms or ideals, its antagonisms, gaps, and absences no longer understood as faults or imperfections but as the necessary and thus intelligible effects of its history. It is to this argument that Macherey points when he asserts an essential link between the normative fallacy (all literary works are judged against a norm that no work can fully realize) and the fallacy of depth (all works appear flawed on the surface, and we must search their depths for what will allow us, through interpretation, to explain away apparent contradictions and supply what is missing in the text).

Finally, it may be an error to speak of the words of scripture "having" a meaning or meanings: the "sacred letters," as he calls them, are sacred not because of the truth they contain, the spirit encased in the flesh of the text, but because of the effects they produce:

> Words acquire a fixed meaning solely from their use; if in accordance with this usage they are so arranged that readers are moved to devotion, then these words will be sacred, and likewise the book containing this arrangement of words. But if these words at a later time fall into disuse so as to become meaningless, or if the book falls into utter neglect, whether from malice or because men no longer feel the need of it, then both words and book will be without value and without sanctity.

> *Verba ex solo usu certam habent significationem, et si secundum hunc eorum usum ita disponantur, ut homines eadem legentes ad devotionem moveant, tum illa verba sacra erunt, et etiam liber tali verborum dispositione scriptus. Sed si postea usus ita pereat, ut verba nullam habeant significationem, vel quod liber prorsus negligatur, sive ex malitia, sive quia eodem non in digent, tum et verba et liber nullius usus, neque sanctitatis erunt.*[24]

Spinoza's language here is striking in its evocation of the simultaneity of thought and extension and mind and body. Words are arranged, placed, distributed in space (the verb is *dispono*), as if they were bodies, impelled not by the idea or intention of the author but by the words' corporeal existence, determined by the regular motions of common use. These bodies, if acted upon by other bodies, will in turn move still other bodies; if not so acted upon, they will remain at rest without the possibility of moving other bodies. Spinoza, too, is a thinker of superficies, having stripped away the entire apparatus of origins, ends, and essences from nature and from scripture understood as part of nature, leaving only the infinite concatenation of singular things, the thin surface of a world without transcendence. It is precisely in this sense that scripture is part of nature: a surface, a crust, segmented, fractured, the possibility of its having any meaning at all dependent on encounters that may not happen or that, having happened, will never happen again.

In Macherey's *Theory*, we see what Deleuze, in the passage cited earlier, referred to as the movement of "returning to the surface," that is, a "paradox . . . that appears as a destitution of depth, the display or dispersion of events on the surface," above all, enunciative events that scatter horizontally across surfaces, indifferent to the vertical, hierarchical order of denotation. For Macherey, the destitution of depth, which is the precondition of theorizing what he calls the specificity (that is, the singularity) of the literary work, begins with the recognition that the "language [*langage*] instituted by the writer's act, in the form given to the statement by this act, is irreducible."[25] The concept of irreducibility played an important role in Macherey's project, as well as in the Althusserian endeavor more generally, above all in the postulation of the materiality proper to ideology—not only the necessary existence of ideas in apparatuses, practices, and rituals, but the materiality of the discourses embedded in them. Thus, when Macherey repeats, near the end of the first section of *Theory*, that the literary work is "irreducible" to anything outside of itself, he endows it with a material existence, effectively ruling out any explanation of the work as the realization of an authorial intention or a preexisting form.

To declare the work irreducible to something more primary than itself and thus to recognize the materiality specific to it, is not, however, to render it indeterminate, outside of any causal process. On the contrary, the irreducibility of the literary work means that it cannot be explained by notion of expressive or emanative causality according to which the meaning and truth of a given phenomenon can be determined only through a reduction to that of which it is the expression. Macherey's critique thus extends beyond old or new historicist readings that collapse literary texts into a reality external to them to recover their meaning and truth. It also represents a critique of a reduction of the work to the structure or form immanent in it, a form that, to the extent it is not coincident with the entirety of the work itself, is a refusal of what is regarded as the imperfection of the surface by a reduction not to a hidden meaning but to a hidden form, structure, or system: for the various formalisms, "to understand is to *reduce*, by returning to that structure deposited in the work's interior from which literary discourse has only apparently distanced itself: it distorts this structure the better to contain and preserve it" (*Comprendre c'est réduire, en revenir à cette structure déposée à l'intérieur de l'œuvre, dont le discours littéraire ne s'est éloigné qu'en apparence: il la travestit pour mieux la renfermer, pour mieux la garder*).[26]

Irreducibility, then, rules out certain forms of causal explanation, thereby allowing "a new type of necessity to be defined: by absence, by lack."[27] It is important to note that Macherey, who had earlier criticized the notion of structure as insufficiently differentiated from the ideas of order and totality, reintroduces the notion of structure but in a recast form: "If there is a structure, it is not in the book, concealed in its depths: it inhabits the book but is not its content. Thus, the fact that the book can be related to a structure does not imply that it is of a homogeneous substance; the structure sustains the work in so far as the work is diverse, scattered and irregular."[28]

Drawing on Spinoza, and to a certain extent Lacan, Althusser in *Reading Capital* calls this an absent cause of effects, not

> *because it is outside them. The absence of the cause in the structure's "metonymic causality" on its effects is not the fault of the exteriority of the structure with respect to the economic phenomena; on the contrary, it is the very form of the interiority of the structure, as a structure, in its effects.* This implies therefore that the effects are not outside the structure, are not a pre-existing object, element or space in which the structure arrives to *imprint its mark*: on the contrary, it implies that the structure is immanent in its effects, a cause immanent in its effects in the Spinozist sense of the term, that *the whole existence of the structure consists of its effects*, in short that the structure, which is merely a specific combination of its peculiar elements, is nothing outside its effects.[29]

To follow this argument is to arrive at the conclusion that what Althusser and Macherey call the silences, absences, gaps, and fissures, and Spinoza the empty spaces and *loca truncata*, exhibited by texts are also irreducible and cannot be understood as mysteries or signs of a distant presence held back from the common reader. To acknowledge them, to let them stand without explaining them away or overlooking them, has proven nearly impossible for interpreters (and in the case of scripture, translators). Because they fix the work in a state of incompleteness and insufficiency, the existence of silences or absences in the text calls into question its unity, whether formal or thematic. It is not that they demand interpretation, but on the contrary they constitute irremovable obstacles to any interpretation that assumes the unity and closure of the text. For this reason, the history of criticism and commentary is overwhelmingly dominated by denial, negation, and active concealing of the gaps and fissures in texts in order to show a unity that, if not exactly hidden, is in danger of escaping the attention of readers.

Thus far, the efficacy of concept of surface as deployed by Macherey has been understood negatively, its importance derived from what it is not, from the attributes it does not possess and the theoretical operations it excludes: it is resistant to reduction, without depth, and therefore without the capacity to conceal either meaning or form. The notion of the literary work as surface prevents theoretical regression by postulating the necessity of explaining inconsistency and conflict rather than reducing them to functions of an ingenious and intricate order hidden beneath the surface of the text. But to begin to explore the idea of the surface of the text in its positivity, Macherey turns to that peculiar surface known as a mirror and the mode of transformation proper to it: reflection. It is not difficult to see the strategic value of rehabilitating the concept of surface in a theoretical conjuncture characterized by the struggle between materialism on the one side and phenomenology (and hermeneutics) and formalism on the other. Indeed, Macherey's text bears the imprint of this struggle on every page. But the "image" of the mirror and the idea of reflection would appear to embody both a norm (realism) against which literary works are measured and thereby deprived of their reality and a theory of literary imitation or reflection (above all in the form of realism broadly defined) as a passive exhibition of reality or life as they are or— and herein lies the problem—as they appear to be. Macherey's recourse to the mirror (or more precisely to the literary mirror as seen by Lenin) might appear to be a kind of compromise formation: the mirror is pure surface but a surface distinguished from other surfaces by virtue of the fact that it offers a reflection or copy of an original upon which it depends. Macherey, however, demonstrates that both the notion of the mirror and that of reflection are transformed by the uses to which they are put and by the discursive contexts, literary, political, aesthetic, and philosophical, in which they appear.

It is perhaps for this reason that Macherey chooses to examine the case of the mirror and the activity of reflection, not in abstraction, as isolated concepts, but in a historically and textually specific form, namely Lenin's articles on Tolstoy, all of which were written between 1908 and 1910 (the year of Tolstoy's death) and therefore after the failed revolution, later called the "dress rehearsal," of 1905 and before the revolution of 1917. The title of the first of Lenin's brief pieces on Tolstoy refers to the latter "as the mirror of the Russian revolution." From this we might expect Lenin to praise the scope of novels like *War and Peace*, as if they were modern versions of a Speculum Mundi, the mirror of the world, whose reflective surface, gathered into a single panoramic view, presented to the reader the profusion of particulars whose magnitude otherwise exceeded the ability of the mind to apprehend it. This is the mirror that in Lenin's time served as an allegory of the realist narrative. But, as Macherey notes, Lenin's opening gesture does exactly the opposite: "To identify the great artist with the revolution which he has obviously failed to understand, and from which he obviously stands aloof, may at first sight seem strange and artificial. A mirror which does not reflect things correctly could hardly be called a mirror."[30] Tolstoy—that is, his discourse—not only does not reflect things as they are but reflects them inaccurately, offering an image that does not correspond to the historical reality of the revolutionary process set into motion by the reforms of 1861 and concretized in the revolution of 1905. Here, the reflective surface, despite the absence of an interior or a capacity to conceal what is reflected, "does not reflect things correctly," as they are; can such a surface be described as a mirror at all? Of course, in addition to the plane mirror or looking glass, there exist convex mirrors, which diminish objects and show a broader area than planar mirrors and concave mirrors, which magnify the images they reflect. But the mirror Lenin identifies with Tolstoy is not simply a distort-ing mirror. The mirror's reflection brings about "a fragmentation of the image," effacing its boundaries but more importantly making visible the unevenness of the contradictions whose fault lines are made visible only by the operation of reflection.[31] Instead of revealing a unity that would other-wise escape the viewer, the mirror Lenin finds in Tolstoy succeeds through its reflection in carrying out an "unmasking of the profound contradictions between the growth of wealth and achievements of civilisation and the growth of poverty, degradation and misery among the working masses."[32] This mirror reflects not only what is present but what is absent, that which is necessary to social transformation but just as necessarily absent from the historical present.

But what kind of mirror, what kind of surface, in its reflection, breaks up, breaks apart, and separates along lines of force the apparent unity of the reality whose image it captures? Macherey asks, "Could it be a broken mirror?"[33] Tolstoy's work and the written forms of his political and social views are fractured by the force of contradictions that no form can resolve or reconcile because, according to Lenin, "the contradictions in Tolstoy's views and doctrines are not accidental" but "express the contradictory conditions of Russian life in the last third of the nineteenth century."[34] But the mirror to which Lenin refers does not simply reflect these contradictions in the form of an image on its surface; the surface—that is, the mirror—is an extension or prolongation of these real conditions rather than an expression external to what it expresses. As Macherey explains in a text written some years after *Theory*, "It is important to understand that the relationship of history to literature is not like the relationship or 'correspondence' of two 'orders,' but concerns the developing forms of an internal contradiction. Literature and history are not constituted externally to each other (even in the form of a history of literature on the one side and social and political history on the other), but are from the outset in an internal relationship but exist in the interwoven and closely linked relation that is the condition of the historical existence of something like literature."[35]

If the mirror is no longer understood as external to what it reflects but rather as its continuation, reflection in turn can no longer be understood as a duplication or doubling that can never reproduce what is reflected with complete accuracy. Indeed, the Latin verb *reflecto* means "to bend backward" and was used figuratively to indicate the action of the mind reflecting upon itself, bending over itself to observe its own thoughts and feelings. For Macherey, however, the mirror insofar as it is the mechanism of reflection signifies the action by which historical reality bends back upon itself. As a part of this reality, the mirror is broken, fractured by the same contradictions and antagonisms. Producing and revealing in one and the same gesture, the mirror is the self-reflection or self-knowledge of historical reality in its dispersion and conflictuality. It is this that confers upon reflection what Macherey calls its objective character: the mirror does not reflect on reality from a position outside of it, but is part of it and thus the self-reflection of the reality in which it is entirely immanent.

Macherey cites Diderot's *Lettre sur les aveugles*: the mirror is "a machine" that simultaneously "puts things in relief far from themselves" and "puts us in relief far from ourselves."[36] If literature can be called a mirror, it is a mirror understood as a kind of machine: it is not only passively affected but affects in its turn. It is thus a machine in two senses: it transforms the images it captures to produce an effect and it is, like the machinery of the stage, the means by which spectators are moved by images. The reflections that take shape on the surface it offers are then projected upon the world. What the mirror projects is not a reproduction of the same but the same prolonged to the point of difference: "The mirror extends the world: but it also seizes, inflates and tears that world. In the mirror, the object is both completed and broken: *disjecta membra*."[37] If the "mirror constructs, it is in an inversion of the movement of genesis: rather than spreading, it breaks. Images emerge from this laceration. Elucidated [*illustrés*] by these images, the world and its powers appear and disappear, disfigured at the very moment when they begin to take shape."[38]

In the image of the mirror we find the beginnings of a conception of the materiality of the literary work and the process of literary production. A surface, irreducible to anything internal or external to it, is thereby abandoned to the disorder proper to it, its silences and empty spaces, its incompleteness. The figure of the mirror allows us to grasp the movement of a surface already fractured and continuing to crack, moved by the same forces that move what it reflects and whose fissures it captures. Sometimes, one fragment captures another in its reflection, the mirror mirrors itself, and the world caught in its movement is deprived of itself and scattered to infinity. But when that world, freed from reflection, returns to itself, every sliver and fragment in place, it is no longer the same world, but a world given to us to know.

Notes

1. Terry Eagleton, *Criticism and Ideology: A Study in Marxist Literary Theory* (New York: Verso, 2006 [1976]).

2. Rita Felski, *The Limits of Critique* (Chicago: Chicago University Press, 2015), 67–68.

3. Pierre Macherey, *A Theory of Literary Production*, trans. Geoffrey Wall (New York: Routledge, 1978), 58.

4. Baruch Spinoza, "Treatise on the Emendation of the Intellect," in *Complete Works*, trans. Samuel Shirley (Indianapolis: Hackett, 2002), 10.

5. Gilles Deleuze, "Michel Tournier and the World without Others," in *The Logic of Sense*, trans. Mark Lester (New York: Columbia University Press, 1990), 301–21; Michel Tournier, *Vendredi ou les limbes du Pacifique* (Paris: Gallimard, 1967).

6. Deleuze, "Michel Tournier," 315.

7. Fredrich Nietzsche, *The Twilight of the Idols*, trans. Richard Polt (Indianapolis: Hackett, 1997), 19.

8. Jacques Lacan, "The Instance of the Letter in the Unconscious, or Reason Since Freud," in *Ecrits*, trans. Bruce Fink (New York: Norton, 2002), 413.

9. Lacan, "The Instance of the Letter," 424.

10. Macherey, *Theory*, 58 (translation modified).

11. Macherey, *Theory*, 58.

12. Macherey, *Theory*, 89.

13. 1 Cor 2:10–16.

14. Macherey, Theory, 76.

15. Pierre Bourdieu and Alain Darbel, *The Love of Art: European Art Museums and Their Publics*, trans. Dominique Schnapper (Cambridge: Polity, 1997).

16. Louis Althusser, "Marx's Relation to Hegel," in *Politics and History: Montesquieu, Rousseau, Hegel and Marx*, trans. Ben Brewster (London: New Left Books, 1972), 174 (translation modified).

17. Macherey, *Theory*, 96.

18. Spinoza, Tractatus Tractatus-Theologico-Politicus, in Complete Works, 457.

19. Spinoza, *Tractatus* 457.

20. Spinoza, *Tractatus*, ch. 7, 456.

21. Pierre-François Moreau, *Spinoza: L'expérience et l'éternité (Paris: Presses Universitaires, 1994,* 334.

22. Spinoza, *Tractatus*, ch. 7, 456.

23. Spinoza, *Tractatus*, ch. 7, 456.

24. Spinoza, *Tractatus*, ch. 12, 505.

25. Macherey, *Theory*, 46 (translation modified).

26. Macherey, *Theory*, 142 (translation modified).

27. Macherey, *Theory*, 155.

28. Macherey, *Theory*, 151.

29. Louis Althusser, Étienne Balibar, Roger Establet, Pierre Macherey, and Jacques Rancière, *Reading Capital: The Complete Edition*, trans. Ben Brewster and David Fernbach (New York: Verso, 2015), 344.

30. Macherey, *Theory*, 299.

31. Macherey, *Theory*, 120.

32. Macherey, *Theory*, 300.
33. Macherey, *Theory*, 120.
34. Macherey, *Theory*, 127.
35. Etienne Balibar and Pierre Macherey, "Literature as Ideological Form (1974)," in *Contemporary Marxist Literary Criticism*, ed. Francis Mulhern (London: Routledge, 1992), 38.
36. Macherey, *Theory*, 134.
37. Macherey, *Theory*, 134.
38. Macherey, *Theory*, 134.

Reading Althusser

Pierre Macherey

By publishing a group of studies under the title *Reading Capital*, Louis Althusser called attention to the importance of reading, understood not simply as an activity of decoding but as an operation of thought: implicitly, he made it the unifying element of his project. In doing so, he attributed to this project a circular movement in whose unfolding reading intervenes not only as a point of departure—an initial flip of the switch—or as an instrument in the service of ends external to it, but as the principal driving force that, from within, impels this project to a permanent recommencement. From this perspective, to read a text—for example, *Capital*, which as its subtitle "Critique of Political Economy" suggests, is presented as a reading of other texts—is to produce a new text, which itself is exposed to a reading, in an interminable process that arises from its own internal logic alone. To echo Michel Foucault's language, it could be said that reading is a surrender to the vertiginous experience of a "thought of/from the inside" [*pensée du dedans*][1] that turns around itself without recourse to an exterior, which seems effectively to correspond to the way Althusser, referring abruptly to Spinoza's thesis according to which "the idea of the circle is not itself circular," thought the autonomy of the theoretical, renamed "Theory." This capitalization signified that the discourse of theory is self-sufficient and develops by the force of its internal dynamic alone. Althusser took this stance without hesitation, and certainly imprudently, as can be seen in the fact that at the outset of the publication of *Reading Capital*, which was at first a collection of studies presented in the context of a graduate seminar, he added a long introductory section titled "From *Capital* to Marx's Philosophy," a reflection on the topic of reading in relation to the original concept of "symptomatic reading," which occupied an important, even crucial, place in a text that fulfilled a foundational or explanatory function. The following, quite revealing phrase appears in the very last paragraph of the introduction: "We have not left the circle of one and the same question," the question raised precisely by means of reading.[2] Fundamentally, "reading Althusser" poses the following question: does this reading consist of taking the dynamic of this cycle a little farther by respecting its immanent principle, or does it necessitate a suspension of this dynamic, which requires us to find an entirely different way of reading, or of not reading, thereby breaking with it?

By assigning a central function to reading and grounding it in his project of refounding Marxist philosophy on a nonideological basis, Althusser exposed himself to a fundamental objection that was not long in coming. First and foremost, in the framework of the tactical alliance with Lacan, a circumstantial alliance that was based to a significant extent on things left unsaid and misunderstandings, he had to reformulate his approach for inclusion under the general rubric of "a return to," presenting it in the form of one of the rereadings of texts by Marx and Freud, understood as partners in the same theoretical struggle who confronted identical forms of resistance. At the end of his 1969 lecture "What Is an Author?" just four years after the publication of *Reading Capital*, Foucault proposed the concept of "founder of discursivity" to account for the paradoxical modality of the author function, to which the bizarre intellectual activity specifically presented in the terms of "a return to" referred. Marx and Freud, constructed as "founders of discursivity," functioned in this capacity as the primary references to which one returned, in a backward movement, in order to innovate, to move forward, based on the discursive dynamic the founders had "founded," and therefore initiated, but which was destined to be carried on after them. To do this required a progressive reshaping of its appearance through a series of "recastings," to take up the term coined by François Regnault in a paper presented in 1967 in the course in philosophy for scientists organized by Althusser at the École Normale Supérieure. In this way, by carrying out a return to these primary references, one progressed by giving oneself the means to move one's inquiry beyond the preliminary results recorded in the primary and supposedly founding texts. Seen from this perspective, reading was not limited to a mechanical repetition of what had already been said, but became an authentically creative and innovative procedure. Lacan, who had come to hear Foucault's lecture, declared himself satisfied with this argument in the discussion that followed. For convenience's sake, he pretended not to understand that, for Foucault, the lecture included a critical dimension. In fact, the latter had insisted that the sciences, like math and physics, did not require founders of discursivity in order to progress. To be Galilean, Newtonian, or Einsteinian did not signify a meticulous rereading of the writings signed by Galileo, Newton, or Einstein with the aim of recovering from the writings themselves an inducement to leap forward. Thus, the fact that "disciplines" such as historical materialism or psychoanalysis, whose scientific status was far from established, needed the kind of guarantee furnished by the textual operation of the "return to," in reference to founders of discursivity like Marx and Freud, reinforced the feeling of their precariousness. Reading texts signed with the names of these key authors, whoever they were, was in fact an undertaking of which Foucault was extremely suspicious from the start. He diagnosed this as the manifestation of thought caught in the trap of the discursivity of a pure statement doubled back upon itself, autotelic, inaccessible to the violence of the event, and therefore to the true historicity that is precisely that of the event, uniquely accessible to the "thought of the outside." This criticism converged with that which Pierre Bourdieu, later and not mincing words, directed against the proponents of a "scholastic reason" that grew out of academic rumination on authoritative texts, whose authority was derived from the unique assurance of the *auctoritas* attached to their signature. According to him, the *lectores*, who were content to recite monotonously, "Marx said," "What Marx really said," were trapped in the closed order of an abstract intellectuality, cut off from the real that they claimed to be transforming; they were only, in the end, would-be revolutionaries who had taken refuge between lines of sacred texts to avoid seeing the misery of the world.

The key question here is to know whether these critiques—which, ten years after the publication of *Reading Capital*, took on particularly vehement forms, to the point of attributing a hidden agenda to the work—were accurate, and whether the reading Althusser proposed to put into practice was not in fact, despite its "materialist" pretentions, the bearer of an idealist theoreticism without any relation to reality. And it is obvious that this question, beyond the way Althusser himself practiced the reading of texts, raises the issue of how his own texts ought to be reread today. At the end of the opening section of *Reading Capital*, having remarked, "We have therefore not left the circle of one and the same question," he continued with the following: "If, without leaving it, we have avoided turning round in this circle, it is because this circle is not the closed circle of ideology but the circle perpetually opened by its closures themselves, the circle of a well-founded knowledge."[3]

A "circle perpetually open by its closures themselves": this formula, with an oxymoronic appeal that confers upon it an almost magical tone, was meant to summarize the spirit of the original approach, motivated and oriented by the concept of "symptomatic reading." It is to this concept that we must now turn in order to examine its objectives, keeping in mind the following concern: Does reading Althusser today mean applying the procedures of symptomatic reading to him, or does it necessitate approaching his heritage under an entirely different angle, in response to the summons of his "specter," in a sense close to the one Jacques Derrida gives it in speaking of the "specters of Marx"?[4] Is Althusser's procedure inscribed in the framework of a process of founding a discursivity, and if so, what sort of discursivity is it?

If we make our way across the totality of the introductory section of *Reading Capital,* in which, as Althusser writes at the beginning of paragraph 10, "there can be no question here of making any other claim than to take theoretical bearings on what we obtain from our reading of *Capital*," we see that very different kinds of questions, approached here by means of a succession of "detours," a procedure of which Althusser was particularly fond, are connected to one another through a return to a major categorical opposition:

that of the intellectual posture that consists of *seeing*, according to the modality of the *gaze*, and more precisely the specular gaze whose mirror records the reflections that have come from the real, and another posture, of a completely different nature, which consists of *reading*. To read is for Althusser initially an operation that rejects the immediacy of the gaze directed at the real, and thus makes it possible to escape what he calls "the empiricist illusion." Under this generic term he calls up a whole series of interventions by philosophers from Plato to Husserl, by way of Descartes and Hegel, who by means of the most diverse paths succeeded in opening the way to a representation of knowledge as direct contact with the real, or at least with a real. To take the side of reading against vision is consequently to move toward an intervention whose objective is the development of a new image of thought purged of the paradigm of the gaze.

From this perspective, reading is not a mechanical process, an entrenched habit of intellectuals confined in the offices they hesitate to leave because they fear a confrontation with the things themselves; rather, it is the choice of a new posture whose objectives are in the last instance philosophical. In fact, at the moment he published *Reading Capital*, Althusser was convinced that it was necessary to intervene on philosophical ground, and in particular to give to Marxism the philosophy it lacked, and whose lack explains why Marx himself, despite the power of his intuitions (intuitions: another modality of the gaze), was most frequently misunderstood, which has contributed to the confusion over his notion of ideology. It is what distinguished Althusser from the start from people like Foucault and Bourdieu, who, for their part, took the position of distancing themselves from philosophy to participate in other fields of struggle to better understand the reality of their time. The decision to intervene in the field of philosophy was one Althusser never questioned afterward, even if the modalities of its implementation changed. This was because, according to the interpretation of this intervention that he proposed and sought to put into practice, in the last instance, philosophy alone could bring about the conjunction of theory and politics, which made it an essential link and one of the fundamental stakes of the conjuncture. Reading is precisely the practice that, situated at that point of conjunction, which is also a point of rupture, serves as the weak link whereby radical change may take place.

The adversary Althusser attacks, using the weapon of reading to "shake things up" [*faire bouger les choses*] in the field of philosophy, is what he calls the "theory of knowledge," in which are concentrated all the effects produced by the exploitation of the paradigm of vision that is key to the empiricist illusion. By "theory of knowledge" he understands the schema in which a subject and an object posed at the outset as given entities, immediately endowed with the reality proper to them, are set face to face. The goal of the theory of knowledge, whose traditional formula presents the truth as *adaequatio rei et intellectus*, is to account for the conditions in which a relation between these distinct entities develops, a relation that inevitably takes the form of an external relation: direct contact. The all too famous doctrine of "reflection," as part of the Marxist vulgate, was finally merely an avatar of this theory of knowledge, impregnated with ideology, which refers all operations of thought to the presupposed double of subject and object, and hence to the gaze directed by a subject at an object and to the reflection of the object in a subject. Following the same reasoning, Althusser also criticized the notion of "worldview," which also operates within the specular system of the theory of knowledge insofar as it imputes to a collective being, a historical people, or a social class the position of a subject before an objective reality, the world, that its gaze reflects. In the presentations given two years after the publication of *Reading Capital* in the context of the course on philosophy for scientists, a part of which was published under the title *Philosophy and the Spontaneous Philosophy of the Scientists*, Althusser once again targeted the "theory of knowledge," whose effects are all the more harmful because they are disseminated spontaneously, which is the ultimate form of ideological domination. And when on this occasion he stated the "thesis" according to which "philosophy has no object," it was, among other reasons, for the purpose of rejecting philosophy's status as "worldview," which was implicitly tied to the theory of knowledge and, through it, to the paradigm of vision.[5]

Behind the misleading image of thought contained in the theory of knowledge and of worldviews, there exist the categories of immediacy and of origin, from which is constructed the representation of subject and object as foundational instances facing each other, irrespective of the modalities of the gaze that links them. Reading is one way—perhaps neither the sole nor the best—to obstruct the scopic drive that governs the mental system specific to ideology. What authorizes us to oppose the fact of reading to that of seeing? It is the following argument: seeing refers to the originary or the immediately given, for example, the world at which the gaze directs its aim. Reading is a process without beginning or end, a circle that turns on itself indefinitely and produces difference by repeating itself, as one might put it in the language of Gilles Deleuze, who, like Althusser, had turned to Spinoza to elaborate a new image of thought. Indeed, as noted earlier, to read is to take into consideration texts that present themselves as readings of texts; and we read these texts to compose others, which are also destined to be read. The process of discursivity materially consists of the cycle that generates itself without having to leave itself, which thus never takes the form of a simple vision turned toward external things, seeking that which in them bears the marks of origin and meaning. At issue here is a practice of reading of a particular type, one that does not consist of bringing a direct gaze to bear on a text, with the aim of extracting or receiving a "meaning," already deposited within it, which would be another way of seeking an origin. It is not an all-encompassing reading subject to a demand for totalization, but rather a surface, horizontal reading that proceeds by way of detours, condemned to obtain only temporary and partial results destined to be constantly revised. Considered in this way, reading takes note of the fact that in the text it takes as its object something happens, something is moving, an event is taking place, an event in whose wake the operation of reading is called to make a place for itself. To take up again the metaphor Althusser habitually employed to characterize political action such as he understood it through his intersecting readings of Machiavelli and Lenin, it is a question of catching a moving train, even of missing it or falling on one's face, and therefore of taking risks. In this sense, it may be argued that there are only partisan readings conscious of being caught in the developing cycle from which the text on which they provisionally work has emerged—a cycle whose renewal they bring about, following a direction that, not being contained in incipient form in an origin, is not established in advance. For these reasons, the circle in which it poses its questions, namely the circle of Theory, is a good circle that opens the perspective of a dynamic whose immanent logic cuts short the empiricist illusion that nourishes ideology.

Does the circle that proceeds by returning from text to text, deviation to deviation, and detour to detour turn with perfect circularity? No, as it happens. This is what the concept of "symptomatic reading" is meant to indicate. Such a reading operates by inserting itself into a textual dynamic, not taking it as it is at first glance, as an external gaze that claims to see it face to face might, but by insinuating itself into its fault lines and putting the texts into play to show the disequilibria in them that bear the mark of the event and push us farther along a trajectory that develops without beginning or definitive end. Symptomatic reading is an infinite process advancing by means of its weak links, as is the case for any historical conjuncture. To account for this singular process, Althusser takes up the paradigm of vision again while attempting to turn it to another use. The symptomatic reading, he explains, determines in the text to which it applies the ratio between the visible and the invisible, between the manifest and the latent. To understand the relation between the manifest and the latent is to undo the tie with which the scopic drive artificially wove them together, presenting the latent as the potentially manifest, and the manifest as the latent actualized. The latent revealed by a symptomatic reading has nothing to do with a hidden meaning waiting to be deciphered or interpreted. It is not the already-there of an original meaning, but rather nonmeaning, the labor of the negative that is at work throughout the production of meaning and tips it toward another meaning that is not prefigured in what precedes it. To translate this analysis into the language of Derrida, to whom Althusser here appears very close, symptomatic reading consists not of deconstructing a text through an external operation of decomposition and analysis, but of revealing the traces in it which indicate that, even at the level of its literal inscription, a process of deconstruction is at work. It deconstructs and deconstructs itself, and in so doing, encourages a different mode of construction that proceeds indefinitely.

We now begin to understand the orientation of the formula that presents the circle of Theory as a "circle perpetually opened by its closures themselves." These closures are the internal limits into which it bumps, impelling the movement of its renewal. The circle of Theory thus presented is not a closed circle but rather an open circle, or even better a circle "perpetually opened." And it is here that Althusser's analysis runs up against its own limits, and by itself, according to its own internal logic, tips in another direction. For if the good circle of Theory is protected from turning back upon itself in a perfect circle by the fact that it must remain perpetually opened, it's because no magical operation, even a miraculous epistemological break, can lead it to a terrain where, without standing still, it would be destined to remain forever, definitively established there. Or, more precisely, the notion of an epistemological break, which Althusser borrows from the history of the sciences, must be, if there is a place to inscribe it in a circle destined to remain perpetually open, declined in the plural. It is an operation that may take place once and only once. Its scope and effectiveness are conditioned by the fact that it is destined to be indefinitely taken up again on new grounds through a process without beginning or end, the same sort of process of discursivity that shapes the practice of symptomatic reading.

The Spinozist formula to which Althusser often referred, *verum index sui et falsi*, insisting each time on the fact that we must take the phrase in its entirety instead of presenting it in the abbreviated form *verum index sui*, as it too often was, an amputated presentation that essentially idealizes the truth, this formula affirms and illuminates in a striking way this manner of conceiving and practicing symptomatic reading. It signifies that truth only affirms itself by reproducing each time the dividing line that separates it from what is false, or rather from a falsehood, its falsehood, having a falsehood only in the movement in the course of which truth is produced in partial forms. Similarly, in every discursive statement the schism between that which in it becomes visible and that which it renders invisible is both effectuated and made legible in the search for a precarious equilibrium for which there is no ideal guarantee. The representation of a naked truth, absolutely sufficient in itself, whether its manifestation is original or terminal, is an avatar of the empiricist illusion from which, by engaging in the circle of Theory, philosophy seeks to demarcate itself. Yet, just as there can be no naked truth, so there can be no pure theory permanently purged of the miasmas of ideology, with which it wages an unending battle. In the same way, there are no good concepts separated once and for all by an intangible border from bad concepts. This is why to read Althusser today cannot consist of reading what he has said to the letter, but must go farther by seeking in what he has written the indications of a division between the true and the false, the visible and the invisible, of which his texts, by simultaneously saying more or less than they appear at first sight to do, bear the mark.

To conclude, I will outline the perspectives that a symptomatic reading applied to Althusser might open up. And for that, I take what he himself cites

as an example in the fifth paragraph of his introduction to *Reading Capital*.
In this paragraph we find the analysis of a reading, expressly presented as a
"detour" for, according to the terms used by Althusser, the purpose of showing "a necessary invisible connection between the field of the visible and the
field of the invisible, a connection which defines the necessity of the obscure
field of the invisible, as a necessary effect of the structure of the visible field,"
which is in turn a translation of the content of the formula *verum index sui
et falsi* as Althusser read it.[6] This analysis refers to a passage from the introductory chapter of the sixth section of volume 1 of *Capital*, devoted to wages
(chapter 17 in the original German edition, chapter 19 from Roy's French
edition cited by Althusser). The importance of this passage had already been
underlined by Engels, who writes in the preface to his edition of volume 2
of *Capital*: "By substituting labor-power, the value-producing property, for
labor, he solved with one stroke one of the difficulties which brought about
the downfall of the Ricardian school, viz., the impossibility of harmonizing
the mutual exchange of capital and labor with the Ricardian law that value
is determined by labor."[7] In this same preface, Engels treats this theoretical
innovation as analogous to that carried out in chemistry when it rejected the
theory of the phlogiston: "Marx stands in the same relation to his predeces-
sors in the theory of surplus-value as Lavoisier stood to Priestley and Scheele
(the last disciples of the doctrine of the phlogiston at the end of the eighteenth
century)." What drew Althusser's attention in Engels's text was precisely this
comparison, and the sense in which it opened the way to a presentation of
Marx's theoretical innovation in *Capital*, on the basis of models of analysis
appropriated from the history of the sciences in a prefiguration of the concept
of the "epistemological break." Consequently, he began to study Marx's text
by reading over the shoulder of Engels, who had already added to Marx's
message in the course of his own reading. Further, Marx's own text is presented as a reading aimed at classical political economy, above all, Ricardo.
Marx's reading showed the "misunderstanding" (*quiproquo*, the term used in
the French edition by Roy, but which does not appear in the original German
text) on which this analysis rests. It is that of confusing "labor" and "labor
power," which are surreptitiously rendered identical, while according to the
result obtained on the basis of Marx's new conception of wage labor, they are
two completely different things. Taking a position himself in this discursive
cycle, Althusser pays particular attention to the way Marx explains his way
of seeing in order to exorcise the error on which classical political economics
rests, and offers this extraordinary commentary:

> What classical political economy does not see, is not what it does
> not see, it is *what it sees*; it is not what it lacks, on the contrary, it is
> *what it does not lack*; it is not what it misses, on the contrary, it is
> *what it does not miss*. The oversight, then, is not to see what one sees,
> the oversight no longer concerns the object, but *the sight* itself. The

oversight is an oversight that concerns *vision*: non-vision is therefore inside vision, it is a form of vision and hence has a necessary relationship with vision.[8]

When we ourselves, today, dwell on what Althusser writes here, we can only be struck by the insistence with which he again calls into question the fact of seeing, declaring it responsible for the oversights and misidentifications that Marx avoided by distancing himself from classical political economics. The latter's error did not consist of "seeing" things badly but, more profoundly, of trying too hard to "see" them, thereby yielding to the scopic drive that generates the empiricist illusion. As Althusser argues, in the crucial passage of *Capital* that caught his attention, Marx makes a "change in terrain," not concerning the things themselves but the manner of seeing them, and even more profoundly, the belief in the fact that it is by directing a lucid and perceptive gaze at them that they can be known in their truth.

If, as Althusser did not do, we return to the context of the passage from *Capital* on which this discussion is based, "a new attempt at reading that takes up where the previous left off," we realize that beyond the identification of an error, Marx intervened by means of the relationship between philosophical categories, the relation between appearance and essence. The error, as he describes it, consisted of mistaking appearance (labor) for essence (labor power), which leads to a transfer to labor of a property, value, which it does not have as such because value pertains to labor power. In the paragraph that immediately precedes the passage quoted by and commented on by Althusser, Marx writes (in the original version of chapter 17 from volume 1 of *Das Kapital*:

> In the expression "value of labor," the concept of value is not only completely erased but transformed into its very opposite. It is as imaginary an expression as, for example, the value of the earth. Nevertheless, these imaginary expressions have their own source in the relationships of production themselves. These are the categories corresponding to the phenomenal forms of essential relationships. It is fairly well known in all the sciences, except evidently for political economics, that in their phenomenal manifestation, matters often occur in reverse.[9]

It is easy to see that the reasoning developed in these terms makes use of a way of thinking that ultimately refers to a theory of knowledge as turning a gaze on things: the "categories corresponding to the phenomenal forms of essential relationships" privileging an external vision, which only grasps superficial appearances, "manifestations," unable to discover below this surface the essential underlying relationships that the true knowledge must attempt to determine. Presented in this way, the discrepancy between the phenomenal manifestations and the essential relationships emerges, not between things but between ways of "seeing" things. While the one decorates the envelope that contains them, the other opens it to reveal what is within it; the alternative is between seeing the surface (partial vision) and seeing into the depths (total vision). Considered from the point of view of symptomatic reading, this explanation leans in the direction of the theory of knowledge with which, according to Althusser, Marx is in the process of breaking when he denounces the confusion between labor and labor power from which classical political economics does not escape. Hence the necessity of carrying out an intervention within philosophy that definitively eliminates the fantasy according to which knowledge [*connaissance*] consists of a more or less accurate vision of things, a fantasy in which Marx remains entangled even as he opens an entirely new path to the knowledge of economic reality.

I will attempt to go still farther: symptomatic reading, taking the terms employed by Althusser, aims to identify in a text not what it says without saying, and thus in veiled words, opening the way to an interpretive procedure whose objective is to reveal a hidden meaning, but instead something completely different, what it does not say in saying it. Symptomatic reading seeks to show between the lines not the hidden presence of a content—the essence hidden beneath appearance, which requires only that it be brought into the open and placed before our eyes—but a lack waiting for the means that would permit it to be filled, means which materially are lacking. When Marx says that the error in which classical political economics remains permanently confined concerns the relationship of essence/appearance, he does not say something without saying it, that is, without completing the expression of his thought, but instead says something by not saying it, or by saying something different. The nature of the thing toward which he turns is not implicitly contained in what he says, but remains entirely to be determined, which is precisely what the ambiguous way he presents it without presenting it incites us to do. This why we can say that in his text, which does not develop complete knowledges in a definitively proven form any more than it is the bearer of a latent meaning that would need only to be brought to light to be seen in the proper sense of the word, something happens, an event of thought is in the process of being produced, or at least has begun to be, in the wake of which we must situate ourselves, taking hold of it in flight in order to perpetuate its momentum.

Clarifications. When Marx says that political economy misunderstood the nature of the system on which capitalism rests because it confused the appearance, labor, with the essence, labor power, he transposes the terms of his own discovery to the plane of a metaphysics of knowledge governed by the specular paradigm of the gaze, which constitutes a theoretical regression on his part. But this does not prevent his intervention, the scope of which he does not entirely control, from completely modifying our view of the field of political economy by showing the function this view fulfilled. This disruption depends on the use of a completely new instrument of analysis, the concept of "labor power," which nothing in the analyses of political economy, and in particular of Ricardo, anticipated. What is original in this conception is the reference to the old idea of "power" [*force*] with a view to reinterpreting the system of wage labor. Power here is the Aristotelian *dunamis*, that is, this mysterious, one might be tempted to say supernatural, entity that exists potentially before existing actually: as long as it is not activated, in other words employed, it is as if it did not exist, at least not yet, until the means are found for it to assume an effectively real form. Descartes refused to include this notion in his physics precisely because its ambiguity led it to be counted among "hidden qualities," and only with Leibniz and Newton would it be reintegrated into the system of scientific rationality. Marx's discovery is that capitalism exploits an ambiguity related to that on which the notion of "power" is based; it is made possible by the ambiguity proper to a reality that may exist both potentially and in actuality at the same time, and from which it has found the means to draw the maximum profit, in the two forms of the extraction of absolute surplus value (an extension of the working day) and of relative surplus value (an increase in the productivity of labor power). When Marx speaks of the relation between essence and appearance, he speaks without knowing it, because, in fact, he does not speak of it, all the while speaking without speaking of the relation between the potentiality and actuality, which is the secret of the function of labor power and of its exploitation by the capitalist who pretends to buy labor, and to pay what it is worth, as Ricardo insisted, while in fact he has rented the right to make use of it at a certain place and time, transforming it from the potentiality to the actuality of labor power. This being understood, the mistake that drew Althusser's attention when he studied the chapter from volume 1 of *Capital* on wages presents itself differently: it is not only a theoretical mistake that concerns a way of knowing things, of "looking" at them, either by stopping at their appearance or by penetrating to their essence; it is an error concerning the things themselves, a practical error on which the real operation of the capitalist economy depends; it pretends to pay for work at its price, while in fact it sets the rent of a labor power that gives it the means to exploit it, by playing on the fact that this power exists at the same time on the two planes of potentiality and actuality.

By advancing the concept of labor power, Marx indeed fundamentally changed the manner of treating a problem of political economy, that of the labor contract. At the same time, he leads us to understand that this problem to which political economics pretended to offer a solution—namely, how to know whether the work was paid according to its value or not—is not only inadequately resolved by political economics but concealed under a purely economic treatment. To interpret the regime of wage labor in the light of the concept of labor power is not to pass from the realm of appearance to the realm of essence, but to leave the closed field of political economy; it is to show in practice that the real solution to economic problems is not only economic. Why? Because "labor power" is not, as might be imagined from the use of the word "power," a natural given the worker would possess from birth, just as every individual is supposed to possess from birth an identity as a subject that adheres to him for life. It is an artificial reality, an invention, historically constituted under those conditions proper to the capitalist system. Labor power does not preexist the employment contract that registers hiring by the entrepreneur; it is an effect or practical result of this contract, a contract which, by establishing the confusion between labor and labor power, fabricates labor power in its entirety.

Before becoming a so-called natural given of economics, the existence of labor power rests on the relationship of domination, a constraint whose actual nature the legal form of the employment contract eludes by exploiting the confusion that is key to its operation. In fact, if the worker were not forced, not only would he not offer his labor power for hire to the capitalist, but he would not possess this very force, which is a fiction completely fabricated by the regime of wage labor, a potential reality assumed to exist separately from the conditions of its realization. It is basically what Lafargue wanted to make clear in writing his pamphlet on "The Right to Be Lazy": this right, denied by the capitalist system, is that of not being constituted as the bearer of a labor power destined to be rented for its value, that is, the cost of its maintenance and its reproduction. If the worker were truly free, not only would he have the possibility of exploiting his labor power for his own benefit, but he would not have labor power divided along the lines of potentiality and actuality, this division being the condition of the capitalist entrepreneur's profit. This is the thesis Marx formulates with clarity in his "Notes on Wagner" from 1880: "The capitalist is not confined to removing or to stealing, but extorts the production of a surplus, that is to say he contributes first to creating what he will remove."

Yet this "creation," which results in the existence of labor power, does not arise from economic laws alone because it involves a whole system of a social power, or the regime of governmentality proper to what Foucault calls the "society of normalization." If we take the project of a symptomatic reading of Marx to its conclusion, we discover that the reason for the economy, and the social system that organizes it, exceeds the limits proper to the economy: we are given the means to formulate an antieconomistic analysis of the economy. Althusser, a fierce defender of the "determination in the last instance by the economy," did not go so far; he continued to affirm, with an energy born of despair, that the economic infrastructure, with its "forces," constitutes a separate reality unto itself, which must be viewed with lucidity. In this regard, he was himself still a prisoner of the specular metaphysics whose phantasm he had attempted to exorcise. But if we apply the protocol of symptomatic reading to him, we may begin to understand that perhaps he too does not say something while saying it; his objective is not to be taken as a result or a conclusion, but as the beginning of a movement of thought whose task, beyond what he says and what in saying he does not say, is to know that the theoretical revolution carried out by Marx consisted of showing that the only way to resolve the problems of political economy is to reveal the real equivocities on which it rests, which leads both to an interrogation of its system as a whole and to a change of terrain by drawing all the consequences from the fact that society does not function solely by the economy and its forces, but involves "relations" of a completely different order. Even if the detours of symptomatic reading do not help us better "see" the real, they lead us back to it without seeming to, and permit us to explore its fault lines.

Translated by Warren
Montag and Audrey Wasser

Translators' Notes

This text was originally given as a paper on June 6, 2015 at the École Normale Supérieur, rue d'Ulm, at the conference entitled "Althusser 1965, La découverte du continent histoire." See Pierre Macherey, "Lire Althusser," https://philolarge .hypotheses.org/1651. Accessed January 20, 2022.

1. Macherey echoes the title of Michel Foucault's "La pensée du dehors," a 1966 essay on Blanchot reprinted in *Dits et écrits: 1954-1975*, vol. 1 (Paris: Gallimard, 2001), 518–39.

2. Louis Althusser, Étienne Balibar, Roger Establet, Pierre Macherey, and Jacques Rancière, *Reading Capital: The Complete Edition*, trans. Ben Brewster and David Fernbach (New York: Verso, 2015), 72.

3. Althusser, *Reading Capital*, 72.

4. Jacques Derrida, *Specters of Marx*, trans. Peggy Kamuf (New York: Routledge, 1994).

5. Louis Althusser, "Philosophy and the Spontaneous Philosophy of the Scientists (1967)," trans. Warren Montag, in *Philosophy and the Spontaneous Philosophy of the Scientists and Other Essays*, ed. Gregory Elliot (New York: Verso, 1990), 77.

6. Althusser, *Reading Capital*, 18.

7. Friedrich Engels, Preface, *Capital: Volume II*, trans. I. Lasker (Moscow: Progress Publishers, 1956), np. Open access at https://www.marxists.org/archive /marx/works/1885-c2/index.htm.

8. Althusser, *Reading Capital*, 19.

9. Karl Marx, *Capital: Volume I*, trans. Samuel Moore and Edward Aveling, ed. Frederick Engels (Moscow: Progress Publishers, 1887), ch. 19. Open access at https://www.marxists.org/archive/marx/works/1867-c1/index.htm. Translation modified.

Between Literature and Philosophy

✦

An Interview with Pierre Macherey by Joseph Serrano

Your interest in Spinoza preceded your work with Althusser, as your master's thesis [*maîtrise*], "Philosophie et politique chez Spinoza," which you completed in 1961 under the supervision of Georges Canguilhem, demonstrates. What initially drew you to Spinoza? Did Spinoza lead you to Althusser? To put it another way, did Spinoza figure in the collective project that began in 1961 with the seminar on the early Marx?

In October 1960, the beginning of my third year of study at the École Normale Supérieure (ENS), which I started in 1958, I sought out Georges Canguilhem, whose classes I had attended during the previous two years (and it was to these classes that I owed a large part of my philosophical training), to ask if he would supervise my *maîtrise* on the topic of philosophy and politics in Spinoza. I had earlier spoken to Althusser, who, in his capacity as adviser (or *caïman*, in the jargon of the ENS), oversaw the work of philosophy students at the ENS; it was he who had suggested that I focus on the "political" aspect of Spinoza's work. This theme had been largely overlooked by French commentators, and for me it was an opportunity to explore a little-known domain, which was particularly exciting for a young student.

My interest in Spinoza dates back to my years at the *lycée* and then at university, where, in 1958, I took courses with Dina Dreyfus, the assistant professor working under Vladimir Jankélévitch (and Lévi-Strauss's first wife, who accompanied him on the journeys recounted in *Tristes tropiques*). She was extremely energetic and eloquent, and introduced me to the demonstrative system of the *ordo geometricus* of the *Ethics* in the context of my certification in moral and political philosophy [*philosophie morale et politique*]. For her, Spinoza was not a more or less neatly assembled package of general ideas to be taken in at a glance (which was typically how he was taught at the time, in a summary and cursory way) but a demanding and rigorous experience of thought that had to be followed word by word, as we later learned to do systematically from [Martial] Guéroult's lectures (whose major works on Spinoza were published in 1968, which, by reading the texts in minute detail and paying close attention to the stakes of the argument

179

they contained, completely changed the way Spinoza was read in France. Thanks to her, I came to understand that Spinoza's philosophy was not simply one doctrine among others, but rather represented a different way of doing philosophy (or "true philosophy," a phrase that appears in the *Letters*, when, in response to Albert Burgh, Spinoza says, "I do not maintain that my philosophy is more true than others, but that it is true philosophy, *vera philosophia*").

This idea was later confirmed by Althusser, who was himself convinced of the exceptional, essentially anomalous character of the rigorous dynamic set in motion by Spinoza, which in fact marked a point of rupture in the history of philosophy. My first few years of study at the university were also marked by the teachings of [Gilles] Deleuze (then responsible for the courses in the history of philosophy at the *Faculté des Lettres,* under the auspices of Ferdinand Alquié), which I found fascinating. At the time, however, he was not teaching Spinoza (I took the unforgettable courses on Nietzsche and Kant), and it was only later, when he published his thesis on the problem of expression in Spinoza,[1] that I learned the extent to which he had privileged the study of Spinoza. The exemplary singularity of Spinoza's contribution had been at the center of his discussions with Althusser from 1965 on, some of which I attended.

At first, my proposal for the *maîtrise* was not well received: Canguilhem, well known as a difficult person, became angry and said to me, "You are mocking me. I know nothing about Spinoza!" (his official areas of specialization were the history of the sciences and epistemology). But finally he agreed: I later learned that what had convinced him of the validity of my proposal and persuaded him to support it was precisely the emphasis on Spinoza's political thought, which up to that point had been neglected. Canguilhem deliberately refrained from becoming an adherent of any philosophical system (he had never been a Platonist, Aristotelian, Cartesian, Kantian, or anything else of this type), but was interested in them all on the condition that they were true philosophy [*de la vraie philosophie*]. Immediately behind Spinoza's name was that of [Jean] Cavaillès, who had been the origin of Canguilhem's own political commitment during the war, against both the Vichy regime and the German occupation, and who remained for him a model of thought and action, as Canguilhem explained in the commemorative pieces he devoted to Cavaillès. The latter expressly declared himself a Spinozist, including in his philosophy of mathematics, inspired by phenomenology. It was thus the syntagm "philosophy-and-politics" (a formulation I owe to Althusser) that had captured Canguilhem's attention: he undoubtedly saw in it a projection and prolongation of Cavaillès's militant activity, a reference that, while not formally academic in character, was nevertheless at the heart of his own philosophical position.

The year during which I wrote this work (a thesis of a hundred pages) was spent reading and studying, and represented a threshold in my philosophical formation. It was also a time of political agitation, the epoch of OAS [Organisation de l'armée secrète][2] and the final paroxysms of the Algerian War, which had been particularly violent during the first years of the Gaullist regime. I was very active politically, and it was difficult to reconcile my academic research with my activism, but I managed one way or another, and at the same time found myself fully involved in "philosophy-and-politics," at the heart of the question. Canguilhem understood this and did not disapprove; quite the contrary. That was also the year I met Étienne Balibar, with whom I often worked subsequently. He was younger than I and had just entered the ENS; very soon he shared my passionate interest in Canguilhem's courses, which he too attended (two years later, he wrote a master's thesis on the idea of labor in Marx, also directed by Canguilhem). Canguilhem followed my work quite closely, which at the time was very unusual for a *mandarin* [an ironic term denoting senior faculty who wield institutional power] at the Sorbonne. Generally, his colleagues paid little attention to their students' work, regarding which they were negligent and condescending. He advised me with increasing benevolence and was satisfied with the results I had achieved, which greatly encouraged me and determined the future direction of my studies.

I do not recall that Althusser particularly helped me in this work, although he had given me the idea for it initially. I believe he was often absent that year because of health problems that only worsened over time. I entered into a closer working relation with him two years later, after I had successfully passed the *agrégation*[3] in philosophy (Canguilhem was one of the examiners): my passing, which was by no means a mere formality, given the fact that the exam was particularly competitive, allowed me to engage in an additional year of study at the ENS. This additional year had no obligations attached to it and was devoted to one's own inquiries (in France at this time the practice of sabbatical leaves was unknown and was adopted later only very gradually and incompletely). When he was present at the École, Althusser was very involved with the philosophy students, "preparing" and advising them; he taught some courses and corrected dissertations in his very original and stimulating way. This did not go on for much longer, however, and I do not recall having had any really fundamental discussions with him before the start of fall term in 1962, and therefore the beginning of my fifth and final year as a student at the ENS. Before I left to do my military service in 1963 at Prytanée de La Flèche (where Descartes had been taught by the Jesuits!) Étienne Balibar and I spent part of our summer vacation preparing a translation of Engels's "*Esquisse d'une critique de l'économie politique*,"[4] a text that had not yet been translated into French. When school resumed in fall 1962, we went to Althusser's office to show him the results of our labor, and from there, things developed very quickly. We proposed organizing a course of study focused on Marx, something that had never been done in France in an academic context. That a request of this type had been formulated by students who had not yet finished their studies was striking to him, especially because it coincided with a long-standing desire of his own that had never been concretized. He soon acted on our request, launching a series of seminars, of which one in particular, the seminar devoted to the young Marx, led to the collective labor of which the two volumes of *Reading Capital* represent the visible form. This was followed in 1967 by the Course in Philosophy for Scientists, which had a large audience.[5] At that time, I had thought of writing a thesis on Marx (I do not recall the topic I had proposed: it must have concerned the method of reasoning at work in *Capital*, and therefore the dialectic). It was to have been directed by Jean Hyppolite, who was very close to Canguilhem and in whom Althusser had great confidence. But the project, accepted in principle, never came to fruition. At that time, Althusser advised those close to him not to play the academic game and thus not to write a thesis. He himself only defended a thesis ten years later at the Université d'Amiens.

I had thus provisionally put Spinoza to the side, but he remained a back-drop to my concerns, as well as those of Althusser, who thought that the elements of Marx's philosophy, a philosophy that Marx himself had not elab-orated and that remained to be developed, were to be sought in Spinoza, on the condition, of course, that his concepts were reworked and their content enriched by means of knowledges acquired later on new terrains, essentially the history of the sciences, psychoanalysis, anthropology, political economy (rethought from a critical perspective), and above all political experience linked to workers' struggles. I myself returned to the study of Spinoza ten years later in the context of the courses I taught at the university where I was an assistant professor when I wrote my book *Hegel or Spinoza*, one of the last titles published in Althusser's Théorie collection with Maspero, in 1979. By that time, the practice of collective work that Althusser had initiated and which, for those who continued to work with him, was one of his principal contributions, had ceased: the political and intellectual context had com-pletely changed with the arrival of the "New Philosophers," the resurgence of interest in the philosophy of "human" rights, from the perspective proper to a humanism understood from an institutional and juridical point of view. In this context, to be regarded as "Althusserian" was not a compliment but a mark of opprobrium.

You asked if my somewhat precocious orientation to Spinoza had led me to Althusser. This was certainly one of the essential motifs of our alliance, above all when we judged that it was possible to graft him onto larger con-cerns that were less narrowly doctrinal and academic. Althusser said that it was necessary to do philosophy differently and judged that the passage through Spinoza would help us do so. I say the passage through Spinoza, for there was no question in his mind of focusing on a theoretical totality closed on itself and consequently fixed, which we would only need to turn upright in order to restore the identity of its systematic content. It was instead—to bor-row an image that Deleuze often uses—a matter of employing Spinoza like an optical instrument that can be turned in different ways, thanks to which it becomes possible to see in a new way domains that had not attracted the attention of professional philosophers.

What was the influence of Althusser on your political activity? You left the French Communist Party, of which Althusser remained a lifelong member, early on. Did this affect your relationship to Althusser? What was the significance of Maoism?

In 1967, I left the Communist Party, which I had joined five years earlier and in which I never held any position of responsibility. I felt less and less at ease there and could not put up with the workerist atmosphere, based on a foundation of economism, that dominated it. The young "intelllectuals" like me who joined and became active most often found themselves facing a climate of distrust hidden under a veneer of comradeship and were carefully marginalized. It was difficult to think and to express oneself freely there without provoking unstated suspicions. Further, the increasingly opportunist political orientation of the organization, which emphasized electoral maneuvers over long-term political strategy, was discouraging to me. The party, instead of being an instrument of class struggle, had become an end in itself, to the detriment of the development of an authentically internationalist line. It was enclosed in a narrowly nationalist perspective that prevented it from addressing the problems connected to colonialism and imperialism that had become uncomfortable given its corporatism. In brief, I could no longer see what I was doing there and on impulse submitted a letter of resignation. As soon as he learned what I had done, Althusser was very unhappy and tried to make me revisit my decision and withdraw my resignation, thereby avoiding its consequences. But I held firm, and we never spoke of it again; we worked together as if nothing had happened, and I was relieved not to have to intervene personally in the party's seemingly endless internal debates. If he had disapproved of my actions, it was because, by leaving the party in which I had never really participated except in a haphazard way, I had called into question and compromised the somewhat torturous and subterranean strategy he had adopted, which allowed him to maintain, for a number of years, formal ties to the organization and those of its leaders willing to listen to him. But these ties loosened over time, with the result that in a few years, he found himself in open opposition to the party. In truth, he never maintained any illusions concerning the downward slide of the PCF into irreversible decline. In twenty years "the first party of France" was transformed into a groupuscule whose existence as a closed circle, a cult of the distant past, was maintained only with extraordinary effort by its adherents. But, on the one hand, Althusser thought that his task as a philosopher who produced theoretical innovations and not as a pious preserver of immutable doctrinal acquisitions (the eternal "Marxism" whose fixed formulas party functionaries were content to repeat without really reflecting on their content, while preventing with all the means at their disposal any authentic reflection on these formulas, which to them led to destabilization and "deviation") consisted precisely in intervening in this conjuncture by injecting into it the elements of knowledge that it lacked. The absence of these elements in his eyes was one of the causes of the short-sighted political choices that finally made the PCF a party like the others, bogged down in struggles between politicians, for which Marxism served as no more than a moral justification, a position Althusser tried in vain to change until the moment he recognized that this was an impossible task. On the other hand, he understood that he, as an intellectual of bourgeois origins and educated in the academic institutions put into place and controlled by the bourgeoisie, had no way of establishing and maintaining contact with what he called "the masses" other than through the intermediary of the party of the working class (or reputed to be, given that in reality it was the party of its own members whose primary task was to maintain itself by engaging in constant maneuvers, compromises, and unprincipled alliances). It was for this reason that he thought it necessary to maintain his membership at any cost, whatever price he had to pay, a sacrifice that became increasingly difficult to accept. In this way, he was caught in a contradiction whose weight he bore like a cross: his attitude was at once lucid, perfectly free of any illusion, and haunted by an obsession whose religious dimension was clear—for the famous "masses" with which he had to maintain a quasi-mystical tie were for him an object of faith, perhaps even a fantasy that, associated with those proper to him personally, tormented him. Althusser never completely rid himself of the behavioral patterns and reflexes of the Catholic training that, to a certain extent, marked his Communist engagement.

The question of Maoism you raised intervened in this context in a fundamentally ambiguous way. Althusser, taking a big risk, judged that it was possible to maintain a lucid and open relation with the thought of Mao Zedong and the political decisions it inspired. Even more, it was necessary to renounce the demonization of his thought characteristic of the leadership of the PCF, who, for purely opportunist reasons, did not want to displease the Soviet party, under whose discipline the PCF remained and from which it attempted only clumsily and timidly to distance itself. As was the case with Stalinism, it was necessary to attempt to understand the process then under way without being limited by ready-made explanations or simplistic slogans (like the "cult of personality," which addressed a political problem from the perspective of psychology in its vaguest forms) that served to justify blind adherence to a system, as well as its condemnation, in the absence of a serious examination of the question and its stakes. In his preface to the Chinese edition of Althusser's writings published in 2015, Balibar offers a precise and detailed analysis of Althusser's relation to Mao, which clarifies ambiguities that initially appear overwhelming. I will summarize this analysis, whose examination of the problem is separated into two periods. First, at the moment he was writing his article "Contradiction and Overdetermination," one of the most important pieces in *For Marx*, Althusser drew primarily from the philosophical text Mao devoted to the question of contradiction: he adopted its argument to separate Marx's dialectic from its Hegelian covering, to which a long tradition of readings had confined it, on the basis of a finalism sustained by the thesis of the negation of the negation and sublation, a thesis set aside by Mao in an admittedly very elliptical way (it would be necessary to read his text very closely to bring out this point). Althusser attached particular importance to Mao's text, for it made it possible to place at the center of historical materialism the analysis of conjunctures and the unevenness they perpetually inject into the course of events, thereby furnishing political action with the matter proper to it. At the same time, this repoliticization of the dialectic allowed him to distance himself from the structuralism of the time and from the formalist tendency that was dominant within it. This quasi-Machiavellian reading of Mao scandalized the party's official thinkers, who diagnosed it as the symptom of a serious deviation. This only increased their distrust of Althusser's project, which impressed but did not convince them. When this initial discussion took place (in an admittedly surreptitious way), no Maoist current then existed in France; it came into existence and developed only with the events of 1968, the interpretation of which was immediately projected on what was known about the Cultural Revolution, an event that certainly marked a dramatic change, without anyone having a clear sense of the direction of the movement it had unleashed. It is in this way that, in a context that was no longer merely theoretical and speculative but tied to directly political and practical stakes, a fact that concretely obliged him to move beyond alliances and choose sides, Althusser confronted Mao's heritage for the second time and in particularly difficult conditions. He was caught in the crossfire: on one side, there was the party with which he would not break no matter what the cost and which totally condemned the Chinese experience without any attempt to understand its objectives and outcomes, content to align itself in the most servile way with the positions of the Soviet bloc; on the other, there was a radicalized segment of the French student movement that, in the course of the events of 1968, became a separate political force with a spontaneous obsession, just as lacking in rational justification and information, with "the Great Cultural Revolution," which was hailed as a miraculous turning point that would redirect, in a good way, the course of history. Thus, Althusser made use of the means at his disposal (the information circulating in France on this subject was fragmentary and biased) to untangle all of this without yielding to pressure from either side. This placed him in a difficult and equivocal position, at odds with both sides: for one side, he was too Maoist, while, for the other, he was not Maoist enough, with the result that his position satisfied no one. The debate on the Chinese question coincided with the campaign against "Althusserianism," diagnosed on all sides as a resurgence of Stalinist dogmatism. Althusser's denunciation of the ambiguities that characterized the PCF's abandonment of the dictatorship of the proletariat provided them with an additional argument, and the pressure to which he was subjected increased in the atmosphere of growing tension. The result of all this is well known; what is surprising is that in the periods of remission allowed him by the personal torment that at a certain moment took a tragic turn, he unfailingly resumed his effort to trace the lines from which a new way of doing philosophy might begin. That these lines, as he came, for better or worse, to sketch them, appear incomplete, hesitant, and faltering is hardly surprising in such circumstances. Jacques Rancière has described this as a spectacular failure, although we must not forget the other aspect of this failure: it represented an experiment, a test. That this experiment did not achieve definitive and irrefutable results is clear, but this does not mean that it was not carried out from the perspective of an authentic inquiry that, in the final analysis, is "theory" as Althusser understood and practiced it. This is why, it seems to me, it is still possible even today to be interested in Althusser's work, without blind devotion and therefore on the condition that it become the object of a critical reading that identifies both its weaknesses and the points with which they coexist that deserve philosophical attention. Althusser did not leave behind a completed doctrine, but sought the resonances on the basis of which philosophy might begin again in order to go farther and, eventually, differently.

Can you say a little about the early days of your work with Althusser (as well as with the others in the group)? For example, how did the "return to Marx" come about? Étienne Balibar has said that it was initially the students who prodded Althusser into the collective project of rereading Marx. What was your role in this?

Althusser's initial intuition was that, in France, Marx was referred to in a formal and distant manner, replete with approximations and simplifications, without ever having been really studied. It was enough to extract elements from some of his writings and set them end to end in a vulgate composed of a vague, dogmatic language, a kind of intellectual ready-made passkey, incoherent and all-purpose. It is for this reason that he took as his first and primary task the production of the introduction to Marxism that had not yet been undertaken and whose absence had affected the orientation of the French workers' movement from the outset. By virtue of the theoretical deficit that marked its formation and accompanied its development, this movement had never freed itself completely from the influence of bourgeois thought and its interpretive schema, such as, for example, humanism, whose moralizing foundation runs counter to a comprehension of the real movement of history and of truly revolutionary political action. For Althusser, to undertake seriously reading Marx in the original text, tracing its actual development, instead of taking it en bloc as if it constituted a definitive system of thought closed upon itself, was finally a political intervention, the condition of a change of terrain and not simply an academic occupation restricted to erudite and speculative tasks. It was in this spirit that, with his encouragement, the careful examination of both the early and later work of Marx and Engels in their historical context was undertaken, with the aim of identifying their true philosophical and political stakes, these being inseparable from one another. To work with Althusser meant taking part in a long-term endeavor that had never been undertaken in France and that could not lead immediately to definitive results, achieved without debate and discussion.

It is often said, concerning this endeavor, that Althusser preached a "return to Marx" according to the model of what Lacan for his part presented as a "return to Freud." This comparison is not completely invalid, given that in the sixties Althusser and Lacan were fellow travelers in the margins of the official institutions and the dominant intellectual currents, though they took their distance from one another more and more after 1968. In truth, their alliance had always been essentially tactical in nature and rested on a certain number of misunderstandings and silences for which both were responsible and which should have been clarified at some point. In any case, it is necessary to keep in mind that for both the theme of the "return" was not to be understood in the usual sense of a return to the past that, out of either disinterested curiosity or cultish devotion, consisted solely of recapturing Marx or Freud "as they really were," according to the written text, by leaving it unchanged and by adopting toward it the purely contemplative and passive attitude characteristic of antiquarianism turned toward a past that by definition no longer exists. Instead, for them, the "return" was a matter of intervening actively in the present conjuncture by exploiting the new elements it brought forth that were conducive to its transformation.

There is no question that, after Althusser, it was no longer possible to read, as before, the fundamental texts of Marxism in a careless way that proceeded through an arbitrary homogenization of the content and an expurgation of the difficulties and of what Balibar has called the points of heresy, which are also, if one manages to identify them, occasions of a recommencement. It is on the basis of this tendentially creative rather than retroactive approach that Althusser advanced the idea of a "symptomatic reading," directing our attention to what protrudes from the texts as an indication that something is happening which pertains to the order of the event and dissuading us from taking texts as uniform, complete, as if, having from the beginning arrived at the end of the trajectory they initiated, they were cut off from the movement of transformation that traverses and may come to lacerate them, tearing them from within, thereby propelling them beyond what they seem to say at the moment. To perform a symptomatic reading, therefore, consists in inserting oneself into a textual dynamic to explore its creases, inserting oneself into its fault lines, for there its real stakes are lodged in the form of points of instability that trigger a process of rupture and the constitution of events. It is therefore no longer a matter of interpreting—that is, of bringing to light a hidden meaning already present, awaiting its revelation, which needs only to be rediscovered. The objective is to go farther, without being afraid to subvert truths assumed to be untouchable dogmas, established and sanctified.

Seen from this perspective, Marx's work takes on a fundamentally "historical" character, in the sense not of a past history but of a history taking its course in and through this work. The dialectic is not simply an external object of thought, but the material out of which the work is made in the most intimate sense, its very texture. For Althusser, the name Marx was not the indication of an "author function," formally the bearer of finished doctrinal positions that we may survey from the outside by understanding them as belonging to the past. He did not take Marx's work as a toolbox that had only to be opened to yield the keys, ready to be put to use, to an explication of the real. Instead it represented a knot of still unresolved problems that, once taken into account, provoked an indefinitely open movement of inquiry in the present, both creative and free of all prejudice. To cite a phrase of which Althusser was particularly fond and that he had taken from Lenin: "We will advance and then we will see" [*On avance et puis on voit*]. This invitation to take risks, even to the extent of changing course when necessity demands it, frightened the guardians of the temple, who, for their part, practiced Marxism as a religion to which they were blindly and mechanically devoted, a cult, whose supposedly unchangeable order they were careful not to disturb. It simultaneously proved disconcerting to those in the opposing camp, who were satisfied with a simplistic and reductive reading of Marx's thought that authorized its definitive rejection. In the properly theoretical realm, as in the realm of his political choices, Althusser was caught in the cross fire, attacked both by those who reproached him for expecting too much from Marx and by those who thought he had subverted Marx and was thus guilty of a serious "deviation." It was on the basis of this unresolvable dilemma that the attacks on his "theoreticism" were launched.

What were the conditions that led to your first book, *A Theory of Literary Production*? More specifically, what was it about Jules Verne's oeuvre that led you to carry out a reading of it?

I undertook the study of literature for a number of reasons. Some of them can be traced back to the beginning of my studies at the university, where I was torn between two areas of interest. One led me to the examination of literary texts that, because of my family history, had fascinated me since childhood. The other oriented me to philosophical reflection, a field I discovered in my last year at the *lycée*, and whose richness and complexity stupefied and attracted me. In the French educational system, which, since Napoleon, has been strictly codified and structured by inviolable disciplinary boundaries, it is necessary at a certain point to choose one's direction. For example, either—to use the current expression—"one does philosophy," which means becoming enclosed in a kind of speculative bubble, or one takes up literary studies, which calls for an entirely different training. It is, however, impossible to pursue at the same time both areas of study, whose requirements are completely distinct. When I entered the ENS in 1958, I was quasi-officially enrolled, by virtue of my scores on the entrance examination, in the section that prepared students for the degree in classical literature. I stayed there for a few months, long enough to convince me that the prospect of spending the rest of my life teaching French, Latin, and Greek through their canonical texts was not going to work for me. I therefore took it upon myself to request a transfer to be incorporated into the very small, closed group of students preparing for the *agrégation* in philosophy, a frightening test, a kind of Holy Grail, access to which was reserved for an elite quasi-predestined or touched by grace. This was the occasion of my first contact with Althusser, who was in charge of the student "philosophers." He did not really encourage me to pursue this change of orientation: it seemed to him, as well as to Jean Hyppolite, the director of the École, that my efforts were very likely to fail. I was not "made" for philosophy, an intellectual vocation of the highest kind, which required particular gifts that I did not possess and without which I could aspire only to the status of unqualified amateur. I held firm, and despite some initial difficulties, things sorted themselves out. The year I worked under the direction of Canguilhem was very helpful in this regard, and I ended up, thanks to his support, being judged capable of pursuing the course of study upon which I had imprudently intruded. I succeeded in passing the *agrégation* in philosophy, which led me to envision pursuing research in this domain set apart and restricted in both theory and practice, which I had forced my way into. In doing so, however, I had not abandoned the "literary" interests that it would have been, it seemed to me, regrettable and even absurd simply to give up.

When I began to work with Althusser in 1962, I talked to him about this problem, and at that moment he understood and supported my desire to bring together two approaches that the organization of the French university system presented as formally separate and mutually exclusive. He approved of my efforts as part of the simultaneous development of a philosophical culture oriented to Marx (and Spinoza) and a reflection on the subject of what at that time was beginning to be called "literariness" [*littérarité*], that is, the set of conditions that led to the identification of certain artistic productions as "literary," the consequence of a process that was not simply formal and ideal but socially determined as well. This was a relatively new terrain on which to work: on the one hand, at that time, although things would later change thanks primarily to figures like [Michel] Foucault, Deleuze, and [Jacques] Derrida, it was neither common nor obvious to link philosophical reflection to an investigation of literary works, except to understand the latter as situated at "the height of thought" (Hölderlin, Mallarmé, . . .); on the other, after

[Georgi] Plekhanov and [Georg] Lukács, Marxism had contributed nothing really significant to literary theory (an exception was Lucien Goldmann, with whom, to my regret, I did not have a substantive discussion). In the PCF, the high priest of all things literary, [Louis] Aragon, who for purely opportunist reasons formed a brief alliance with [Roger] Garaudy, the philosophical advocate of the "humanist" position in philosophy, to which Althusser was directly opposed, had restricted the debate to an examination of the question of "socialist realism," which on the stated pretext of putting them back on the solid ground of the "real," infused these discussions with a crippling sterility, even if they they did not take refuge in the false pretenses and contortions that accompanied the theme of "truthful lying" [*mentir vrai*] cultivated by Aragon, who represented official doctrine. This is why Althusser encouraged me to pursue my project, which in his mind fit perfectly into his endeavor to recast and expand Marxist theory. Accordingly, it was at his request that I wrote my first book, *A Theory of Literary Production*, in 1966, the third title to appear in his Théorie collection, launched with the publisher Maspero the previous year.

This publication to my surprise had a certain resonance and was translated into a number of foreign languages. In France, however, its reception remained very limited. In the PCF, those responsible for addressing cultural questions maintained a weighty silence, which amounted to censorship. This was not surprising, for they habitually reacted this way when something disturbed them. At the same time, the people around [Roland] Barthes, [Philippe] Sollers, and [Gérard] Genette, who developed the program of what had just begun to be called "literary theory" and who formed the closed circle of an avant-garde, did not pay attention to a project that doubtless appeared at odds with the formal imperatives imposed by the structuralist ideology then dominant. This ideology saw value only in discourses that presented a degree of technical sophistication that I admit without hesitation my work did not possess. Only the analysis of *Les paysans*, Balzac's unfinished novel, which Marx had been interested in, attracted the attention of some specialists. Nevertheless, my book enjoyed a certain success, primarily through word of mouth, and went through a number of editions until 1985, when it was withdrawn by the publisher, with whom, in the meantime, I had published a second, very different, book, *Hegel ou Spinoza*, which addressed a different audience. Later, I again devoted several works to the problems of literature, specifically to what I called "exercises" in literary philosophy: *A quoi pense la littérature?* (1990, reissued in 2013 under the title *Philosopher avec la littérature*), *Proust entre littérature et philosophie* (2013), and *Études de philosophie littéraire* (2014). Throughout the course of a fifty-year period, I thus remained situated between philosophy and literature, and the questions that I posed at the outset have continued to occupy my attention.

When I happened to reread the book Althusser had asked of me, *A Theory of Literary Production*, I must admit that I experienced a certain . . .

perplexity. I saw it as the expression of an inquiry that had then just begun and was in search of its bearings, a quest that, in my view, has to this day not yielded definitive results. What really bothers me today about my first book is the rather brutal imposition of the notion of "production," supposedly less "idealist" and more "materialist" than that of "creation," on a domain in which I lacked the means sufficient to give this notion an explanatory value: it served very broadly to refer to a framework of thought but did not go much farther than that. I later regretted not having paid sufficient attention to another aspect of the question, that of "literary reproduction." This seems to me to come closer to the operation proper to literature, in as much as it does not simply gather what [Jean-Paul] Sartre called "fruit that must be eaten on the spot" in the sense that it is so "engaged" with its own epoch, to which it adheres so closely (a way of restaging the theory of "reflection") that it will not survive beyond it. Why continue to read Balzac today, in the sense of a reading in the present that is not merely an antiquarianism, given that the forms of socialization to which he responded and to which he bore testimony are far behind us? An interrogation of this type adds a supplementary dimension to the notion of production. It not only refers to the conditions in which works liable to being identified as literary are originally produced by the labor proper to the writer in the conditions proper to his or her time, but also directs our attention to the effects these works produce over time, once they have come into existence and have begun to circulate. In carrying out this type of interrogation, we confront an aspect of the problem that literary analysis, without ceasing to be indispensable at the initial stage, cannot resolve. In short, I now see in this first book from 1966 the beginning of a project that remains only partially explored, which is why I have continued to return to it.

At the core of this project is a long study of Jules Verne's novel *The Mysterious Island*, which I had written a few years earlier and tried in vain to publish, but which, when I showed it to Althusser, interested him. Why Jules Verne? There were several different clusters of reasons. First, a personal interest going back to the years of my youth that never left me. I just now finished correcting the proofs of a work that will appear in a few months, titled *En lisant Jules Verne* [Reading Jules Verne], in which I attentively examine four of the first "extraordinary voyages": *Five Weeks in a Balloon, The Adventures of Captain Hatteras, Journey to the Center of the Earth,* and *Twenty Thousand Leagues under the Sea.* These novels, apart from their indisputable literary qualities, seem to me to illuminate in an original way a question that for me currently presents significant philosophical interest and that I began to examine in my book *S'orienter* (2017), part of which, once again, I dedicated to a consideration of one of Verne's other novels, *Around the World in Eighty Days.* Julien Gracq, an acute reader of Jules Verne, says that what Balzac did for history by making society as such a literary object in the fullest sense, Verne did for geography by treating "the face of the earth" as the subject of a novel that he had worked on for a long time. Verne detailed by means of fictional narrative the multiple forms that the occupation of space may take, a concrete activity that in a certain way echoes what Spinoza theorized in a more abstract manner with the concept of conatus, "the tendency to persist in its being" characteristic of every existing thing in the world and, in particular, those beings that we are. Living, existing—as much as these are temporal destinations (a theme that has particularly nourished religious speculation), they also consist in taking a position among places, in changing places and asking what it is to be "somewhere," in wondering if it is legitimate to have a given place, an interrogation that may on occasion provoke anxiety. Jules Verne, in his way, addressed these problems and, by constructing narratives out of precise details concerning the means available in his time to traverse space (for example, to travel "around the world," no mean feat in his epoch) made intelligible the urgency of these problems. This is why it is worth the trouble to examine them closely by following the lines of reflection his novels initiate. These lines intersect with those that, in the real world, are followed by anthropologists or those interested in psychoanalysis, and I believe that philosophers have an interest in taking such lines of reflection into account. I don't think there is something like "the philosophy of Jules Verne," any more than there is a "philosophy of Balzac" or a "philosophy of Proust." If something of this nature is nevertheless to be found in a few discrete corners of their writings, it would not be sufficiently original to be of interest. But— and this is quite different—by recounting imaginary histories that we should not too quickly classify as anticipations of scientific discoveries, because their importance lies elsewhere, a writer like Verne encounters along the way, without noting them and without having any intention of doing so, preoc- cupations and schemes of thought that allow philosophers to expand the perspective from which they grasp these discoveries, with the rational and conceptual means available to them. In particular, it seems to me that literary texts, or at least certain among them, permit an apprehension of the question of ideology from a new angle: they are not content to replicate the ideologies to which they relate—in Verne's case, the scientist positivism cultivated by industrialized societies—but they put them in perspective, rework them, and allow them to be seen with a certain distance; they reveal the fault lines on which they were constructed and which lead to their destabilization.

There was an additional reason I granted an importance to an author ordi- narily assigned to the unflattering and generally slighted category of "genre fiction," in this case, educational literature written for the edification of (exclusively male) youth, a narrow category that Jules Verne's oeuvre, which continues to surprise me with its intellectual innovation, exceeds. I have always been bothered by the barrier separating "great" and "minor" literature, given that the latter, in the forms perhaps less finished and less sophisticated proper to it, is as (or more) creative and revealing of events in formation than what is referred to as the literature of ideas, events that are not purely intellec- tual in nature, belonging only to the atmosphere of the time or to superficial opinions. It is not by chance that when Marx arrived in Paris in 1843, he was so struck by Eugène Sue's *Les mystères de Paris*, which had just been published in serial form (Sue's novel initiated this form, which has subsequently had a long and rich history) that he devoted to it no fewer than two chapters of *The Holy Family*, where, with Engels, he settled accounts with the Hegelian Left in Berlin, to which he owed his initial intellectual formation. Twenty years later, [Victor] Hugo understood what great literature, of which he was supposed to be the representative, could take from the model of Sue's novel's composition. He made use of it himself in the writing of *Les misérables*, where he gave it a quasi-metaphysical resonance. In our time, Marguerite Duras came to rework the ordinary thematics of the melodrama and the photo novel, giving them, through the alchemy of style, a greater scope. In contemporary literary production, it is the detective novel or noir fiction, derived from the serial novel, that seems to me to be the most inventive in this domain. Turned toward social reality in the manner of an optical instrument, it furnishes a partial and distorted vision of this reality that underscores its blind spots and contradictions. There is much work to be done here.

We know now that Althusser was influential in your decision to write the theoretical sections that became the first part of the work. Why did Althusser find this was necessary?

When this book project was first proposed, the section on Jules Verne had already been written. Without knowing it, I had practiced a kind of symptomatic reading before the concept had been established by Althusser. In any case, it was what drew his attention. He then suggested that the book be organized around the study of Verne, which would occupy its center on the condition that its presuppositions were explained, which would allow me to emphasize its properly political dimension. In his mind, the book he had requested from me was supposed to be a weapon in a struggle whose stakes would be made clear. I therefore wrote, just as he desired, the "theoretical" section, which contained theses of a general nature. This is the part of the book that seems the most dated to me today. I am convinced that the best way to approach the problems posed by literary texts is to engage in exercises in reading that permit us to enter into the details of their composition and illuminate that which in them constitutes an event and stimulates a process of reflection. This is the aspect that appears in the third section of the book, in the studies of Balzac and Tolstoy that had already been published as articles. I was also very attached to the text on Borges.

Recently, Warren Montag has documented the role you played in the development of Althusser's thought, particularly around the notion of structure. In letters exchanged between you and Althusser in May 1965, he asks you to develop your criticism of his use of "structure" and above all of latent

structure in his contributions to *Reading Capital*. It appears that Althusser
could see certain of the silences and lacunae proper to his contributions only
after reading your essay on structuralism, "Literary Analysis: The Tomb of
Structures" first published in *Les temps modernes*. Can you speak about this
exchange and about the related question of your suggestion to replace contradiction with décalage?

At the time, attention was focused in a quasi-obsessional way on structuralism, a generic term that covered intellectual movements that were in reality
quite diverse and of unequal significance. They had in common nothing more
than the fact that they called into question a certain number of previously
held convictions, above all, those connected with Sartre's humanist existen-
tialism, which dominated the intellectual scene in the postwar period up to
the end of the fifties. They made it possible to challenge the foundations on
which the philosophies of consciousness were based. Between the "structuralism" of [Claude] Lévi-Strauss, [Jacques] Lacan, [Georges] Dumézil, [Martial]
Gueroult, and the linguists inspired by [Ferdinand de] Saussure, there were
more than differences of nuance. It is for this reason that it would be better
to speak of structuralisms in the plural, given that they do not form a perfectly homogeneous and harmonious whole, definitively organized around a
systematic methodology that could be accepted or rejected en bloc. In particular, it is important not to confuse investigations carried out on different
terrains, the understanding of which they fundamentally recast (in fact, these
investigations represented effective advances and fundamentally changed
everything related to problems as diverse as those of knowledge, power, subjectivity), with what might be called the ideology of structuralism, a catchall
term or journalistic invention that amalgamates these projects, referring only
to their most external and formal aspect, thereby encouraging the cult of
formalism, at the expense of the contradictions of the real, in particular by
excluding any consideration of the irregularities and conflicts engendered by
the uneven development of social relations. Althusser exercised extreme vigilance in relation to this tendency, which was only coherent in appearance: he
sought by every possible means to demarcate himself from it. The difficulty
did not simply lie in the fact that this tendency was dominant—everything
that seemed even slightly new was labeled "structuralist"—but in Althusser's
judgment that it was just as necessary to wage a struggle simultaneously on
another front: the Hegelianism, and the historical teleology for which it serves
as a guarantee, that renders meaningless and suppresses political action by
depriving it of the ground on which it is materially compelled to intervene.
The question of contradiction was at the heart of this difficulty, which eluded
both the reigning structuralist ideology and the humanist ideology that it
claimed to oppose. It was necessary to work on two fronts: to struggle at
the same time against the thesis of dialectical overcoming [*dépassement*],
an essential part of the Marxist vulgate that had the effect of derealizing

historical contradictions by removing class struggle, and against the unifying formalism of structures that in a different way also emptied revolutionary action of its effective content. It was for this reason that Althusser accorded a particular importance to the notion of *décalage* he borrowed from Mao's *On Contradiction*; this notion led to a new understanding of the relation between the principal contradiction and secondary contradictions in the analysis of a social formation by showing that this relation does not develop by magic in a single straight line toward its destination, but is subject to permanent displacements, most of which, while governed by the principle of the concatenation of causes, are unpredictable by virtue of the multiplicity and complexity of the conditions they encounter. From this is derived the priority granted to the analysis of concrete conjunctures and the turbulence that destabilizes them from within, without it being possible to plan in advance the outcome of the conflicts provoked by their disequilibrium. This is also what explains the theoretical importance that Althusser accorded to Machiavelli, in whom he saw the greatest theoretician before Lenin of the conjunctures that furnish the terrain in which political action intervenes in the present, without inscribing it in the ideal perspective of a History whose trajectory is already completely plotted out. From this perspective, Althusser's most important text in this period is incontestably "Contradiction and Overdetermination," in which all these questions are concentrated.

My text "Literary Analysis: The Tomb of Structures" is in part inscribed in this context. It is an attack less on the notion of structure in itself, which it characterizes in fairly broad terms (the suspension of everything referring to the myth of interiority), than on the attempt to unite domains of investigation that are in reality very different, by forcing on them the notion of structure elevated to the status of a universal paradigm and by this means reducing them to a single plane or parallel planes linked to each other by relations of a one-to-one correspondence. This was the means by which a fusional (or confusual) regime of equivalences was established in which everything finally resembles everything else and vice versa. My primary target was the thesis, circulating everywhere and adopted without discussion, concerning the fashionable commonplace that everything is reducible to language, that everything "is" language, which was elevated to the position of sole explanatory model. This simplistic perspective, which in the end reduced social relations to relations of communication endowed with a functional efficiency, effaced with the wave of a magic wand the contradictions, real conflicts, and struggles or acts of resistance to which these relations give rise and that are difficult, if not impossible, to reduce to effects of structure. This led to an antihistoricism whose conclusions ended up converging with those reached by the teleological dialectic of sublation [*dépassement*]: the two sides found themselves engaging in the same denial of the conjunctural faults, gaps, and ruptures that condition the active taking of positions in the sense that they materially transform the order of things.

In the conclusion to your book *Hegel or Spinoza,* you argue that "to read Spinoza following Hegel, but not according to Hegel, allows us to pose the question of a non-Hegelian dialectic." Although this work was written in a different conjuncture than that of the essays of Althusser's *For Marx,* the question of a non-Hegelian dialectic seems to link these two works. Is there a way in which *Hegel or Spinoza* responds to problems first delineated by Althusser in *For Marx,* especially in "Contradiction and Overdetermination"?

Effectively, it is the project of formulating a dialectic purged of the finalist presupposition that Hegel had imparted to it by means of his conception of absolute negation (which contained in its premises the promise and guarantee of its resolution), which was at the core of the refounding of Marxist theory undertaken by Althusser. In his eyes, this was the condition of a return to historical processes grasped in their effective conjunctural unfolding and of situating political struggles on solid terrain by removing the prejudice of progression toward destiny. I find this project more pertinent and indispensable today than it has ever been. Marx and Engels believed that it was enough to "reverse" Hegel's "idealist" dialectic to rematerialize it, by setting it on its feet, as they put it. In doing this, they took up, without a clear sense that they were doing so, the Feuerbachian scheme of the specular reflection proper to ideological representation that supposedly reverses things, with the result that it would suffice to turn this representation around to see the real, of which it presents a deformed image. As Althusser explains, such a reversal conserves, exactly reproduces, more than it transforms. This is why the dialectic it reveals is finally the same as it was at the outset. The human essence in which Feuerbach believed he saw the truth of the religious representation of the divine, which would be no more than man's deformed and inverted image, remains, once it is set right, invested with the ideal character that this representation attributed to it: real Man, or God seen upside down, remains now and forever God, or a God—that is, a fiction adorned with the prestige of necessity and universality, to the detriment of the actual contradictions internal to the tangled network through which revolutionary action must force open a path—a path, to be precise, whose end cannot be fixed in advance and toward which it cannot move along a single, ideally straight, line.

If Spinoza may be presented as an alternative to Hegel, it is by virtue of his radical critique of finalism. Such a critique requires a rethinking of the nature of things on a new basis, on the two simultaneous planes of substantial reality (*natura naturans*) and modal reality (*natura natutata*), which are, in fact, one and the same reality seen in its two aspects, which correspond exactly to each other. Because of its extreme concentration, a result of its mode of argumentation—that is, the *ordo geometricus* through which the complex network of arguments is realized—Spinoza's thought is difficult to grasp and liable to interpretations that I believe lead away from its true meaning.

Too often we see a tendency to present it as a set of certitudes arranged in a closed unit that can only be accepted or rejected as such. Having gone through it in every sense over the course of decades, I am more than ever aware of the unevennesses and contrasts that work it and destabilize it from within. It is precisely these difficulties that most forcefully stimulate reflection and encourage us not to be satisfied with ready-made ideas. I am thus far from seeing Spinoza's work as a finished system of incontrovertible answers, which, having resisted the ravages of time, would be directly applicable to contemporary problems. This is doubtless why we are never done with Spinoza, the representative par excellence of a critical philosophy permanently open to being called into question, if only through a confrontation with historical facts that it could not have foreseen, which in turn discourages us from sacralizing it or regarding it as an absolute and unsurpassable limit. This is precisely what makes it what Spinoza himself called "true philosophy," not a discourse on or about reality but an activity of thought that, no longer aspiring to occupy a position above reality, maintains contact with it, is modified by this contact, and in this way works toward its transformation. The result is the obligation to read Spinoza, like Marx, in and through the present, in opposition to the approach proper to a "return to," that is, a return to the past whose inspiration is essentially conservative. [Antonio] Negri, in relation to Marx, proposed this beautiful formula: Marx beyond Marx. I think that this is equally applicable to Spinoza: to seek to understand Spinoza by pushing Spinoza beyond himself, confronting him with questions that he could not, or did not have the occasion to, formulate.

That said, I would also argue that it is not productive to set Spinoza and Hegel back to back, as if they constituted the terms of an alternative whose dividing line is clear. The formulation "Hegel or Spinoza" that I made the title of my book does not signify a decision to choose Spinoza over Hegel by banishing the latter to a kind of speculative hell. Reread in the light of Spinoza, Hegel himself appears "beyond Hegel," traversed from within by a dynamic of thought that challenges the limits of his system, in the spirit of "true philosophy," which is an undertaking perpetually tested and begun again and not a rumination on ideas or truths established once and for all. If it is still worth reading Althusser today, it is precisely because, even in his hesitations and failures, he represents that effort at reworking and refoundation, in which he encourages us to participate, even by going, if necessary, "beyond Althusser."

In your essay on Althusser and [Frantz] Fanon, "Figures of Interpellation," you argue that the notion of a specific subject, particularly the black subject, escaped Althusser. Why was Althusser unable to see this, especially considering that Fanon's book was published in 1952? Is it possible to link Althusser's insistence that every individual is "always already" a subject to the situation-specific notion of the subject developed by Sartre and Fanon? Further, does

race theory have anything to gain by taking seriously Althusser's proposition
that ideology exists only in material apparatuses?

I do not recall hearing Althusser speak of Fanon. He may not have known
Fanon's work, or at least was not really interested in it. This ignorance may
be explained by his desire to remain close to the PCF at any price, and the
party, holding up the banner of "the first party of France," approached with
extreme reticence anything that touched on the colonial question and anti-
imperialist struggles for liberation. They did so in the name of the absolute
priority given to the specific interests of the working class, understood as the
"French" working class. From this followed an ambiguity or difficulty that
continued even after the end of the Algerian War, and that was one of the
reasons the organization, whose visceral workerism confined it to a kind of
corporatism, broke with its student group. The latter was much more open
to the outside world and in any case less inclined to engage in the preserva-
tion of narrowly national values. Fanon, who was wholeheartedly committed
to the FLN,[6] was profoundly disturbing to those who claimed to be official
adherents of Marxism. Moreover, in the intellectual sphere he was seen as a
"Sartrian," whereas in fact he knew how to detect the part of Sartre's oeuvre
that, once separated from the speculative logorrhea that blunts its sharp edge,
is truly innovative. His caustic reading of *Anti-Semite and Jew*, which, with
Transcendence of the Ego, is among Sartre's best philosophical texts, allows
problems of identity and subjectivation to be posed in new ways.

  These were precisely the problems that lay at the heart of Althusser's pre-
occupations in that he had diagnosed the insufficiencies and lacunae in the
conception of ideology inherited from Marx. This conception was inadequate
from the start because of its inscription in the base and superstructure model,
which, by subjecting mental phenomena to a narrowly causal explanation,
made these phenomena, in their double—individual and collective—forms
dependent on mechanisms external to the order proper to them, thus dematerializing them. It was precisely with the aim of rematerializing the figures
of consciousness that govern what Althusser called the "always-already subjects" socially produced according to determinate norms that he proposed
the concept of the ideological state apparatus. This concept, which in fact
identified but did not solve a problem, compels us to reintegrate ideological
processes into the play of social relations instead of placing them in a purely
representational, ideal sphere (according to the model of the spirit moving
across the surface of the water). It is therefore on the plane of conduct, or
what [Pierre] Bourdieu, from a similar perspective, called "habitus," and not
in some one's head, that the attitudes of thought which orient individuals in
a given way, before they have become conscious of them, are formed in practice. I myself proposed the notion of "infra-ideology" as a way of separating it
from the superstructural conception of ideology to which it stands opposed.
This is the meaning of the thesis according to which ideology interpellates

individuals as subjects, at least as I understand it. But it also seems to me that while he began to recast the problems of subjectivity, Althusser did not reach the end of the path he had opened. The process of interpellation on which he based his approach was, in the best of cases, metaphorical and, once again, foregrounded the communicational networks of language at the expense of the aggressive and potentially violent forms in which the processes of subjection are embodied. These forms were at the forefront of certain inquiries conducted by Foucault, who, although he expressly repudiated the concept, created the possibility of posing the problem of ideology in a new way.

And these are precisely the forms of domination that Fanon—from his position as one of the colonized—privileged, with the result that the mechanisms of ideology were removed from the foundation of simple determination and were literally overdetermined, opened up to play [*d'en ouvrir le jeu*]. This is why the confrontation between Althusser and Fanon, which did not take place at the time, enlarges and enriches, it seems to me, the investigation initially driven by the thesis concerning interpellation and permits a correction of its weaknesses, allowing us to understand better the phenomena of subjectivity that constitute the essential stakes of practical philosophy. My hypothesis is that the notion of norm as it was utilized by Canguilhem and Foucault, given its double inscription in the vital and the social, which inevitably generates conflicts, gives privileged access to what is at issue, there at the intersection of the ethical and the biopolitical. It was from this perspective that I proposed the concept of "the subject of norms" [*le sujet des normes*], understanding it in two senses of the genitive case: being subject to norms and the product of norms, exposed to their domination, but also being the subject of norms, capable accordingly not of freeing itself once and for all from them but of pushing against them by adopting an active and not only passive attitude toward them. To be a subject of norms is precisely to occupy an intermediary position between activity and passivity, and to be permanently compelled to manage the conflicts to which this position is exposed, by virtue of the ambivalent and, by definition, unstable status that condemns it to incompleteness and instability. In my book *S'orienter*, published in 2017, I sought to reflect on this incompleteness, using examples from philosophy and literature. Another work, *À l'essai*, which appeared in 2019, continued this reflection on the basis of references taken, this time, from the history of the sciences and from anthropology, which shed a new light on such questions as that of crisis and the common as the latter takes shape in difficult conditions, which for better or worse, equivocally and therefore dialectically, offer opportunities to be grasped. To me, all of this is linked to and continues the work I began fifty years ago. Of course, this undertaking could not have proceeded in a straight line. It pushed up against difficulties that forced it at certain moments to change direction and try different paths. But despite its irregularities and, in a way, because of them, it represents a project that has remained basically the same, the pursuit of which I have never renounced, except to start again elsewhere, when to do so proved necessary.

In your "Soutenance" [Defense],[7] which you presented in May 1991, you refer to Althusser's "fearlessness" and the "inexhaustible fecundity" of many of the paths opened by his thought. What are these paths, and which seem the most relevant to the current conjuncture?

In retrospect, what strikes me about Althusser's project is its impetuousness, in which inventiveness is combined with a certain disorder that prevented it from establishing a closed and definitively complete system. With concepts like over-determination, which required a rethinking of the dialectic on new grounds, and ideological interpellation, which reinscribed the question of subjectivation in a field other than psychology, he opened a number of areas of investigation that, even today, are worth exploring. But this requires a critical rereading of his writings that will allow us to separate out, perhaps brutally and in the spirit of provocation, what in them was a direct response to conjunctural necessities that today have no meaning, or at least do not have the same meaning. It is indisputable that the exclusive valorization of "Theory" that Althusser initiated in the sixties for essentially tactical reasons, that is, to legitimate his intellectual position within the workers' party in the service of which he had placed himself, does not make sense today, at least when formulated in this way. The idea of a radical and definitive break with ideology that situates the latter entirely on the side of error establishes the representation of a truth that is pure, self-referential, and ideal, which is mythical. One of Althusser's "theses" was that the condition of engaging in Theory was to have only good concepts. It was in the name of this principle that he mercilessly hunted down bad concepts, such as alienation, to take one example. But what I learned as I attempted to pursue the work of reflection that began with his encouragement and required being carried out on the different terrains to which I happened to have access, was that to reason with good concepts and only with them is an inaccessible ideal. To believe that theory can ever be extracted from the terrain of ideology is a pious wish, and to entertain this wish is ultimately to render theoretical reflection sterile and cut it off from any possibility of development or innovation.

According to Spinoza, truth is *norma sui et falsi*, a formula often interpreted in an abusively simplistic way, as if truth were the "norm of itself," meaning sufficient to itself, having an autotelic character that definitively encloses it in its own order. But this is not what Spinoza says: what he affirms is that truth is the norm "of itself and of the false." At the same time as it reveals itself and imposes its power as truth, it continues to maintain a relation to the false, which, in the same gesture, it also reveals; this is a way of saying that there is no truth without error. Pascal would say that we were caught in the vicious circle of truth and error, that is, placed permanently at the point of their intersection; the most we can hope for is to shift the point at which they meet. This constitutes the effective history of our knowledges, which, as history, is presented as an uninterrupted movement that cannot be reduced to a single line. Althusser was very attached to another of Spinoza's formulas, found in the *Treatise on the Emendation of the Intellect: Habeo enim ideam veram* [For we have a true idea]. He insisted on the fact that its interest (and its theoretical force of truth) lay above all in the little word *enim* (for), to which a careless reading does not pay sufficient attention, even though it constitutes the formula's pivot. Once it is taken into account, it becomes clear that the true idea does not stand alone on ground that belongs exclusively to it: for it to manifest itself, for one to be able to "have it," a series of conditions must converge. Because this unity is conjunctural, that is, contingent, which signifies that it is not established in advance.

Everything is a matter, here as in politics, of the *Kairos*, the opportune moment that, given the impossibility of our creating it from scratch, must be identified for us to be able to intervene in the course of events with the hope of "moving things along" [*faire bouger les choses*], to use another expression of which Althusser was fond. He also liked to say that we must learn how "to catch a moving train." The train is history, which has already started and will continue on, without anyone knowing exactly where it is going. There is nothing to do but catch it along the way and leap on board as well as one can. We can acknowledge the courage with which Althusser, in the determinate conjuncture with which he was confronted, executed a perilous leap of this type, at the risk of falling on his face, which did not fail to happen to him. This is why, even if his efforts did not produce definitive results that might serve as the achievements around which a cult might blindly be maintained, they have left traces, some of which have yet to be effaced. I cannot see any reason to forget Althusser.

Translated by Warren
Montag and Audrey Wasser

Translators' Notes

1. The thesis was published as *Spinoza et le problème de l'expression* (Paris: Éditions de Minuit, 1968). Translated as *Expressionism in Philosophy: Spinoza* by Martin Joughin (New York: Zone Books, 1992).

2. L'Organisation de l'armée secrète (Secret Army Organization) was a far-right, terrorist group opposed to Algerian independence.

3. Highly competitive, subject-specific examination required for obtaining a position in secondary or higher education in the French system.

4. Translated in English as "Outlines of a Critique of Political Economy" by Martin Milligan, in Karl Marx and Frederick Engels, *Collected Works*, vol. 3 (London: Lawrence & Wishart, 1975).

5. Published as *Philosophie et philosophie spontanée des savants (1967)* (Paris: François Maspero, 1974). Translated by Warren Montag in *Philosophy and the Spontaneous Philosophy of the Scientists* (New York: Verso, 1990).

6. Front de Libération Nationale (National Liberation Front), the nationalist political party in Algeria that emerged during the Algerian War.

7. This was a defense of his entire corpus, presented to an academic jury for the title of Docteur ès Lettres, the highest academic degree awarded in France.

WORKS BY PIERRE MACHEREY

Books

Pour une théorie de la production littéraire. Paris: Maspero, 1966. Reissued with a new postface by the author, Lyon: ENS Éditions, 2014. Open access at https://books.openedition.org/enseditions/628. Translated by Geoffrey Wall as *A Theory of Literary Production* (New York: Routledge, 1978; reissued 2006).

Hegel ou Spinoza. Paris: Maspero, 1979; La Découverte, 1990. Translated by Susan M. Ruddick as *Hegel or Spinoza* (Minneapolis: University of Minnesota Press, 2011).

Gebroken Spiegel: Over de realistiese illusie. Nijmegen: SUN, 1981.

Hegel et la société (with Jean-Pierre Lefebvre). Paris: Presses Universitaires de France, 1984.

Comte: La philosophie et les sciences. Paris: Presses Universitaires de France, 1989.

À quoi pense la littérature? Exercices de philosophie littéraire. Paris: Presses Universitaires de France, 1990. Reissued as *Philosopher avec la littérature* (Paris: Hermann, 2013). Translated by David Macey as *The Object of Literature* (Cambridge: Cambridge University Press, 1995).

Avec Spinoza: Études sur la doctrine et l'histoire du spinozisme. Paris: Presses Universitaires de France, 1992. Partial translation by Ted Stolze in *In a Materialist Way: Selected Essays,* ed. Warren Montag (New York: Verso, 1998).

Introduction à l'Éthique de Spinoza, la cinquième partie: Les voies de la liberation. Paris: Presses Universitaires de France, 1994.

Introduction à l'Éthique de Spinoza, la troisième partie: La vie affective. Paris: Presses Universitaires de France, 1995.

Introduction à l'Éthique de Spinoza, la quatrième partie: La condition humaine. Paris: Presses Universitaires de France, 1996.

Introduction à l'Éthique de Spinoza, la deuxième partie: La réalité mentale. Paris: Presses Universitaires de France, 1997.

Introduction à l'Éthique de Spinoza, la première partie: La nature des choses. Paris: Presses Universitaires de France, 1998.

Histoires de dinosaure: Faire de la philosophie. 1965–1997. Paris: Presses Universitaires de France, 1999. Partial translation by Ted Stolze in *In a Materialist Way: Selected essays,* ed. Warren Montag (New York: Verso, 1998).

Marx 1845: Les « Thèses » sur Feuerbach. Traduction et commentaire. Paris: Amsterdam, 2008.

Petits Riens: Ornières et dérives du quotidien. Bordeaux: Le Bord de l'eau, 2009.

De Canguilhem à Foucault: La force des normes. Paris: La Fabrique, 2009.

De l'utopie! Paris: De l'incidence éditeur, 2011.

La parole universitaire. Paris: La Fabrique, 2011.

Escritos sobre el arte (with Louis Althusser, Étienne Balibar, and Warren Montag). Madrid: Tierradenadie Ediciones, 2011.

Proust entre littérature et philosophie. Paris: Éditions Amsterdam, 2013.

Il soggetto produttivo: Da Foucault a Marx. Postface by Antonio Negri and Judith Revel. Verona: Ombre Corte, 2013.

Études de philosophie "française": De Sieyès à Barni. Paris: Publications de la Sorbonne, 2013.

Identités. Paris: De l'incidence éditeur, 2013.

Querelles cartésiennes. Lille: Presses Universitaires du Septentrion, 2014.

Geometria dello spazio sociale: Pierre Bourdieu e la filosofia. Edited by Fabrizio Denunzio. Verona: Ombre Corte, 2014.

Le sujet des normes. Paris: Éditions Amsterdam, 2014.

Études de philosophie littéraire. Paris: De l'incidence éditeur, 2014.

S'orienter. Paris: Éditions Kimé, 2017.

En lisant Jules Verne. Caen: De l'incidence éditeur, 2018.

À l'essai. Paris: Éditions Kimé, 2019.

Sagesse ou ignorance? La question de Spinoza. Paris: Éditions Amsterdam, 2019.

Articles and Other Writings

1964

"La philosophie de la science de G. Canguilhem." *La Pensée* 113 (February 1964): 62–74. Translated by Ted Stolze in *In a Materialist Way: Selected Essays*, ed. Warren Montag (New York: Verso, 1998), 165–87.

1965

"À propos du processus d'exposition du *Capital*." In *Lire le Capital*, by Louis Althusser, Étienne Balibar, Roger Establet, Jacques Rancière, and Pierre Macherey, vol. 1, 213–56. Paris: Maspero, 1965. Revised version in *Lire Le Capital*, Presses Universitaires de France (Quadridge), 1996. Translated by Ben Brewster and David Fernbach as "On the Process of Exposition of *Capital* (The Work of Concepts)," in *Reading Capital: The Complete Edition* (New York: Verso, 2015), 175–213.

"'Marxisme et humanisme': À propos de la rupture." *La nouvelle critique* 166 (June 1965): 131–41. Reprinted in *Histoires de dinosaure*, 9–34 (Paris: Presses Universitaires de France, 1999). Translated by Ted Stolze as "On the Rupture," *Minnesota Review*, no. 26 (Spring 1986): 118–27.

"L'opéra ou l'art hors de soi" (with François Regnault). *Les temps modernes* 231 (August 1965): 289–331.

1966

"A propos de *L'amour de l'art*." *Cahiers Marxistes Léninistes* 12/13 (July/October 1966): 8–14.

1969

"Lire le Capital." In *Le centenaire du Capital: Actes d'un colloque tenu à Cerisy en 1969, 53–67*. Paris: Mouton, 1969. Reissued by Éditions Hermann, 2012.

1974

"Sur la littérature comme forme idéologique" (with Étienne Balibar). *Littérature* 13 (February 1974): 29–48.

Preface to *Le Français national: Politique et pratiques de la langue nationale sous la Révolution française* by Renée Balibar and Dominique Laporte (with Étienne Balibar). 9–30. Paris: Hachette, 1974.

1975

"Dialectique," "Epistémologie," "Matérialisme dialectique," "Plekhanov" (with Étienne Balibar). In *Encyclopedia Universalis*. Paris: Encyclopedia Universalis, 1975. Online at https://www.universalis.fr.

1977

"Problems of reflection." In *Literature, society and the sociology of literature: Proceedings of the Conference held at the University of Essex, July 1976*, edited by Francis Barker, 41–54. Colchester: University of Essex, 1977.

"Debussy et Maeterlinck." *L'Avant-scène Opéra* (March/April 1977): 4–12.

"An Interview with Pierre Macherey," edited and translated by Colin Mercer and Jean Radford, *Red Letters* 5 (Summer 1977): 4.

1979

"Histoire et roman dans *Les Paysans de Balzac*." In *Sociocritique*, edited by Claude Duchet, 137–46. Paris: Éditions Nathan, 1979. Translated by Warren Montag as "History and Novel in Balzac's *The Peasants*," *Minnesota Review* 26 (Spring 1986): 102–11.

1982

"Hegel et le présent." *Cahiers philosophiques* 13 (December 1982): 7–19. Translated by Frederico Lyra de Carvalho and Rodrigo Gonçalves as "Hegel and the Present," *Crisis and Critique* 4, no. 1 (March 2017): 239–51.

"Spinoza présent." Preface to *L'anomalie sauvage: Puissance et pouvoir chez Spinoza* by Antonio Negri, translated from the Italian by François Matheron, 13–17. Paris: Presses Universitaires de France, 1982.

1983

"In a Materialist Way." In *Philosophy in France today*, edited by Alan Montefiore, 136–53. Cambridge: Cambridge University Press, 1983. French version: "En materialiste," in *Histoires de dinosaure*, 87–106. Paris: Presses Universitaires de France, 1999.

Review of *Le récit utopique* (*Droit naturel et roman de l'État*) by Pierre François Moreau. *Revue internationale de philosophie* 37, no. 144 (October 1983):
228–38.
"Dialettica della natura," "Dialettica materialistica," Leggi della dialettica,"
"Materia," and "Materialismo." In *Dizionario Marx-Engels*, edited by Fulvio
Papi. Bologna: Zanichelli, 1983.

1984

"Le grand voyage." *Oui la philosophie* 3 (May 1984): 27–30.

1985

"Leroux dans la querelle du Panthéisme." In *Spinoza entre Lumières et Romantisme: Actes du Colloque de Fontenay aux Roses*, 215–22. Fontenay: ENS
Fontenay/Saint-Cloud, 1985.
"Le leurre hégélien." *Le Bloc Note de la Psychanalyse* 5 (September 1985): 27–50.
Translated by Ted Stolze as "The Hegelian Lure: Lacan as Reader of Hegel," in
In a Materialist Way: Selected Essays, ed. Warren Montag (New York: Verso,
1998), 55–75.

1986

"Aux sources de l'*Histoire de la folie*: Une rectification et ses limites." Special
issue on Michel Foucault, *Critique* 471–72 (1986): 753–74. Previously published as "Nas origens da Historia da Loncura: Una retificaçao e sens limites,"
in *Recordar Foucault*, 47–71 (Sao Paulo: Brasiliense, 1985). Reprinted in
*"Histoire de la folie à l'âge classique" de Michel Foucault: Regards critiques
1961–2011* (Caen: Presses Universitaires de Caen, 2011), 231–61. Translated
by Ted Stolze as "At the Sources of *Histoire de la folie*: A Rectification and Its
Limits," in *In a Materialist Way: Selected Essays*, ed. Warren Montag (New
York: Verso, 1998), 77–95.

1987

"Bonald et la philosophie." *Revue de synthèse* 1 (January–March 1987): 3–30.
Review of *Broussais et le matérialisme: Médecine et philosophie au XIXe siècle*,
by Jean François Braunstein, *Revue de synthèse* 1 (January–March 1987):
111–15.
"Foucault avec Deleuze : Le retour éternel du vrai." *Revue de synthèse* 2 (April–
June 1987): 277–85.

1988

"Les yeux de Ligéia: Pouvoirs de la fiction." *Digraphe* 43 (March 1988): 75–82.
"Hegel occulte," *Digraphe* 45 (September 1988): 94–106.
"Foucault: Éthique et subjectivité." *Autrement* 102 (November 1988): 92–103.
Translated by Ted Stolze as "Foucault: Ethics and Subjectivity," in *In a Materialist Way: Selected Essays*, ed. Warren Montag (New York: Verso, 1998), 96–107.

"Eins teilt sich in zwei." *Kulturrevolution* 20 (December 1988): 19–22. French version in *Histoires de dinosaure* (Paris: Presses Universitaires de France, 1999), 64–73.

1989

"Eins teilt sich in zwei." In "Denken an den Grenzen: Althusser zum 70. Geburtstag," special issue of *Kulturrevolution* 20 (December 1988): 19–22. French version in *Histoires de dinosaure* (Paris: Presses Universitaires de France, 1999), 64–73.

"Vers le social." In "L'individualisme: Le grand retour," special issue of *Magazine Littéraire* 264 (April 1989): 38–40.

"Pour une histoire naturelle des normes." In *Michel Foucault philosophe: Rencontre internationale Paris, 9, 10, 11 Janvier 1988*, 203–21. Paris: Éditions du Seuil, 1989. Translated by Timothy Armstrong as "Toward a Natural History of Norms" in *Michel Foucault Philosopher* (New York: Routledge, 1992).

1990

"La révolution dans la contre-révolution: De Bonald à Lamennais." In *La révolution française et la philosophie: Échanges et conflits*, 217–23. Poitiers: Centre Régional de Documentation Pédagogique, 1990.

"Comte" and "Foucault" in *Dictionnaire encyclopédique Quillet*, supplement to vol. 1, 244–45, 369–71. Paris: Librairie A. Quillet, 1990.

"Le conseil de Newton: Une utopie scientifique." *Alliage* 3 (Spring 1990): 23–26.

"La philosophie à la française." *Revue des Sciences Philosophiques et Théologiques* 74, no. 1 (January 1990): 7–14.

"Kojève et les mythes." *Les Lettres Françaises* 1 (July 1990): 18–19.

"Une nouvelle problématique du droit: Sieyès." *Futur Antérieur* 4 (Winter 1990): 29–50.

1991

"Soutenance." In *In a Materialist Way: Selected Essays*, ed. Warren Montag, trans. Ted Stolze (New York: Verso, 1998), 17-27.

"La sociologie entre guillemets." Review of *Les trois cultures: Entre science et littérature, l'avènement de la sociologie*, by Wolf Lepenies. *L'Ane* 46 (April–June 1991): 10–11.

"Lacan avec Kojève, philosophie et psychanalyse." In *Lacan avec les philosophes*, 315–21. Paris: Albin-Michel, 1991.

"Philosophies laïques." *Mots* 27 (June 1991): 5–21.

"Le positivisme entre la révolution et la contre-révolution: Comte et Maistre." *Revue de Synthèse* 112, no. 1 (January–March 1991): 41–47.

"Réflexions d'un dinosaure sur l'anti-anti-humanisme." In *Le gai renoncement*, supplement to *Futur Antérieur*, 157–72. Paris: L'Harmattan, 1991.

"Kojève l'initiateur." In "Hegel et la Phénoménologie de l'Esprit," special issue of *Magazine Littéraire* 293 (November 1991): 51–54.

"Les débuts philosophiques de Victor Cousin." *Corpus* 18–19 (1991): 29–49.

1992

"Marcel Broodthaers: Une pensée négative." Interview by Jean-Christophe Royoux. *Galeries Magazine* 48 (April/May 1992): 60–63, 128.

"Un philosophe de la République." Preface to *La morale dans la démocratie*, by Jules Barni. 7–27. Paris: Kimé, 1992.

Review of *Hegel et les libéraux* by Domenico Losurdo. *Liber* 12, supplement to *Actes de la Recherche en Sciences Sociales* 95 (December 1992): 18–19.

"Connaître la littérature, connaître avec la littérature." Interview with Claude Amey. In "Le texte et son dehor," special issue of *Futur Antérieur* (June 1992): 159–67.

"Foucault/Roussel/Foucault." Preface to the re-edition of *Raymond Roussel*, by Michel Foucault, i–xxx. Paris: Gallimard, 1992.

"L'idéologie avant l'idéologie: L'École normale de l'an III." In *L'institution de la raison: La révolution culturelle des idéologies*, edited by François Azouvi, 41–49. Paris: Vrin/Éditions de l'EHESS, 1992.

"Aux sources des rapports sociaux: Bonald, Saint-Simon, Guizot." *Genèses* 9 (1992): 25–43.

1993

"De Canguilhem à Canguilhem en passant par Foucault." In *Georges Canguilhem, philosophe et historien des sciences: Actes du colloque de décembre 1990*, 286–94. Paris: Albin-Michel, 1993. Translated by Ted Stolze as "From Canguilhem to Canguilhem by Way of Foucault," in *In a Materialist Way: Selected Essays*, ed. Warren Montag (New York: Verso, 1998), 108–15.

"Pascal dans le *Cours de philosophie positive*." In *Pascal au miroir du XIXe siècle*, edited by Denise Leduc-Fayette, 81–87. Paris: Mame Éditions Universitaires, 1993.

"De l'univers infini au monde clos: Le système d'A. Comte et ses limites." *Annali della scuola normale superiore di Pisa* 22, no. 1 (1992): 199–226.

"La révolution dans le miroir de la contre-révolution: Le cas de Joseph de Maistre." In *La philosophie et la Révolution française: Actes du colloque de la société française de philosophie*, 221–25. Paris: Vrin, 1993.

"Renan philosophe." In *Actes des Journées d'étude Ernest Renan, 13–15 mars 1992*, 133–40. Saint-Brieuc: Ville de Saint-Brieuc / Lycée Ernest Renan, 1993.

"Peut-on encore aujourd'hui lire *Le disciple* de Paul Bourget?" *Le Trimestre Psychanalytique* 2 (1993): 63–70.

"Sobre um tom irreligioso em filosofia." *Discurso* 22 (1993): 167–82. French version: "D'un ton religieux en philosophie," in *Gérard Lebrun philosophe* (Paris: Beauchesne, 2017), 21–34.

"L'essai sur les révolutions de Chateaubriand, ou le laboratoire d'un style." *Europe* 775–76 (November/December 1993): 29–45.

1994

"Spinoza est-il moniste ?" In *Spinoza: Puissance et ontologie*, 39–53. Paris: Kimé, 1994.

"Marx dématérialisé ou l'esprit de Derrida." *Europe* 780 (April 1994): 164–72. Reprinted in *Histoires de dinosaure*. Translated by Ted Stolze as "Marx Dematerialized, or the Spirit of Derrida," in *Ghostly Demarcations: A Symposium on Jacques Derrida's "Specters of Marx,"* ed. Michael Sprinker (New York: Verso, 1999), 17–25.

"Philosophie et littérature" and "Spinoza et la littérature." In *Dictionnaire universel des littératures*, edited by Béatrice Didier, vol. 3, 2819–20 and 3605–6. Paris: Presses Universitaires de France, 1994.

"Entre la philosophie et l'histoire: L'histoire de la philosophie." In *La philosophie et son histoire: Colloque de l'Université Laval, Quebec, 1993*, edited by G. Boss, 11–45. Zürich: Éditions du Grand Midi, 1994.

"Pour une théorie de la reproduction littéraire." In *Comment la littérature agit-elle?*, 17–28. Paris: Klincksieck, 1994. Translated by Ted Stolze as "For a Theory of Literary Reproduction," in *In a Materialist Way: Selected Essays*, ed. Warren Montag (New York: Verso, 1998), 42–51.

"Quand dire la création c'est l'effectuer." In *Dire la création*, edited by Dominique Budor, 21–25. Lille: Presses Universitaires de Lille, 1994.

"*Ethique* IV, propositions 70–71: La vie sociale des hommes libres." *Revue de Métaphysique et de Morale* 4 (1994): 459–74.

1995

"Le *Lysis* de Platon: Dilemme de l'amitié et de l'amour." In *L'amitié*, éd. *Autrement*, série Morales, 17 (February 1995): 58–75.

"Spinoza lecteur et critique de Boyle." *Revue du Nord* 77 (October–December 1995): 733–74.

"A Production of Subjectivity." Translated by Roger Celestin. *Yale French Studies* 88 (1995): 42–52.

1996

"Sympathie." In *Dictionnaire de philosophie politique*, edited by Philippe Raynaud and Stéphane Rials, 656–60. Paris: Presses Universitaires de France, 1996.

Review of *Esquisses de dialogues philosophiques*, by Gilbert Boss. *Revue Canadienne de Philosophie* 35, no. 2 (1996): 396–99.

"Auguste Comte." In *Dictionnaire d'éthique et de philosophie morale*, edited by Monique Canto-Sperber, 279–83. Paris: Presses Universitaires de France, 1996.

"The Encounter with Spinoza." In *Deleuze: A Critical Reader*, edited by Paul Patton, 139–61. Oxford: Blackwell, 1996. French version: "De l'expressionnisme en philosophie: Gilles Deleuze et la rencontre avec Spinoza," in *Gilles Deleuze: Politiques de la philosophie* (Genève: MetisPresses, 2015), 57–84.

"Georges Canguilhem: Un style de pensée." *Cahiers philosophiques* 69 (December 1996): 47–56.

1998

"Spinoza: Une philosophie à plusieurs voix." In "Spinoza," special issue of *Philosophique* (1998): 5–22.

"Choses, images de choses, signes, idées." *Revue des Sciences Philosophiques et Théologiques* 82, no. 1 (January 1998): 17–30.

"Lire aujourd'hui l'*Ethique*." *Magazine Littéraire* 370 (November 1998): 35–40.

"Normes vitales et normes sociales dans l'*Essai sur quelques problèmes concernant le normal et le pathologique* de G. Canguilhem." In *Actualité de Georges Canguilhem: Le normal et le pathologique: Actes du Xe colloque international d'histoire de la psychiatrie et de la psychanalyse*, 71–84. Paris: Le Plessis-Robinson / Institut Synthélabo pour le Progrès de la Connaissance, 1998.

"Pouvoir et passions: Sade politique." In *Politiques de l'intérêt*, edited by Christian Lazzeri and Dominique Reynié, 377–80. Besançon: Presses Universitaires Franc-Comtoises, 1998.

1999

"Y a-t-il une métaphysique du positivisme comtien?" In *Positivismes, philosophie, sociologie, histoire, sciences*, edited by Andrée Despy-Meyer and Didier Devriese, 53–62. Turnhout: Brepols, 1999.

"Spinoza, lecteur de Descartes." *Bulletin de l'Association des Professeurs de Philosophie de l'Académie de Poitiers* 16 (June 1999): 35–47.

"Descartes et Spinoza devant le problème de l'usage des passions." In *Spinoza: Puissance et impuissance de la raison*, edited by C. Lazzeri, 93–114. Paris: Presses Universitaires de France, 1999.

2000

"Faire de la philosophie en France aujourd'hui." *Singulier/Pluriel* 8 (Spring 2000): 37–45.

Science, philosophie, littérature." In "Où en est la théorie littéraire?," special issue of *Textuel* 37 (2000): 133–42.

"Les philosophes français de l'après-guerre face à la politique: *Humanisme et terreur* de Merleau-Ponty et *Tyrannie et sagesse* de Kojève." In *Materia actuosa: Antiquité, Age Classique, Lumières. Mélanges en l'honneur d'Olivier Bloch*, 717–30. Paris: H. Champion, 2000.

"Un chapitre de l'histoire du panthéisme: La religion saint-simonienne et la réhabilitation de la matière." In *Philosophies de la nature*, edited by Olivier Bloch, 357–66. Paris: Publications de la Sorbonne, 2000.

2001

"De la philosophie à la politique: Jules Barni traducteur de Kant." In *Traduire les philosophes*, edited by Jacques Moutaux and Olivier Bloch, 393–406. Paris: Publications de la Sorbonne, 2001.

"Francis Wolff, *Dire le monde*." *Les Études Philosophiques* (January–March 2001): 109–16.

2002

"Le Mallarmé d'Alain Badiou." In *Alain Badiou: Penser le multiple*, edited by C. Ramond, 397–406. Paris: L'Harmattan, 2002. Translated by Marilyn Gaddis

Rose and Gabriel Riera as "The Mallarmé of Alain Badiou," in *Alain Badiou: Philosophy and Its Conditions*, edited by Gabriel Riera (New York: New York University Press, 2005), 109–15.

"A partir de Bourdieu: Penser la pratique." *La Pensée* 330 (April–June 2002): 137–45.

"Althusser et le jeune Marx." *Actuel Marx* 31 (2002): 159–75.

2003

"Sur l'histoire de la philosophie." *Le Philosophoire* 20 (Spring/Summer 2003): 7–20.

2004

"Comte dans la Querelle des Anciens et des Modernes: La critique de la perfectibilité." In *L'homme perfectible*, edited by Bertrand Binoche, 274–92. Seyssel: Champ Vallon, 2004.

"En marge d'un livre possible." Special issue on Jacques Derrida. *Europe* 901 (May 2004): 96–106.

"Penser la pratique." In *L'action en philosophie contemporaine*, 17–24. Paris: Ellipses, 2004.

"Y a-t-il une philosophie littéraire ?" *Bulletin de la Société Française de Philosophie* 98 no. 3 (2004): 1–4.

2005

"Marx et la réalisation de la philosophie." *Actuel Marx* 37 (2005): 127–44.

"Quel doit être aujourd'hui l'objet de la philosophie?" *Atala: Cultures et sciences humaines* 8 (2005): 13–24.

"Sur l'action." *Archives de Philosophie* 68, no. 4 (Winter 2005): 629–35.

"*Verum est factum*: Les enjeux d'une philosophie de la praxis et le débat Althusser-Gramsci." In *Sartre, Lukàcs, Althusser: Des marxistes en philosophie*, edited by Eustache Kouvélakis and Vincent Charbonnier, 143–55. Paris: Presses Universitaires de France, 2005.

"Between Pascal and Spinoza: The Vacuum." In *Current Continental Theory and Modern Philosophy*, edited by Stephen H. Daniel, 58–59. Evanston, IL: Northwestern University Press, 2005.

2006

"Penser la pratique." *Le Temps Philosophique* 12 (2006): 53–66.

2007

"Histoire des savoirs et épistémologie." *Revue d'Histoire des Sciences* 60–61 (January–June 2007): 217–36.

"Penser avec la littérature" (interview with Aliocha Wald Lasowski). *Agenda de la pensée contemporaine* 8 (Fall 2007): 69–88. Reprinted in *Pensées pour le nouveau siècle*, edited by Aliocha Wald Lasowski, 257–72. Paris: Fayard, 2008.

"Petit dialogue des morts entre Pascal, Spinoza et Fontenelle." In *Pascal et Spi-
noza: Pensées du contraste: De la géométrie du hasard à la nécessité de la
liberté*, edited by Laurent Bove, Gérard Bras, and Eric Méchoulan, 29–37.
Paris: Amsterdam, 2007.
Contribution to the roundtable *La raison sans l'Histoire* by Bertrand Binoche.
Philonsorbonne 2 (2007–8): 163–69. https://journals.openedition.org
/philonsorbonne/201.
"Spinoza lu par Victor Hugo." In *Spinoza au XIXe siècle*, edited by André Tosel,
Pierre-François Moreau, and Jean Salem, 255–67. Paris: Éditions de la Sor-
bonne, 2007.

2008

"Le Marx intempestif de Derrida." In *Derrida, la tradition de la philosophie*,
edited by Marc Crépon and Frédéric Worms, 135–54. Paris: Galilée, 2008.
"Entre Weber et Freud: Questions de modernité, modernités en question." *Incidence* 3 (2008): 111–54.
"L'autoportrait en regard de la psychanalyse." Review of *Les démons de Gödel*
by Pierre Cassou-Noguès. *Psychanalyse* 13 (September 2008): 99–115.
"La chose littéraire." Postface to *La production de l'immatériel: Théories,
représentations et pratiques de la culture au XIXe siècle*, 441–55. Saint-Étienne:
Publications de l'Université de Saint-Étienne, 2008. Translated as "The Liter-
ary Thing" by Audrey Wasser. *Diacritics* 37, no. 4 (Winter 2007): 21–30.
"Debord lecteur de Feuerbach." *Héritages de Feuerbach*, 181–95. Lille: Presses
Universitaires du Septentrion, 2008.
"Les mathématiques littéraires de Raymond Queneau." *L'école des philosophes*
10 (December 2008): 11–27.
"Idéologie: Le mot, l'idée, la chose." *Methodos* 8 (2008). https://journals
.openedition.org/methodos/1843

2009

"Un exemple d'émancipation par l'art: Le Galilée de Brecht." *Actuel Marx* 45,
no. 1 (2009): 66–79.
"Actualiser Hegel? Axel Honneth et les *Principes de la philosophie du droit*."
Review of *Les pathologies de la liberté* by Axel Honneth. In *La revue interna-
tionale des livres & des idées* 11 (May–June 2009): 53–58.
"Création spirituelle et production de concepts en histoire de la philosophie."
In *Le concept, le sujet, la science: Cavaillès, Canguilhem, Foucault*, edited by
Pierre Cassou-Nogues and Pascale Gillot, 205–17. Paris: Vrin, 2009.

2010

"Bourdieu critique de la raison scolastique: Le cas de la lecture littéraire." In
Bourdieu et la littérature, edited by Jean-Pierre Martin, 113–41. Nantes: Cécile
Defaut, 2010.